Recent titles in this series:

5. *Discharge of selected rivers of the world.* (Multilingual English/French/Spanish/Russian.) Volume III (Part IV): *Mean monthly and extreme discharges (1976-1979).* 1985.
30. *Aquifer contamination and protection.* 1980. (Also published in French and Arabic.)
31. *Methods of computation of the water balance of large lakes and reservoirs.* (English only.)
    Vol. I: *Methodology.* 1981.
    Vol. II: *Case studies.* 1985.
32. *Application of results from representative and experimental basins.* 1982. (English only.)
33. *Groundwater in hard rocks.* 1985. (Also published in French and Spanish.)
34. *Ground-water models.* Vol. I: *Concepts, problems and methods of analysis with examples of their application.* 1982. (Also to be published in Spanish.)
35. *Sedimentation problems in river basins.* 1982. (Also published in French.)
36. *Methods of computation of low stream flow.* 1982. (English only.)
37. *Proceedings of the Leningrad Symposium on specific aspects of hydrological computations for water projects.* 1981. (Russian only.)
38. *Methods of hydrological computations for water projects.* 1982. (Also published in French.)
39. *Hydrological aspects of drought.* 1985. (Also published in French.)
40. *Guidebook to studies of land subsidence due to ground-water withdrawal.* 1985. (English only.)
41. *Guide to the hydrology of carbonate rocks.* 1984. (English only.)
42. *Water and energy: demand and effects.* 1985. (English only.)
43. *Manual on drainage in urbanized areas.* (English only.)
    Vol. I: *Planning and design of drainage systems.* 1987.
    Vol. II: *Data collection and analysis for drainage design.* 1987.
44. *The process of water resources project planning: a systems approach.* 1987. (English only.)
45. *Groundwater problems in coastal areas.* 1987. (English only.)
46. *The role of water in socio-economic development.* (To be published.)
47. *Communication strategies for heightening awareness of water.* 1987. (English only.)
48. *Casebook of methods for computing hydrological parameters for water projects.* 1987. (English only.)

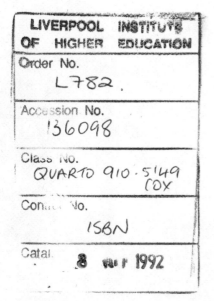

The role of water in socio-economic development

Report 1 of IHP-II Project C1
(on heightening awareness of the
socio-economic role of water)

Prepared for the International
Hydrological Programme by the
Working Group of Project C1 (IHP-II)

Editor: W.E. Cox

Unesco

The designations employed and the presentation of material throughout the publication
do not imply the expression of any opinion whatsoever on the part of Unesco concerning
the legal status of any country, territory, city or area or of its authorities, or concerning
the delimitation of its frontiers or boundaries.

Published in 1987 by the United Nations
Educational, Scientific and Cultural Organization
7, place de Fontenoy, 75700 Paris

Printed by:
Imprimerie de la Manutention, Mayenne

ISBN 92-3-102534-1

© Unesco 1987

Printed in France

Preface

Although the total amount of water on earth is generally assumed to have remained virtually constant, the rapid growth of population, together with the extension of irrigated agriculture and industrial development, are putting stress on the quantity and quality aspects of natural systems. Because of the increasing problems, society has begun to realize that it can no longer follow a "use and discard" philosophy — either with water resources or any other natural resources. As a result, the need for a consistent policy of rational management of water resources has become evident.

Rational water management should be founded upon a thorough understanding of water availability and movement. Thus, as a contribution to the solution of the world's water problems, Unesco, in 1965, began the first world-wide programme of studies of the hydrological cycle — the International Hydrological Decade (IHD). The research programme was complemented by a major effort in the field of hydrological education and training. The activities undertaken during the Decade proved to be of great interest and value to Member States. By the end of that period, a majority of Unesco's Member States had formed IHD National Committees to carry out relevant national activities and to participate in regional and international co-operation within the IHD programme. The knowledge of the world's water resources had substantially improved. Hydrology became widely recognized as an independent professional option and facilities for the training of hydrologists had been developed.

Conscious of the need to expand upon the efforts initiated during the International Hydrological Decade, and following the recommendations of Member States, Unesco launched a new long-term intergovernmental programme in 1975: the International Hydrological Programme (IHP).

Although the IHP is basically a scientific and educational programme, Unesco has been aware from the beginning of a need to direct its activities toward the practical solutions of the world's very real water resource problems. Accordingly, and in line with the recommendations of the 1977 United Nations Water Conference, the objectives of the International Hydrological Programme have been gradually expanded in order to cover not only hydrological processes considered in interrelationship with the environment and human activities, but also the scientific aspects of multi-purpose utilization and conservation of water resources to meet the needs of economic and social development. Thus, while maintaining IHP's scientific concept, the objectives have shifted perceptibly towards a multidisciplinary approach to the assessment, planning, and rational management of water resources.

As part of Unesco's contribution to achieving the objectives of the IHP, two publication series are issued: "Studies and Reports in Hydrology," and "Technical Papers in Hydrology." In addition to these publications, and in order to expedite exchange of information in the areas in which it is most needed, works of a preliminary nature are issued in the form of Technical Documents.

The purpose of the continuing series "Studies and Reports in Hydrology," to which this volume belongs, is to present data collected and the main results of hydrological studies, as well as to provide information on hydrological research techniques. The proceedings of symposia are also sometimes included. It is hoped that these volumes will furnish material of both practical and theoretical interest to water resources scientists and also to those involved in water resources assessment and planning for rational water resources management.

Contents

Contents (*continued*)

III. Managing interactions between water and socio-economic development

Contents (*continued*)   Page

Contents (*continued*)   Page

Foreword

Project Cl, of which this report is part, represents a new direction in the International Hydrological Programme. It is the sole IHP-II project in the field of public information and was established with two objectives:

- "To prepare for planners and policy makers material illustrating the importance of water resources in socio-economic development under varying conditions";
- "To prepare recommendations on other ways in which awareness can be heightened."

The Project Working Group was drawn from a diversity of national backgrounds. Membership was as follows:

> T.B.F. Acquah, Ghana
> P.M. Aristotelous, Cyprus
> W.E. Cox, United States of America
> Q.N. Fattah, Iraq
> M.C. Fuschini Mejia, Argentina
> L.E. Garcia Martinez, Guatemala
> B.S. Sadler, Australia (Chairman)
> G.V. Voropaev, Union of Soviet Socialist Republics

The Working Group approached this project by preparing two major reports, by presenting a set of recommendations for heightening awareness of the role of water, and by planning an abridged report designed for wider appeal. Having decided an outline for the two main reports and having reviewed early draft material in committee, the Working Group assigned responsibility for report completion to two editors elected by the Group. Further contributions and reviews by other members were achieved through correspondence. The project reports are as follows:

> Report 1 — "The role of water in socio-economic development"— Editor W.E. Cox
> Report 2 — "Communication strategies for heightening awareness of water"— Editor B.S. Sadler
> Report 3 — "Water and development: managing the relationship"— W.E. Cox

As a further consequence of this project, extensive materials on the role of water in development of the USSR has been gathered by Professor Voropaev. This material has been presented in an additional independent report issued by Unesco. This and the other Project Cl reports provide a basis for subsequent IHP-III Projects 12.1 and 16.1.

Report 1 is directed toward planners, policy makers, and decision makers, both inside and outside the water sector, and is relevant for consideration in both developing and developed countries. The report examines the relationships between water and socio-economic development, delineating fundamental roles and alternative approaches for optimizing these roles. The report documents an intricate relationship with other sectors of socio-economic development and with social values and customs. The need for communication and coordination between palnning in the water sector and other sectors and the need for maintaining awareness of interacting issues and values among planners and decision makers are made evident. The report emphasizes the following requirements:

- (a) Water planning that is comprehensive, coordinating effectively with general socio-economic planning and recognizing that water development will fail to achieve its goals without corresponding action in other sectors;
- (b) Realistic assessment of the social, economic and environmental effects, whether beneficial or adverse, of proposals for water development;
- (c) Proper consideration of the effects of land use and development of other sectors on water resources management;
- (d) Adoption of an integrated approach, inside the water sector, to water resources planning, development, and management.

These fundamental requirements in turn led to an emphasis on the following more specific needs:

- (a) Establishment of appropriate mechanisms to achieve effective inter-sectoral and intra-sectoral comunications in the socio-economic and land-use planning processes;
- (b) Development of an adequate organizational structure for decision-making and implementation which is continuously adaptive to the changing demands and circumstances associated with socio-economic progress;
- (c) Scientific evaluation and continuous assessment of water resources as prerequisites for well-balanced water resources planning, development, utilization, and protection;
- (d) Effective incorporation of information of social and cultural issues and values into decision processes and the related need to adopt the use of public participation for this purpose.

Report 2 deals with communication of the message of Report 1. It reviews the need for communication; examines the problems and techniques of communication; and discusses means for heightening awareness in planners, decision makers, and the general public. The report examines public and professional awareness and motivation as rational and political prerequisites for initiation of appropriate problem-solving actions. Communication problems and processes for communicating awareness are reviewed from the viewpoint of water planners and managers acting as the prime communicators. Some general observations are made in relation to principles and strategies of communication which might be adopted by national water agencies and by international programs such as the International Hydrological Programme.

Report 3 is an abridged version of Report 1 intended to convey its primary message to a broader audience.

I. Introduction

Socio-economic development processes are closely related to the water resource because of the diverse range of interactions between water and human activities. Water serves as a positive input for many activities: it serves essential biological functions, as a basic element of social and economic infrastructure, and as a natural amenity contributing to psychological welfare. Water also serves in negative roles such as flooding and disease transmission. The significant magnitude and pervasive nature of these positive and negative attributes create a close relationship between water and human welfare. Human history contains a continuing series of water management activities intended to upgrade the quality of life through enhancement of water's positive functions and control of its negative functions.

The precise nature of the relationship between water and socio-economic development is obscured by several factors. A major factor is the complexity of the development process itself. Development is the result of many interacting factors, and isolation of the influence of any single factor is difficult. Another complication in understanding the overall role of water is the interdependent nature of the several individual impacts of water on human welfare. These interactions can become especially significant whenever water resource development activities are undertaken. The beneficial impacts of different water project purposes can be cumulative but may involve some degree of conflict; thus, achievement of an acceptable combination often requires trade-offs among the individual functions. In addition, negative impacts, which can occur simultaneously with beneficial effects, may at least partially offset project benefits. The net effect of a project of this type on the affected population may be difficult to determine.

Another basic dimension of the interactive relationship between water and socio-economic development is the potential for development to impact the water resource. Many socio-economic development activities involve modification of the quality and flow characteristics of water. As a result, the characteristics of the water resource must be viewed as dynamic along with the development process itself.

This report analyzes relationships between water and socio-economic development to delineate fundamental roles and evaluate alternative approaches for managing interactive relationships. The remainder of this introductory section provides background by briefly considering the historic role of water in socio-economic development and providing an overview of current water problems.

The second section explores the interactive relationship between water and development. To provide the necessary perspective, general consideration is given to a relatively wide range of development problems and issues. An inherent danger in focusing on any single factor in development is the tendency to neglect interrelationships with other factors. This tendency can serve as a significant impediment to understanding the development process since no single factor is likely to be adequate to produce development by itself. The pervasiveness of conflicts and complementarities among the individual factors in development dictate that their interdependence be viewed as a major characteristic. Thus the report, while emphasizing the roles of water in the development process, attempts to present these roles in proper context by focusing on interactions between water and other factors.

The third section of the report is devoted to consideration of issues associated with managing water as a factor in socio-economic development. Attention is focused on institutional aspects of management, with emphasis on law, policy, and administrative organization that define the decision-making framework through which management activities are planned and implemented.

1. History of water in socio-economic development

A history of man's activities relating to water would constitute a relatively comprehensive history of civilization itself. Indeed, some historians believe that the emergence of civilization was associated with organized efforts to control water supplies necessary for irrigation. Water management activities, particularly irrigation, played a central role in the development of the earliest known civilizations in the valleys of the Tigris and Euphrates, Nile, Indus, and Yellow Rivers. In Mesopotomia, along the Tigris and Euphrates, irrigation was established at least as early as 4000 B.C. Although irrigated agriculture was the economic base of the Mesopotamian civilization, navigation and flood control were also significant water management objectives (Fukuda, 1976, p. 21). Problems with maintaining irrigation systems may have been a factor in the shifting of the centers of power (Bennett, 1974, p. 43), and problems related to water management appear to have been instrumental in the ultimate decline of Mesopotomia. Of primary significance were salinization and waterlogging of soils and the siltation of water supply systems resulting from abuse of watershed areas (Teclaff and Teclaff, 1973, p. 31).

Irrigation also played a major role in the development of the Egyptian civilization along the Nile. The left bank of the Nile was under irrigation by 3400 B.C. (Teclaff and Teclaff, 1973, p. 31), and irrigation has been practiced with little change until recent times. The technique of basin irrigation provided both nutrients in the form of fertile silt and moisture for crop production.

Irrigation development was initiated only slightly later in time in the Yellow and Indus River valleys. Irrigation in the Yellow River Valley began about 3000 B.C. (Fukuda, 1976, p. 25) and may have been preceded by flood control efforts, which have long been a major water management activity in the Yellow River Basin. In the 400-200 B.C. period, floodwater diversion by means of dike construction has been reported to have seen frequent use as an instrument of war by the feudal states of the Yellow River Basin, a somewhat unique integration of water management into social processes (Greer, 1979, p. 25).

In the western hemisphere, an example of an early irrigation civilization is that of the Incas of Peru, which dates back to 1000 B.C. Irrigation was practiced extensively after 700 B.C., and irrigated agriculture was well developed at the time of the Spanish conquest in 1532 (Fukuda, 1976, p. 29-30).

Irrigation played a major role in the socio-cultural development of these early civilizations. The need for communication and coordination in connection with irrigation operations influenced the development of institutions for water management and constituted an important factor in social organization. This role of irrigation has been emphasized by Wittfogel's (1957) concept of "hydraulic societies." According to this theory, the rulers of certain ancient civilizations were able to use control over hydraulic facilities such as irrigation works as a base for establishing absolute political power. In this view, control over water and the associated development of organization and communication leads to expansion of power into other areas of activity and ultimately results in totally centralized control over the society involved.

While disagreement exists over the validity of some of the aspects of Wittfogel's theory, most agree that intensive use of irrigation creates a tendency toward centralized control and produces far reaching social consequences (Downing and Gibson (ed.), 1974). The importance of water management in the socio-cultural development of these early fluvial civilizations is indicated by the incorporation of related requirements into law. For example, early Chinese and Indian law controlled the use of wells. Chinese law also specified the duties of local officials with respect to the maintenance of facilities such as dikes, dams, canals, and ditches. The code of Hammurabi imposed liability for resulting injury on any party neglecting the upkeep of water control facilities (Teclaff and Teclaff, 1973, p. 30).

Later in history, water management was a prominent achievement of the Roman Empire. One accomplishment was the spread of water resource development technology of the Middle East to other areas. Another development was the water-powered grain mill, which was first used around 100 B.C. (Teclaff and Teclaff, 1973, p. 29-33). Perhaps the most notable water-related achievement of the Romans consisted of extensive aqueduct construction. At the end of the first century A.D., the water supply system of Rome included nine aqueducts with a combined length of over 421,000 meters. An abundant water supply was a central feature of the Roman social system as indicated by the prominent social role of the elaborate public baths. Although Roman water systems exhibited defects relative to current standards, improvements in design were not made until the modern era (Hansen, 1983, pp. 264-269).

More recent history is also replete with examples of the fundamental role of water in socio-economic development. Prior to its displacement by the steam engine, water power was an important factor in early industrialization and influenced patterns of industrial location. Water-borne transportation has also served as a major factor in socio-economic development. The importance of navigation is one of the reasons why many of the major cities of the world are located on navigable waters. In addition to the locational influence of naturally navigable waterways, canals and other navigation improvements also have influenced patterns of economic growth (Miller, 1977, p. 100).

Recent history provides numerous examples of governmental use of water resources development as a primary mechanism for achieving socio-economic goals. In the Union of Soviet Socialist Republics, for example, multipurpose water resources development has played a major role in achieving such objectives as industrialization and increasing agricultural output. Water development has been an important measure in the settlement and assimilation of outlying regions in such forms as hydroelectric power development, provision of irrigation and industrial water supply, and improvement and maintenance of navigation (Voropaev, 1986; Kuznetsov and Lvovich, 1971; Karaulov, 1971; Averyanov, Minayeva, and Temoshkina, 1971). India provides another example of a nation according high priority to water development within national development plans. Agricultural development has played a major role in the program to achieve higher standards of living and national self sufficiency; irrigation development has been fundamental to increasing agricultural output due to irregular precipitation patterns over much of the area suitable for cultivation (Varma, 1978; Murthy, 1978).

A well known example of the use of water resources development as an integral aspect of a comprehensive program for regional socio-economic development is the case of the Tennessee Valley Authority created within the Tennessee River Basin of the eastern portion of the United States of America. Although extensive water resources development projects may be the most visible function of TVA, achievement of the regional development objective of the Authority has involved a broad range of activities. In addition to multipurpose development of the Tennessee River and its tributaries for such purposes as flood control, navigation, and electric power production, TVA programs have included such diverse goals as controlling erosion, introducing better fertilizers and farming practices, promotion of the forestry industry, industrial development, and community improvement. Per capita income in the TVA region has grown from approximately 45 percent of the national average at the time of creation of TVA to nearly 80 percent of the national average (TVA, 1982).

Although a wide range of other examples of the role of water in socio-economic development could be given, these illustrations suggest the fundamental nature of the relationship. From the origins of civilization to the present, many of man's major achievements have involved improvements in water resource utilization. Similarly, notable setbacks in the advancement of civilization, such as the decline of Mesopotomia, often have been directly related to the inability to overcome water-related problems. With these examples as background, the report now undertakes a brief consideration of current water problems potentially constraining further socio-economic development.

2. Contemporary water problems

Just as water historically has played a significant role in socio-economic development, water is an important factor in currently ongoing development processes. Water management problems constraining development range from inadequacies in supply of water for purposes such as domestic and agricultural use to inadequate control over such negative impacts as flooding and soil erosion. Serious water shortages at certain geographic locations may be simultaneously accompanied by major flooding at other locations. The disruption of the world's weather during 1983 by the climatic event known as El Niño provides an example. Widespread devastation by flood and drought resulted. Associated deaths have been estimated at 1100 and damages placed at 8.7 billion United States dollars (Canby, 1984).

Other relatively recent water problems have reached catastrophic proportions in a variety of situations. Especially catastrophic in terms of human suffering and death have been the drought-related famines in Sub-Saharan Africa during the 1970s and 1980s. The 1970s drought produced substantial food and livestock losses resulting in serious food shortages. Despite a major international relief effort, the death toll from starvation was substantial. The 1980s famine was even more severe.

Although these recent African famines were triggered by drought, their underlying causes include a variety of social factors. Per capita food production has declined for a number of years because of rapid population growth, land degradation and loss of productivity, and social policies acting as disincentives for food production. In the case of the 1970's famine, recognition has been given to the contributory effect of the limited nature of water management infrastructure (M. Biswas, 1978, p. 13). Mismanagement of drought-related problems during the 1970s contributed to far-reaching social and political consequences

(Carlson, 1982, p. 13). The Sahelian experience indicates that the effects of drought, as well as those of other catastrophies, are not solely the product of nature but arise from interaction between natural and social systems (Hewitt (ed.), 1983).

The recent period also provides examples of catastrophies related to excess water. Bangladesh is an area that suffers catastrophic flooding losses on a frequently recurring basis, both from overflowing rivers and from cyclones that inundate low-lying coastal areas. During the 1960s, eight cyclones caused the loss of as many as 50,000 lives and extensive property damage. The most devastating cyclone of the century occurred in 1970, with the death toll estimated to be at least 250,000 (O'Donnell, 1984, pp. 9, 84-85). The extent of the disaster has been attributed at least in part to the lack of an adequate warning system in much of the affected area. More recently, at least 15,000 deaths resulted from a 1985 cyclone (Iyer, 1985). Although effects vary among nations, flooding is a widespread problem with major adverse effects on human welfare.

Although public attention is likely to focus on water-related disasters, many other less dramatic problems currently pose significant impediments to socio-economic development. For example, the fact that two-thirds of the cultivated land in Bangladesh is subject to flooding (Islam, 1978, p. 1) is important to the welfare of that nation's citizens along with the loss of life and direct suffering resulting from floods. These less publicized water problems can be significant in terms of their chronic nature, and the large number of people affected.

One of these chronic problem areas involves inadequacies in domestic water supplies and sanitation. A survey covering 90 percent of the population of developing countries exclusive of China (conducted by the World Health Organization) showed that, at the end of 1975, 76 percent of the population of urban communities and 22 percent of the population of rural areas of these countries had reasonable access to safe water. On a combined basis, 35 percent of the urban and rural populations was being adequately served. The same survey indicated that 75 percent of the population of urban communities and 14 percent of rural communities were served by sewage disposal facilities, or 32 percent of the combined urban and rural populations (United Nations Water Conference Secretariat, 1978, pp. 25-26). To summarize the situation another way, 1,200 million people lacked safe drinking water and 1,400 million people were reported to have inadequate sanitary waste disposal facilities (Biswas, 1978, pp. xiv-xv).

Subsequent to this survey, the United Nations International Drinking Water Supply and Sanitation Decade, a major effort to improve water supply and sanitation conditions worldwide during the 1980s, has been implemented. At the midpoint of the Decade, prospects that overall conditions will be substantially improved appear poor (Wiseman, 1985). Although water and sanitation services have been extended to a substantial number of additional people during the first half of the decade, some have estimated that a smaller percentage of the world's population now enjoys such services than at the beginning of the Decade in

1980 (Gunnell, 1984). This lack of progress can be attributed to two principal factors: lower than anticipated funding due to world economic conditions and rapid population growth that has expanded the number of people without service.

The absence of reasonable access to a safe domestic water supply has two direct impacts on the population affected: (1) excessive time and energy expenditures associated with water collection and (2) health problems associated with water collection and/or use. Women and children of families in developing countries may spend several hours each day collecting water to meet family requirements. This effort is estimated to be up to 25 percent or more of daytime calorie needs in mountainous regions (Biswas, 1978, p. xiv). Health problems associated with inadequate domestic water supply include diseases caused by ingestion of infective organisms; diseases associated with inadequate quantities of water for consumption, personal hygiene, and other purposes; and those transmitted by biting insects that frequent water collection sites.

An even wider range of diseases are water-related when disease-transmission mechanisms not associated with domestic water supplies (for example, widespread disease-transmission by aquatic insects such as mosquitoes) are considered. Approximately 20-30 diseases have been identified as having some relationship to water (ITDGL, 1978, p. 1114). The magnitude of the total water related health problem is illustrated by the following data concerning annual occurrence of some of the water-related diseases as presented at the 1977 United Nations Water Conference: 400 million cases of gastroenteritis, 200 million cases of schistosomiasis, 200 million cases of filariasis, 160 million cases of malaria, and 20-40 million cases of onchocerciasis (Biswas, 1978, p. xiv).

Water supply deficiencies and other water-related health problems produce impacts extending beyond direct effects on individual members of society. Water supply is a component of socio-economic infrastructure and therefore affects various elements of development. For example, industrial growth, which generally is considered to be a key component of development, depends to some extent on water (as well as on a variety of other factors). Industrial water demand is often met in urban areas from public supplies, with the result that deficiencies in such supplies have potential to impede the industrialization process. Widespread health problems of the type often associated with water-related diseases also impede development by lowering the productivity of the affected population.

Another chronic water-related problem is hunger. The world's permanently hungry were estimated to number 460 million in 1974. Expansion in agricultural output through such means as improved crop varieties has reduced the magnitude of the problem, but hunger continues to be a major social concern. Water management is an essential factor in maintenance and expansion of agricultural production to meet food needs (FAO, 1978, p. 907-910). Management activities needed include rehabilitation and improvement of existing irrigation projects, expansion of irrigated acreage, provision of drainage for reclaiming waterlogged lands, provision of community supply to allow establishment of agricultural settlements, and protection of agricultural lands from flooding.

Existing or projected water resource problems and limitations have resulted in proposals for additional water resource development projects in many nations. Among those of greatest scope are plans of the Soviet Union for major diversions of northern rivers for use in the water scarce southern regions of the country where water deficits by the end of the century have been estimated at over 100 cubic kilometers per year (Voropaev, 1978). Water diversions of continental scale have also been proposed in North America. Such plans generally have involved movement of water from the northwestern part of the continent to drier areas of Canada, the United States, and Mexico (Biswas (2), 1978; Simons, 1969). In the People's Republic of China, projects have been undertaken for large-scale transfers of water from the southern part of the country to the North China Plain (Yiqiu, 1981). A large-scale development project for increasing the yield of the Nile River by control of swamps in the upper watershed and other hydrologic modifications has been proposed (Mohamed, 1978). Although most are of smaller scale than the above examples, proposals for additional water resources development exist in most nations as a basic part of the continuing socio-economic development process.

Existing simultaneously with interest in additional water resources development is an increasing concern for protection of environmental values associated with water in its natural setting. The potential for water projects to produce adverse environmental effects is now generally recognized (Ackerman, White, and Worthington (eds.), 1973; Goldman, McEvoy, and Richerson (eds.), 1973). Due to the potential severity and often unanticipated nature of these effects, water project construction has become a controversial activity in many countries. The increased concern for environmental protection has been a factor in the reduction of investment in water development projects occurring in some nations in recent years. Achievement of a proper balance between developmental and preservationist interests currently is a major water management issue.

A special aspect of the environmental issue is the water quality problem facing many areas. Rapid urban growth often outpaces measures to treat resulting wastewater adequately, with the result that the urban area and downstream areas are adversely affected by water pollution (UNECLA, 1979, p. 77). Although water quality problems generally are more severe in areas of concentrated population, rural areas also experience water contamination due to such causes as improper disposal of human wastes, uncontrolled erosion, and agricultural runoff. Water quality degradation within a given area is likely to be recognized first as a surface water problem, but groundwater is also subject to contamination by waste disposal and other activities.

Listing examples of current water problems only suggests the many ways in which water may constrain continuing socio-economic development. Additional perspective for evaluating water problems and needs is provided by considering the potential of existing

4

water supplies to satisfy current and future water demands. The nature and extent of water management problems are related to the scarcity or abundance of water within the area under consideration. The next section provides a general overview of the world's water supply relative to demands for the resource.

2.1 Assessment of water supply and demand

Of the approximately 1,360 million cubic kilometers of water on earth, 97.3 percent is contained in the oceans. Although the oceans are important for such purposes as navigation, fisheries, cooling water supply, a source of water for desalination, and their role in climatogical processes, ocean water is not readily available for satisfying many of man's needs. Of greater immediate significance for many water-using activities are fresh-water resources. However, most of the earth's freshwater is contained in ice caps and glaciers. Most of the freshwater with potential for use is in the form of groundwater, with estimates of the amount in storage above 4,000 meters in depth ranging from 8.1 million to 10.5 million cubic kilometers. The greater occurrence of groundwater indicates its importance as a source of future water supply. The quantity of water contained in freshwater lakes and streams is estimated at 0.126 million cubic kilometers (United Nations Water Conference Secetariat, 1978, p. 15-16; M. Biswas, 1978, p. 8; Todd (ed.), 1968, p. 62).

Although the above data are of general interest in defining the physical dimensions of the water resource, the fact that water use is a recurring activity means that the most significant measure of water availability is the rate at which a particular freshwater source replenishes itself through the processes of the hydrologic cycle. Stores of water contained in freshwater lakes, artificial impoundments, and aquifers can be used in excess of replenishment rates, in some cases for substantial periods of time, but such practice cannot be continued indefinitely. The source of water with greatest long term significance for supply purposes is the runoff from the world's land areas (including the contributions of groundwater to stream flow), a quantity estimated at 40,000 to 47,000 cubic kilometers annually (United Nations Water Conference Secretariat, 1978, p. 15). Runoff of the inhabited areas exclusive of the polar zones has been estimated at 39,000 cubic kilometers (Falkenmark and Lindh, 1976, p. 17).

Distribution of this runoff among the continents is highly variable as indicated in table 1. Runoff of the South America and Caribbean region accounts for 30 percent of the world's total while the Australian continent accounts for less than one percent. Distribution of runoff within continents is also highly variable. For example, the Atacama Desert, generally considered the driest area in the world, is located in South America in spite of the abundance of water on a continental basis (UNECLA, 1979, p. 16). Certain South American nations, such as Peru, experience chronic water supply shortages (Falkenmark and Lindh, 1976, p. 124). Variability is also a major characteristic within many individual countries as

illustrated by the fact that about half the total stream flow of Mexico is concentrated in less than ten percent of the land area of the country (UNECLA, 1979, p.19).

The extent to which runoff at a particular location can be used depends to a significant degree on its distribution over time. The above data are based on long-term averages while actual water availability is subject to significant fluctuations both seasonally and over different years. A large portion of runoff occurs in the form of flood flows of relatively short duration. Although fluctuation varies with location, the average low-flow or stable runoff has been estimated to be approximately 35 percent of average annual runoff under a variety of conditions. But the concept of stable runoff has little significance in parts of the world (such as most of the Australian Continent) where dry weather flows are small or nonexistent. Where stable flows do not exist, or where demand for water exceeds the dependable supply, water management activities such as construction of storage reservoirs becomes essential.

Attempts to correlate the need for water management activity and the level of water demand have been undertaken on the basis of European water-use experience. This analysis indicates that few water problems occur and little management activity is needed when water demand is less than 5 percent of total runoff. (Of course, management problems not related to supply such as flooding are independent of water demand.) When demand is in the range of five to ten percent of total runoff, certain areas may encounter supply difficulties although overall conditions are still considered favorable. Water supply commonly will become a significant problem when demand is in the range of ten to twenty percent of total runoff, and a need arises for water planning and investment in water supply facilities. If demand exceeds twenty percent of total runoff, severe water supply problems can be expected that require intensive management activity and increasingly heavy investment in planning and construction of facilities. Under these conditions, water supply may become a limiting factor in economic development (Falkenmark and Lindh, 1976, pp. 34-38). Of course, such generalizations are subject to limitations because of variations in conditions among geographic locations.

Table 1
Average Water Balances of the World

Region	Baumgartner 1975			USSR Monograph 1974			Lvovich 1974		
	P	E	R	P	E	R	P	E	P
Europe	6.6	3.8	2.8	8.3	5.3	3.0	7.2	4.1	3.1
Asia	30.7	18.5	12.2	32.2	18.1	14.1	32.7	19.5	13.2
Africa	20.7	17.3	3.4	22.3	17.7	4.6	20.8	16.6	4.2
Australia	7.1	4.7	2.4	7.1	4.6	2.5	6.4	4.4	2.0
North America	15.6	9.7	5.9	18.3	10.1	8.2	13.9	7.9	6.0
South America	28.0	16.9	11.1	28.4	16.2	12.2	29.4	19.0	10.4
Antarctica	2.4	0.4	2.0	2.3	0	2.3	—	—	—
Land areas*	111	71	40	119	72	47	113	72	41
Oceans	385	425	-40	458	505	-47	412	453	-41
World	496	496	0	577	577	0	525	525	0

P = Precipitation, E = Evaporation, R = Runoff

Source: United Nations Water Conference Secretariat, 1978, p.14.

Projections of water demand are not generally available at a level of detail adequate for meaningful assessments of the adequacy of supply. On a global scale, supplies will remain much in excess of demand. Total renewable supplies have been estimated to be adequate for meeting the needs of five to ten times the existing population (Postel, 1984). Such estimates are essentially meaningless, however, because of nonuniform distribution of water supply and the activities responsible for demand.

General comparisons of projected demand to supply on a continental or more limited geographical basis indicate substantial variation in supply adequacy. Per capita water availability is projected to be low or very very low in much of Africa, South Asia, and the Middle East (United States CEQ and Department of State, 1980, pp. 152-157). Since these regions contain many of the world's developing nations, water resource conditions may be an important factor in future development. Many of the developing nations of Africa are located in areas of low and variable rainfall, and water-related diseases are a major problem in wide areas (Falkenmark and Lindh, 1976, pp. 63-89). In southern Asia, water resources have already been subjected to high levels of use, and significant increases in use for purposes such as irrigation may be necessary. In addition to potential water supply problems, many of the Asian nations are subject to devastation by flooding, both by river overflows and from inundation of low-lying coastal areas (Falkenmark and Lindh, 1976, pp. 90-115).

Identification of these obvious problem areas does not, however, indicate the full extent of future water problems. Generalized consideration of runoff on a continental scale as presented in Table 1 is not an adequate basis for describing the water situation in any individual nation due to significant variation in supply among nations and within individual nations. The appropriate area for water supply analysis is relatively small, and any summation of supply over larger areas obscures nonuniformity in distribution and therefore presents an overly optimistic impression of supply adequacy. The frequent occurrence of local and regional shortages within broader areas of relative abundance indicates that water management will become an increasingly important activity in most nations.

2.2 Water management capabilities

Comparisons of water supply and projected demand and other assessments of physical water resource conditions indicate the potential for water-related problems, but the extent to which such potential problems actually develop depends on water management activities undertaken to realize opportunities or mitigate problems. Management deficiencies are likely to increase the frequency and/or severity of water problems. Such deficiencies can take several forms, including technical inadequacies, funding limitations, and institutional weaknesses.

Technical inadequacies such as limited analytical capabilities and equipment and material constraints can adversely affect all aspects of management. Assessment of the resource requires technical capabilities for collecting, processing, storing, and analyzing hydrologic data. Since information deficiencies jeopardize other management activities, inadequacies in this area can have major adverse consequences. Technical deficiencies can also have a substantial impact on the planning and design of water resources projects and programs. The ability to identify an appropriate range of responses to physical water problems and to select the most appropriate alternative relative to existing policies and objectives is a key management function directly related to technical capabilities. Deficiencies in this area are related directly to deficiencies in education and training programs for providing qualified personnel. Implementation of management programs and projects also requires adequate technical capabilities, including the availability of appropriate equipment and construction materials and techniques.

Technical deficiencies in the various phases of resources management are likely to be closely related to funding limitations. Installation of a hydrologic data collection network and its continuing operation require substantial initial investments and operating funding. Maintenance of a water resources planning program also requires a continuing funding commitment. An even greater financial burden is likely to be imposed where major water management projects must be implemented. Such projects generally require large capital investments that may not be financially feasible.

In addition to technical and financial deficiencies, water management activities are also prone to significant institutional weaknesses. Institutional factors extend from governmental organization, which establishes the processes through which public sector water management decisions are made, to issues such as individual attitudes and incentives, which largely determine the acceptance and effectiveness of many water management efforts. Institutional deficiencies can prevent the application of resources and technical competence to the solution of water problems and realization of opportunities.

These different types of deficiencies occur in varying combinations among nations, resulting in a wide range of water resources management capabilities. Deficiencies related to technical capabilities and funding levels occur more frequently in the developing nations. Institutional weaknesses, on the other hand, are more widespread. They often occur in those countries experiencing technical and funding deficiencies but also may exist in varying severity in countries with adequate technical capabilities and funding levels.

The following statements taken from the summary document prepared for the United Nations Water Conference held in 1977 suggest the pervasive nature of water management deficiencies in the areas of technical, funding, and institutional capabilities:

> Further, the basic data about water supply and its rational use is inadequate for large sectors of the land surface. Decisions about future management for such areas are riddled with uncertainty and frustrated by large margins of error in data derived from inadequate observation networks and

equally inadequate modes of analysis. Also, the gap between scientific knowledge and its application is vast and widening in most parts of the world (Biswas (ed.), 1978, p. 68).

Many countries share problems in educating, training and retaining properly qualified and experienced personnel at all professional and subprofessional levels. There is uncertainty as to the precise extent of these problems and an urgent need to isolate and remedy them. A number ...[of training activities have been undertaken, but] the total impact of all this effort has not been such as to remove the element of the shortage of trained manpower as a critical constraint (Biswas (ed.), 1978, p. 175).

A persistent and recurring problem in many countries is the mobilization and the obtaining of adequate financial resources to implement necessary improvement in the numerous aspects of water resources planning, development and management (Biswas (ed.), 1978, p. 175).

In a number of countries, there is a need for the formulation of a national water policy within the framework of and consistent with the overall economic and social policies of the country concerned, with a view to helping raise the standard of living of the whole population (Biswas (ed.), 1978, p. 165).

Legislation in many countries, though often complex, lags behind modern water management practices and techniques and perpetuates an undesirable fragmentation of administrative responsibilities. Provisions which regulate water management are often contained in different laws and regulations. This may make it difficult to know and apply them. In some instances there are cases of incompatibility between legal provisions of a national character and regulations emanating from regional or local authorities, or between traditional rights and the State's role in controlling water resources (Biswas (ed.), 1978, p. 168).

Whenever large river basins are shared by two or more countries, the tendency towards interrelation encourages international basin management and development. Many international agreements have been signed during the past decades. But for a large number of rivers, either no agreement has yet been reached, even after many years of negotiation in some instances, or the agreements reached have little substance and prove to be ineffective in the solving of difficult problems such as pollution control and the development of large-scale facilities (Biswas (ed.), 1978, p. 68).

The following statement from the introduction to the United Nations Water Conference summary document places water management problems in perspective relative to physical resource limitations:

To conclude, the major problem in the area of water resources is not one of Malthusian spectre of impending scarcity, but one of instituting more rational and better management practices. Water resources of different regions for which adequate data are not available have to be assessed, and based

on such assessments, long-term development and management plans have to be established. Water and land should not appear as constraints in the overall planning process of a country, rather realistic development and production targets should be matched to their availability. What is urgently needed is the formulation of long-term development policies, on a sustaining basis, that reflect changing water supply and demand patterns, consistent with efficient use, and better understanding of the social and environmental implications so that adverse impacts can be minimized (Biswas, 1978, pp. xvi-xvii).

3. References for section I

Ackerman, William C., Gilbert F. White, and E. B. Worthington, eds. *Man-Made Lakes: Their Problems and Environmental Effects* (Geophysical Monograph 17). Washington: American Geophysical Union, 1973.

Averyanov, S. F., E. N. Minayeva, and V. A. Timoshkina. "Increasing Agricultural Productivity through Irrigation and Drainage." In *Natural Resources of the Soviet Union - Their Use and Renewal*. Eds. I. P. Gerasimov, D. L. Armand, and K. M. Yefron. Trans. Jacek. I. Romanowski. English edition ed. W. A. Douglas Jackson. San Francisco: W. H. Freeman and Co., 1971, pp. 131-160.

Bennett, John W. "Anthropological Contributions to the Cultural Ecology and Management of Water Resources." *Man & Water*. Ed. L. Douglas James. Lexington, Ky.: The University Press of Kentucky, 1974, pp. 34-81.

Biswas, Asit K. "Editor's Introduction." In *United Nations Water Conference: Summary and Main Documents*. Ed. Asit K. Biswas. Vol. 2 of *Water Development, Supply and Management*. Series ed. Asit K. Biswas. Oxford: Pergamon Press (for the United Nations), 1978, pp. i-xvii.

Biswas(2), Asit K. "North American Water Transfers: An Overview." *Water Supply and Management*, 2 (1978), pp. 79-90.

Biswas, Asit K., ed. *United Nations Water Conference: Summary and Main Documents*, Vol. 2 of *Water Development, Supply and Management*. Series ed., Asit K. Biswas, Oxford: Pergamon Press (for the United Nations), 1978.

Biswas, Margaret. "United Nations Water Conference: A Perspective." In *United Nations Water Conference: Summary and Main Documents*. Ed. Asit K. Biswas. Vol. 2 of *Water Development, Supply and Management*. Series ed. Asit K. Biswas. Oxford: Pergamon Press (for the United Nations), 1978, pp. 7-23.

Canby, Thomas Y. "El Niño's Ill Wind." *National Geographic*. Vol. 165, 1984, pp. 144-183.

Carlson, Dennis G. "Famine in History: With a Comparison of Two Modern Ethiopian Disasters." In *Famine*. Ed. Kevin M. Cahill, Maryknoll, N.Y.: Orbis Books, 1982, pp. 5-16.

Downing, Theodore E. and McGuire Gibson, ed. *Irrigation's Impact on Society.* Tucson, Ariz.: The University of Arizona Press, 1974.

FAO (Food and Agricultural Organization of the United Nations). "Water for Agriculture." In *Water Development and Management: Proceedings of the United Nations Water Conference.* Ed. Asit K. Biswas. Vol.1 (in four parts) of *Water Development, Supply and Management.* Series ed. Asit K. Biswas. Oxford: Pergamon Press (for the United Nations), 1978, part 3, pp. 907-41.

Falkenmark, Malin and Gunnar Lindh. *Water For a Starving World.* Boulder, Colo.: Westview Press, 1976.

Fukuda, Hitoshi. *Irrigation in the World: Comparative Developments.* Tokyo: University of Tokyo Press, 1976.

Goldman, Charles R., James McEvoy III, and Peter J. Richerson, eds. *Environmental Quality and Water Development.* San Francisco: W. H. Freeman and Co., 1973.

Greer, Charles. *Water Management in the Yellow River Basin of China.* Austin, Tex.: University of Texas Press, 1979.

Gunnell, Barbara. "Time Runs Short for UN Water Supply Decade." *African Business,* (1984), pp. 71-72.

Hansen, Roger D. "Water and Waste Water in Imperial Rome." *Water Resources Bulletin,* 19(1983), pp. 263-69.

Hewitt, K., ed. *Interpretations of Calamity from the Viewpoint of Human Ecology.* Boston: Allen and Unwin Inc., 1983.

ITDGL (Intermediate Technology Development Group Limited). "Water for the Thousand Millions." In *Water Development and Management: Proceedings of the United Nations Water Conference.* Vol. 1 (in four parts) of *Water Development, Supply and Management.* Series ed. Asit K. Biswas. Oxford: Pergamon Press (for the United Nations), 1978, part 3, pp. 1105-62.

Islam, Nurul. *Development Strategy of Bangladesh.* Oxford: Pergamon Press, 1978.

Iyer, Pico. "Trail of Tears and Anguish." *Time,* June 10, 1985, pp. 42-45.

Karaulov, N. A. "Hydropower Resources and Their Use." In *Natural Resources of the Soviet Union: Their Use and Renewal.* Eds. I. P. Gerasimov, D. L. Armand, and K. M. Yefron. Trans. Jacek I. Romanowski. English edition ed. W. A. Douglas Jackson. San Francisco: W. H. Freeman and Co., 1971, pp. 41-52.

Kuznetsov, N. T. and M. I. Lvovich. "Multiple Use and Conservation of Water Resources." In *Natural Resources of the Soviet Union: Their Use and Renewal.* Eds. I. P. Gerasimov, D. L. Armand, and K. M. Yefron. Trans. Jacek I. Pomanowski. English edition ed. W. A. Douglas Jackson. San Francisco: W. H. Freeman and Co., 1971, pp. 11-39.

Miller, E. Willard. *Manufacturing: A Study of Industrial Location.* University Park, Pa.: Pennsylvania State University Press, 1977.

Mohamed, Kamal Ali. "The Projects for the Increase of the Nile Yield with Special Reference to Johglei Project." In *Water Development and Management: Proceedings of the United Nations Water Project.* Vol. 1 (in 4 parts) of *Water Development, Supply and Management.* Series ed. Arit K. Biswas. Oxford: Pergamon Press (for the United Nations), part 4, 1978, pp. 1799-1829.

Murthy, K. S. S. "Interregional Water Transfers: Case Study of India." *Water Supply and Management.* 2(1978), pp. 117-125.

O'Donnell, Charles P. *Bangladesh: Biography of a Muslin Nation.* Boulder: Westview Press, 1984.

Postel, Sandra. "Water: Rethinking Management in an Age of Scarcity." Washington, D.C.: Worldwatch Institutes, 1984.

Simons, Martin. "Long-Term Trends in Water Use." In Richard J. Chorley, ed. *Water, Earth, and Man: A Synthesis of Hydrology, Geomorphology, and Socio-Economic Geography.* London: Methuen and Co., Ltd., 1969, pp. 535-544.

Teclaff, Ludwik A. and Eileen Teclaff. "A History of Water Development and Environmental Quality." In *Environmental Quality and Water Development.* Eds. Charles R. Goldman, James McEvoy III, and Peter J. Richerson. San Francisco: W. H. Freeman and Co., 1973, pp. 26-77.

TVA (Tennessee Valley Authority). "A History of the Tennessee Valley Authority." Knoxville, Tenn.: Tennessee Valley Authority, 1982.

Todd, David Keith, ed. *The Water Encyclopedia.* Port Washington, N.Y.: Water Information Center, 1970.

United Nations Water Conference Secretariat. "Resources and Needs: Assessment of the World Water Situation." In *Water Development and Management: Proceedings of the United Nations Water Conference.* Ed. Asit K. Biswas. Vol. 1 (in four parts) of *Water Development, Supply and Management.* Series ed. Asit K. Biswas. Oxford: Pergamon Press (for the United Nations), 1978, pp. 1-45.

UNECLA (United Nations Economic Commission for Latin America). *Water Management and Environment in Latin America.* Vol. 12 of *Water Development, Supply and Management.* Series ed. Asit K. Biswas. Oxford: Pergamon Press (for the United Nations), 1979.

United States CEQ (Council on Environmental Quality) and Department of State. *The Global 2000 Report to the President: Entering the Twenty-First Century.* Washington: U.S. Government Printing Office, 1980.

Varma, C. V. J. "Efficiency in the Use and Reuse of Water in India." *Water Supply and Management.* 2(1978), pp. 401-423.

Voropaev, G. V. "The Scientific Principles of Large-Scale Areal Redistribution of Water Resources in the USSR." *Water Supply and Management.* 2(1978), pp. 91-101.

Voropaev, G. V. "Socio-Economic Aspects of Water Resources Development in the USSR" (Technical Documents in Hydrology Series). Paris: UNESCO, 1986.

Wiseman, Robin. "Billions Will Still Lack Supply in 1970." *World Water*, 8 (1984), pp. 43-47.

Wittfogel, Karl A. *Oriental Depotism: A Comparative Study of Total Power.* New Haven: Yale University Press, 1957.

Yiqiu, Chen. "Environmental Impact Assessment of China's Water Transfer Project." In *Water Supply and Management.* 5(1981), pp. 253-260.

II. Overview of the role of water in socio-economic development

Any attempt to analyze the role of water in socio-economic development must recognize that the concept of development is not fixed but assumes different meanings at different times and locations. In addition, the individual factors relevant to a particular development process are not independent but interact such that the role of any one factor must be viewed as situationally determined. To provide perspective for consideration of the role of water, this section first examines the meaning of development, including the relative importance of a range of factors. Then the various roles of water are considered, with attention given to possible variations in these roles under alternative circumstances. The section concludes by shifting focus and providing an overview of the impact of socio-economic development on water resources.

1. What is socio-economic development?

The term "socio-economic development" as used in this report refers to general advancement of a given society to a higher level of welfare or well being. Thus the concept of development encompasses all those factors on which welfare depends. While the "economic" part of the term refers to goods and services related to material welfare, the "socio" part of the term includes the full range of socio-cultural characteristics fundamental to welfare.

Attempts to formulate a comprehensive, generally applicable theory of development have had little success. Experience in programs intended to accelerate development in developing nations and lesser developed regions of developed nations has emphasized the complexity of the development process and the uniqueness of individual national and regional situations.

The objectives of development include, at a minimum, a diminution of pain and suffering associated with such factors as inadequate nutrition and health conditions, or a reduction in what has been called "illfare" (Currie, 1967, p. 7). But development objectives generally go beyond bare survival and include other components such as the widespread diffusion of certain goods and services above essential needs and the fulfillment of nonmaterial needs to allow individuals the opportunity for full lives and fulfillment of human potentials. These nonmaterial needs are wide ranging and may include personal liberty, cultural and national identity, national unity, national and personal security,

educational opportunity, and freedom from inequity and dependency (Wilber and Jameson, 1979, pp. 5, 38; Currie, 1967, p. 7). However, views regarding specific objectives to be pursued and their priorities are likely to vary substantially among nations. Consensus on the more fundamental objectives such as adequate nutrition and health standards may be possible, but general agreement with respect to additional objectives is less likely due to their inherent dependency on value judgments.

Since the concept of socio-economic development implies advancement of society on a broad front and includes both material and nonmaterial elements, its scope is more comprehensive than that of economic growth; however, a basic relationship between development and economic growth has been widely recognized. Economic growth traditionally has been seen as the principal means for achieving broad development objectives. In fact, a tendency has existed to view general social progress as an inevitable outcome of an expanding economy (Hunker, 1974, p. 2), and economic growth itself sometimes is viewed as the principal social objective.

Although a positive correlation between economic growth and the broader concept of social development has been widely recognized, acknowledgment has been given to the limitations of such economic indicators as per capita gross national product (GNP) for use as complete measures of socio-economic development (Zukevas, 1979, pp. 14-17; World Bank, 1978, p. 8). A fundamental deficiency of per capita GNP as a measure of welfare is its failure to convey information concerning the types of goods and services produced and, consequently, their impact on welfare. An expenditure to counter the negative aspects of growth such as environmental pollution has the same impact on per capita GNP as does an equivalent expenditure for health, food, or education.

A second weakness of per capita GNP is that it does not reflect distribution of income. Measures based on averages taken over any entire population can obscure the status of individual segments of the population. A rise in per capita GNP may occur while the condition of the poorest segment, which may contain a significant proportion of a population, remains unchanged or even deteriorates.

A third deficiency is the exclusion of goods and services not involving commercial transactions such as self-supplied products. Such transactions can be highly significant, especially in developing countries. The existence of these and other deficiencies indicates the perils of relying on per capita GNP alone as a measure of general socio-economic development.

The fundamental deficiency of the traditional economic indicators as measures of welfare is their inability to reflect a full range of quality-of-life information; thus, several attempts have been made to find other indicators of welfare to provide such information as a supplement or replacement for the traditional measures. Statistics such as life expectancy and literacy rates have been found useful as indicators of social progress. The World Bank (1982, p. 2) has reported that such factors indicate remarkable progress in the developing countries in the past three decades. In other cases, several indicators of social welfare have been combined into single indices of development or quality of life. These comprehensive indices generally show less international inequality than do per capita GNP comparisons (Zuvekas, 1979, p. 24). However, general agreement concerning variables to be included and weights to be assigned does not exist, and other problems such as data inadequacies continue to limit the utility of these approaches.

In spite of the problems associated with measuring welfare, increasing recognition was given during the 1970's to the view that economic growth alone does not always reduce absolute poverty among low income groups at an acceptable rate (World Bank, 1980, p. 32). This view has resulted in emphasis on an approach to development that concentrates directly on the needs of the poor—the "basic needs" approach. This strategy focuses on meeting the minimum needs of all members of a population in essential areas such as nutrition, water supply, sanitation, health, housing, and education (Streeten, 1981). Unlike the traditional approach, the basic needs approach emphasizes direct satisfaction of these needs rather than productivity increases and economic growth as an intermediate means to satisfaction of such needs.

The immediate focus of the basic needs approach differs from that of the economic growth approach to development, but the two approaches are not independent. Proponents of the basic needs approach acknowledge that increasing the productivity and income of the poor is the long range solution to poverty (Streeten, 1981, p. iii). Furthermore, interaction between the two approaches is indicated by the fact that satisfaction of basic consumption needs can itself produce productivity improvements. For example, increases in education and health may have a significant impact on the productivity of those affected. Thus, the choice is not between two exclusive alternatives but instead involves the selection of the desirable mix of the components of the two approaches.

Although continued economic growth generally has been considered central to development, the concept that unlimited economic growth is desirable has been subjected to serious challenge in recent years. A fundamental factor has been the increased recognition that the earth's finite resources cannot indefinitely support continued growth and the associated resource depletion and environmental degradation (Meadows, 1974; Mishan, 1967). This recognition has resulted in greater efforts to control the negative effects of growth and development of a more selective view of what type of growth is desirable, with increased emphasis being placed on the quality-of-life issue (Hamrin, 1980).

But major changes in growth policies have not been adopted uniformly among the nations but have been accepted mainly in the developed countries. Here, a relatively high standard of living has allowed greater attention to increasing adverse effects of growth such as loss of environmental amenities and the dehumanizing aspects of industralized society. The view of the desirability of growth is much different under conditions where even the basic necessities may not be available for much of the population. For example, most delegates from developing nations at the 1977 United Nations Water Conference regarded environmental quality considerations as a secondary issue in relation to development (M. Biswas, 1978, p. 18). Thus, existing inequalities in levels of development among nations is a major factor to be considered in any effort to address the growth issue.

2. Factors in socio-economic development

Although development involves a variety of additional socio-cultural factors, economic growth continues generally to be viewed as a central component of socio-economic development. Therefore, a point of departure for identifying the instrumental factors in socio-economic development consists of the traditional economic inputs to the productive process: natural resources, capital, and human resources. Due to the broader scope of development, however, the range of issues considered must be expanded beyond those traditionally considered in relation to economic growth. This expansion can be accomplished by addition of new factors to the basic list, or, alternatively, by broadening the definitions of the three traditional factors to include the new concerns. In the latter approach, the greatest expansion would be necessary in the human resources category in order to extend consideration to the range of socio-cultural issues that are of fundamental importance in the development process. This is the approach adopted here since the factors underlying economic growth are not isolated phenomena but are closely related to broader socio-cultural factors.

2.1 Natural resources

In order for economic growth and development to be achieved, natural resource inputs must be provided to productive activities producing a range of desirable goods and services. These inputs include such resources as agricultural land, industrial raw materials, power supply, water supply, and a suitable climate and terrain for the activities involved. The existence of certain highly valued resources in abundance can be the predominant factor in the development of a particular nation or region as indicated by the case of the petroleum-producing countries. Furthermore, it would be expected that any nation with a relative abundance of resources would possess a significant development advantage where other factors are equal. Similarly, a scarcity of one or more key resources would constitute a significant relative disadvantage (Zuvekas, 1979, pp. 30-34).

In spite of the potential role of natural resources in growth and development, however, the actual contribution of natural resources is conditional upon several factors. One of the most important determinants is the availability of capital and human resource capabilities for resource utilization. The absence of these complementary factors can produce a situation where abundance of potential resources does not result in substantial development. Another factor tending to reduce the significance of a shortage of natural resources in a particular country is the possibility of international trade to acquire specific resources. A further factor mitigating the significance of resource scarcity is the often substantial potential for substitution of other inputs for the one in short supply. Thus, resource scarcity need not serve as an insurmountable obstacle to development, and several resource-poor nations have achieved high levels of economic growth and development (Zuvekas, 1979, p. 33).

Nevertheless, natural resource deficiencies are a relative disadvantage that may adversely affect development prospects. For example, a nation's shortage of good agricultural land or necessary water for crop production will likely interfere with attainment of self sufficiency in food supply and may contribute to foreign exchange problems. At the least, natural resource deficiencies will require compensatory action in the use of the other factors of production.

2.2 Capital

One of the determinants of the effectiveness with which natural resources are developed is capital investment in the productive processes through which resource development and use take place. Thus, the process of capital formation is a fundamental aspect of the economic growth process. Since capital formation requires sacrifice of current consumption, the process imposes an initial burden on a developing society, especially where levels of income and consumption are very low.

Capital takes a variety of forms extending from facilities and equipment associated with specific productive activities to facilities contributing to a broad spectrum of productive activities simultaneously. This latter form of capital, sometimes referred to as "infrastructure," consists of such facilities as transportation and communication networks, power generation systems, utility services, health and education programs, and water resources development projects. Provision of this form of capital generally has been viewed as the direct responsibility of government, even in nations where capital specific to individual productive activities is subject to private ownership (Zuvekas, 1979, p. 131).

The obvious relationship of capital to the development of natural resources and the productivity of human resources gave rise to the view in the 1940's and 1950's that the shortage of capital was the principal obstacle to economic growth (Zuvekas, 1979, p. 30). During this and the ensuing period, much emphasis was placed on the capital shortage problems of lesser developed regions of developed countries and the developing countries. Attempts to remedy this problem have involved both domestic programs of capital formation and significant international flows of capital funds. A substantial portion of these funds has been invested in elements of infrastructure such as roads and water development projects. While certain beneficial results have been obtained, these efforts often have been disappointing (Currie, 1966, p. 7; Myrdal, 1968, Vol. 2, p. 1284; FAO, 1978, Vol. 1, part 3, p. 924; WHO, 1978, Vol. 1, part 3, p. 980; Widstrand, 1978, p. 279). A primary reason for this disappointment has been the inadequacy of attention to the third factor in growth and development, human resources.

2.3 Human resources and the socio-cultural factor

Increased emphasis has been placed in recent years on the human element in economic growth and development. This additional emphasis is due in part to greater recognition of human development as the direct and immediate objective of socio-economic development. But the shift is also due to recognition that the effectiveness of the other productive factors is determined by the human element and the whole socio-cultural environment within which productive activities take place (Stockwell and Laidlaw, 1981; Wiener, 1972; Myrdal, 1968). When the human element is ignored, potential natural resources can remain latent, and capital can be used ineffectively.

The earlier tendency to neglect the socio-cultural dimension was likely due, in addition to lack of understanding of its significance, to difficulties of incorporating it in economic growth programs and the sensitivity of the issue. Programs to promote economic growth that avoid controversial social issues by focusing solely on investment in physical facilities are simpler to design and may have greater political feasibility even if ultimately ineffective (Myrdal, 1968, Vol. 2, p. 1260). The tendency to avoid the socio-cultural dimension is especially strong in cross-cultural programs due to concern for possible charges of ethnocentricity or imperialism. The danger of cultural bias is always present in such situations since the individual's own cultural background tends to limit objectivity.

In spite of the difficulties involved, however, the socio-cultural dimension cannot be ignored if development is to be enhanced. Inadequate consideration of this factor has been a primary cause of the disappointing results of many development programs. A dynamic, interactive relationship exists between culture and development: culture will influence the development effort and in turn will be affected by the development effort.

Socio-cultural factors will significantly influence the implementation of any development plan. To produce the intended effect, an investment of capital or other development decision must lead to a wide range of complementary decisions by individual citizens, an outcome dependent on the consistency of the initial action with behavioral characteristics as defined by the socio-cultural framework. Culture establishes a range of responses on the basis of cumulative social experience that serves as a limit on individual decision making (White, 1973). Innovative actions are evaluated on the basis of such culturally defined factors as perceptions of effectiveness, desirability in relation to personal habits and tastes, views of social acceptability, and consistency with fundamental values (Ryan, 1969, pp. 213-41). When individual actions needed in association with a particular development decision are inconsistent with these culturally imposed limits, necessary supporting actions are unlikely to be taken, and the success of the development effort itself will be limited.

The interactive nature of culture and development activities creates potential for induced cultural changes whenever development activities are undertaken. The socio-cultural framework is not static but is subject to continual evolution, and development programs can be a major source of change. Socio-cultural change may be an integral aspect of development itself. For example, health improvement is likely to be facilitated by changes in traditional habits regarding personal hygiene and sanitation to supplement other changes of a physical nature such as improvements in water supply facilities (Feachem, 1978, pp. 355-56; Saunders and Warford, 1976, pp. 33-55). Certain types of socio-cultural change that support development appear to occur as a natural consequence of improved living conditions. For example, birth rates generally fall as the standard of living rises (Stockwell and Laidlaw, 1981, pp. 65-107; Zuvekas, 1979, pp. 93-100; World Bank, 1980, pp. 64-70).

Socio-cultural change associated with development can also have undesirable aspects. Review of development efforts indicates examples of negative changes extending from complete disruption of social structures to other less comprehensive socio-cultural impacts (Widstrand, 1978). Although activities causing major socio—cultural disruptions may produce economic growth, such activities are unlikely to constitute development. True development, although likely to produce at least some degree of socio-cultural change, generally must be compatible with basic aspects of the existing socio-cultural framework.

Consideration of the positive and negative aspects of socio-cultural evolution as part of the development process emphasizes the importance of inclusion of socio-cultural factors in development planning. Also stressed is the need to view both the goals and means of development as situationally determined. Development goals and programs must incorporate fundamental values of the affected population and must be established through properly constituted processes for collective decision making by that population. The remainder of this section is devoted to these two issues: the role of values in development and the importance of political mechanisms for making collective decisions regarding value conflict and other aspects of the development process.

2.3(a) The role of values

Evaluating the socio-cultural dimensions of development requires consideration of the role of values. Values are a central component of culture: commonly held values are a basic source of cultural identity and cohesion (Myrdal, 1958, p. 3). Any process of socio-cultural change is intimately associated with value judgments at all points of decision making. In the case of development planning and the design of programs, there has been a tendency for this fact to be ignored in the interests of "scientific" analysis. But the refusal to treat values explicitly leads to implicit value assumptions that may involve the substitution of values not applicable to the socio-cultural environment under consideration.

The most obvious role of values in the development process relates to the determination of development objectives. The ethnocentric tendency may lead an individual to assume that the development objectives of one nation are equally applicable to other nations. This tendency is responsible for the view sometimes held by citizens of the developed countries that the primary objective of the developing countries is to attain the same level of material welfare and other characteristics of the developed countries. But this objective may not be consistent with the values held in certain countries, and other objectives may be more important after some minimum level of material welfare in the form of health, nutrition, and comfort is attained (Shumacher, 1973). Similarly, the choice of a particular environmental quality objective may become largely a value determination beyond minimum standards to protect health and maintain essential ecosystems. Resolution of these and other questions related to selection of objectives cannot be accomplished by resort to scientific analysis independent of value considerations.

In addition to the fundamental role of values in the determination of development objectives, values are a pervasive factor throughout the other aspects of development as well. Another major function relates to selection of means and design of strategies to achieve the objectives chosen. For example, attainment of specified standards of health and nutrition may involve choice between programs of direct provision of food and health care to that part of the population below established standards (the basic needs approach) and programs designed to achieve the desired objectives indirectly by means of increasing average incomes (the economic growth approach). Value judgments, together with other constraints, are an important factor in the decision between alternative means. Adoption of the economic growth strategy implies a willingness to allow continuance of poor health and nutrition among part of the population while necessary investments of capital are made for increasing productivity. Alternatively, selection of the basic needs strategy is a judgement that the condition of the poor is of greater immediate importance than economic growth and its various benefits (Streeten, 1981, p. 38). Values are also important in the design of development programs after an overall strategy is selected. Within an economic development strategy, value determinations are significant in such decisions as the relative attention to be given urban and rural areas in the economic growth process. Within the basic needs strategy, value judgments are central to determinations such as the definition of basic needs. These decisions are also influenced by such factors as limitations of resources, but discretionary decisions within constraints reflect value preferences.

But the role of values extends beyond specification of development objectives and designing strategies for achieving objectives even to include the process of identifying and assessing initial conditions that provide the basis for design of a development program. The process of data collection is generally assumed to be strictly scientific in nature—that is, to consist of the recording of physical facts not subject to value influences. But observation generally is not neutral but instead is affected by prior conceptualizations that serve as a filtering and organizing mechanism. In fact, it has been hypothesized that observation would likely be meaningless outside an organizational framework of preconceptions. Without the order so provided, data would be chaotic (Scheffler, 1967; Myrdal, 1968, Vol. 1, pp. 24-34).

The fact that observation generally is not completely value neutral does not necessarily destroy all potential for objectivity. Observations contrary to preconceptions can be recognized. Science can be seen as a continuing encounter between preconceptions and experience in which each modifies the other. Thus, incorrect preconceptions can be altered by experience rather than remaining static. Of course, the filtering effect of preconceptions tends to resist the acknowledgment of contrary evidence and therefore can result in some degree of systematic distortion in any data collection activity (Scheffler, 1967, pp. 43-44). Expectations can result in failure to see what exists or in "seeing" what does not exist. Open recognition of this defect in the ability of the individual to collect data without the influence of values has been seen as a major defense against associated negative effects on objectivity (Myrdal, 1968, Vol. 1, pp. 32-33).

A major difficulty associated with incorporation of values into development considerations is the existence of multiple value systems within individual societies. Although significant in all nations, this problem reaches its extreme in those countries where a relatively modernized sector exists simultaneously with a large "traditional" sector having substantially different socio-cultural characteristics and different value orientation. Recognition of the need for identifying the range of relevant values, determining priorities, and reconciling conflicts calls attention to the importance of the political component of the socio-cultural framework. This increasingly important component is considered in the next subsection.

2.3(b) The political element

The political element is an especially significant component of the socio-cultural framework since it encompasses the institutional arrangements through which collective decision making is accomplished. The political element is significant to development, both with respect to decisions regarding the internal affairs of an individual nation and also with respect to international relations affecting development.

A wide range of political forms have been developed for purposes of collective decision making and implementation of public programs. These alternative forms of government vary significantly regarding such socio-cultural characteristics as the extent of private property ownership and the form of economic system employed. Examples can be cited indicating significant progress in socio-economic development under a variety of political systems (Gurley, 1979, pp. 214-27), but no particular system appears to guarantee a high rate of development.

The form of government adopted in a particular nation will have significant impacts on water resources management as well as on other natural resource development and economic activity in general. Where economic activity is primarily a function of private enterprise, some water resources development will be accomplished by private firms. Government will be responsible for all such development in those cases where public ownership of productive processes is in effect. In addition, the existence of private property rights in water and other resources is an important institutional factor in water resources development, even where development projects are carried out by governmental entities. Existence of private rights requires that an accommodation be achieved between public and private interests whenever public development activities are undertaken. The existence of private rights therefore creates the need for special institutional mechanisms and can create institutional difficulties not occurring in systems where natural resources are publicly owned.

On the other hand, public ownership and management also create the need for special institutions that may become complex and serve as obstacles to resource management. Financial requirements of public water resources development are also directly affected by political structure. Public expenditures for water rights and other natural resources needed for public projects are necessary only where private property interests exist. The absence of direct expenditure does not, however, mean that such resources are "free" since use for one purpose may displace other uses of those resources, thereby imposing a real cost on society. Thus the ownership issue does not affect the desirability of natural resource development projects although it does have a significant effect on financial considerations.

Regardless of the political system adopted, there appears to be general agreement that government must play a key role in meeting current development needs (Zuvekas, 1979, pp. 182-202; Stockwell and Laidlaw, 1981, pp. 251-96). This role is obvious in political systems where productive processes are publicly owned and in other centrally planned systems, but a significant role for government will also exist in political systems with market economies. Even those nations traditionally advocating limited governmental involvement in economic activities have become increasingly involved in economic affairs through such means as regulation of private enterprise and income redistribution programs (Stockwell and Laidlaw, 1981, p. 253).

A primary development-related role of government in all countries is the provision of infrastructure in the form of essential public facilities and services. Even in those countries where provision of goods and services is primarily a function of private enterprise, many of the components of infrastructure are not likely to be provided through private investment due to such problems as limited marketability of the goods or services involved, the large investments needed, and the long payoff periods involved (Zuvekas, 1979, pp. 132-33). Thus, governments generally will have the responsibility for such investments as construction of roads and major water resource development projects.

In the case of the developing nations, strong central governments appear necessary due to the diversity and magnitude of current problems. Significant development gains in the absence of government-provided stability and direction through planning are unlikely. Economic planning has been seen as especially important in the developing countries due to such problems as defective linkages among individual economic activities.

In addition to the importance of the political element as a factor in resolving a country's internal development problems, a second significant political issue related to development concerns international relations. In the view often referred to as dependency theory, established patterns of world trade and economic activity are seen as the primary constraint on development in many developing countries. In this view, underdevelopment in many nations currently is a direct result of past colonialism and resource exploitation by the developed nations. In addition to the previous social disruption and loss of productive assets, many developing countries are seen as continuing to exist in a state of dependency under the economic domination of the developed countries.

This continuing dependency is seen to result from trade patterns initiated during the colonial period and perpetuated by operations of transnational corporations and direct actions by the developed countries such as restrictions placed on financial aid to developing countries. These trade patterns are seen as exploitive relationships wherein the developing nations continue to supply specialized agricultural products and raw materials to the developed nations while remaining dependent on the developed nations for a wide range of products, including basic foodstuffs. These relationships are seen as destructive of self sufficiency and a major cause of continuing low levels of development (Stockwell and Laidlaw, 1981, pp. 13, 260; Hayter, 1981). This issue has been brought to the forefront of attention by the 1974 adoption of the United Nations General Assembly declaration establishing the New International Economic Order (NIEO). NIEO calls for an international redistribution of wealth and restructuring of the world economic system to reduce the disparity between developed and developing countries.

2.4 Interactions among factors in development

Much effort has been devoted to identification of the predominant factor in development or, alternatively, a singularly important obstacle to development. The view of what constitutes the most significant factor varies with time: for example, physical capital formation has been emphasized in one period, socio-cultural factors in another, and external dependency in a third. But, whatever the prevailing view, there is a basic tendency for attention to be focused on a single factor while all others are relegated to an inferior status.

Although one factor may be predominant in a particular situation, other factors are likely to be operative and a substantial degree of interdependence among factors generally exists. Failure to recognize the multi-faceted, interactive nature of the development process has been a major cause of the disappointing results of many development projects. For example, investment in physical infrastructure facilities such as irrigation works frequently has produced fewer beneficial effects than anticipated due to inadequate attention to socio-cultural dimensions such as institutional infrastructure (FAO, 1978, p. 924). But it is also possible that an approach placing major focus on the human resources factor while neglecting investment in physical capital would produce disappointing development benefits. Similarly, an approach that focuses solely on international relations while neglecting internal obstacles to development may have limited effect. The complexity of the development process suggests that overemphasis on any single factor to the exclusion of others is an oversimplification that overlooks important causative relationships.

2.5 Variation with differing national circumstances

This brief overview of the factors involved in socio-economic development indicates that their relative importance is situationally determined and therefore varies among nations with differing initial conditions and development needs. A major influence regarding the relative standing of the individual factors in a particular country is the current level of development.

Before considering distinctions related to level of development, certain generalizations usually employed in discussions of levels of socio-economic development should be noted. First, this report has adopted the common practice of classifying all nations as either "developed" or "developing." Of course, many different levels exist: the typical approach involves a substantial over-simplification that obscures many distinctions among individual nations. Second, such discussions usually consider each nation to have achieved a single level of development. This approach ignores the multiple levels of development commonly existing among sectors and geographic regions of individual countries. As a result of these factors, a particular "developed" country may have more in common with a "developing" country than the classifications suggest. In spite of its shortcomings, however, the developed-developing categorization is a useful framework for evaluating certain general consequences of existing levels of development on needs and processes relevant to further socio-economic development.

The developed and developing nations exhibit significant differences in each of the three categories of development-related factors considered previously: natural resources, capital, and human resources. In the case of natural resources, many of the developing nations face severe deficiencies relative to most of the developed countries. For example, some have relatively limited supplies of good quality agricultural land in relation to food needs. Another basic resource frequently in scarce supply is water since many of the developing countries are located in relatively arid climates. The previous overview of water supply conditions indicated significant water resource limitations in Asia and Africa, the location of a large proportion of the developing nations. The tropical or semi-tropical location of many of these countries also appears to impose limitations on development. Although the extreme theories of geographical determinism have generally been discredited, problems frequently associated with these areas such as poor soils and the occurrence of a greater range of diseases impose special development problems (Zuvekas, 1979, pp. 30-33).

A relatively low level of capital investment and a limited potential for capital formation generally distinguish the developing from the developed countries. Although substantial industrialization has taken place in several developing countries, general levels of investment in industrial plants remain low, and use of productive technology is limited relative to the developed nations. The low level of capital investment also encompasses basic infrastructure such as transportation, utilities, and water management facilities. The limited potential for capital formation is a direct function of the low productivities and incomes of much of the population of developing countries.

The human resources factor differs substantially between the developed and developing countries in terms of the characteristics of individual citizens and socio-cultural institutions. Characteristics of the individual citizens of developing countries are a function of the low levels of living of much of the population and the associated deficiencies in such areas as education and health. Low income levels result in relatively limited participation in economic processes, a factor constraining the potential for economic growth by holding down the size of markets for products of the economy. Closely associated with low levels of living in the developing countries are birth rates that generally are significantly higher than those in the developed nations. The rate of population growth has been seen by some as the single most important obstacle to development (Currie, 1967, p. 77). In this view, increases in the output of a nation's economy may simply be used to support a larger population at continuing low standards of living.

This view of the population issue is rejected, however, by some who hold that the relationship between population growth and development may be positive rather than negative. Examples exist indicating that rapid population growth has accompanied rapid economic growth in certain developing countries. In addition, economic growth in most of the developed countries has generally been accompanied by population growth although the rate of population increase usually has been less than that occurring in much of the developing world (Birdsall, 1980). Despite these facts, however, a predominance of the evidence appears to indicate a mutually supporting role between rapid population growth and underdevelopment.

Although the view that population growth is the sole cause of underdevelopment oversimplifies the complex nature of development, rapid poplulation growth is likely a major obstacle to development under conditions prevailing in many of the developing nations at present. The net effect of rapid population growth is likely to be negative where food and land for food production is in short supply, where basic health care and other services are inadequate for current populations, where crowding and overall living conditions in urban and other areas prevent suitable socio-cultural conditions from developing, and where subsistence efforts of existing populations are creating serious degradation of the physical environment. Widespread recognition of a negative relationship between population growth and development was indicated recently when the heads of state of a variety of nations signed a document calling for ceasation in population growth in the near future. Signatories represented several of the world's most populous nations, including China, India, Japan, and Bangladesh.

Human resource differences between the developed and developing countries are reflected in socio-cultural institutions. Under conditions currently prevailing in many of the developing countries, socio-cultural institutions generally function less effectively than those of the developed nations. Developing countries span a wide range of political and economic systems, including predominately market systems, centrally planned systems, and mixed systems. The mixed system is common, with elements of the market system existing in combination with substantial amounts of direct governmental involvement in economic activity. But markets in many developing countries function poorly (Zuvekas, 1979, p. 182), and governmental programs are often weakened by ineffective administrative organization and performance. Economic linkages between sectors, and even within sectors, are often weak or nonexistent, with the result that the multiplier effects generally associated with economic activity in the developed nations may not be realized in the developing nations (Wiener, 1972, pp. 136-38; Myrdal, 1968, Vol. 2, p. 1184). This lack of capacity for the economic system to expand and extend the effects of economic activities such as new industrial starts is a major institutional weakness adversely affecting the economic growth of developing nations.

The developing nations also frequently experience special institutional weaknesses that adversely affect attempts to increase agricultural productivity, a key aspect of development. Institutional mechanisms are often inadequate for provision of such services as extension activities for dissemination of information regarding improved farming practices; financial arrangements for acquiring necessary agricultural inputs; and arrangements for transport, storage, and marketing of output. Another class of institutional factors adversely affecting agricultural productivity in many developing countries consists of property-rights systems for land and water. Associated problems can take various forms. For example, land may be subdivided into units too small for productive agricultural operations, or prevailing tenancy arrangements may limit productivity increases due to lack of adequate incentives for farmers to adopt new practices (Zuvekas, 1979, pp. 203-41).

Differences in initial conditions between the developed and developing nations also include international relations. In the dependency-theory view, this factor is the primary obstacle to development. Even without accepting this theory entirely, it is apparent that the developing countries face conditions different from those of earlier periods of national development. Many of the developing nations lack economic self-sufficiency and are substantially influenced by fluctuations in world economic conditions due to dependence on world trade. Established patterns of trade and market restrictions result in less flexibility than existed in the earlier period, thereby imposing additional impediments on the development process (Stockwell and Laidlaw, 1981, pp. 256-61).

The existence of fundamental differences in initial conditions between the developed and developing countries gives the development concept different meaning in the two situations. This difference is reflected in the role of economic growth in the development process. In the developed countries, the current existence of a relatively high level of material welfare has resulted in increased attention to other dimensions of welfare, and significant constraints have been placed on economic growth (or are being considered) to further other social objectives such as maintenance of environmental quality (Hamrin, 1980). Although currently in a minority position, some have questioned the desirability of continued economic growth (Mishan, 1967; Schumacher, 1973). Due to existing lower levels of living, the need for economic growth is less subject to question in the developing nations. Substantial expansion of economic activity is generally seen as an essential component of the effort to raise levels of living and solve a wide range of socio-economic problems (M. Biswas, 1978, p. 18).

Differences in initial conditions also may have implications for the choice of technology to be applied in achieving development objectives. Experience has shown that the transfer of advanced technology from developed to developing countries often has not produced the desired results, and in some cases has produced unintended adverse effects, due to the inappropriateness of the technology to conditions in the developing country. To be appropriate, technology must be physically suitable for environmental conditions to be encountered and must be compatible with the maintenance abilities of the people involved.

Technological appropriateness must also include the socio-cultural characteristics of the intended users. Technology chosen without regard to such characteristics may be rejected by the potential users although functionally capable of performing its planned purpose (ITDGL, 1978, pp. 1105-62). These limitations on technology transfer do not, however, imply that the skills and socio-cultural characteristics of the affected population should be viewed as static. On the contrary, these factors are dynamic and must constitute another dimension to be addressed during the technology transfer process. Education and training programs are central to the success of such transfer and must be considered in defining the scope of appropriate technology.

A somewhat controversial aspect of the appropriate-technology issue concerns the relative proportions of capital and labor to be used in development projects. Since capital usually is scarce in developing countries while labor often is relatively abundant, use of labor intensive rather than capital intensive strategies may be desirable in some situations. Indiscriminant adoption of capital-intensive technology can create or increase problems of employment. However, labor intensive methods are not automatically preferable in developing countries since they impose special management requirements and may not be economically competitive in some situations. Furthermore, use of labor intensive technology rather than advanced technology may be adverse to basic development objectives such as enhancement of national self sufficiency. Choice of technology must be compatible with strategic national goals and not just the requirements of economic efficiency in relation to particular development projects.

Differences in existing conditions generally require development programs in developing countries to have broader scope than would be necessary under conditions existing in a developed country. To expand a statement by Myrdal (1968, Vol. 2, p. 728) in his classic work on South Asia, "very little takes care of itself" in the developing countries. For example, a development effort limited to construction of physical facilities is likely to fail to achieve anticipated increases in production due to failure of socio-economic institutions to provide necessary complementary inputs and actions. The existence of such weaknesses in socio-economic processes means that development programs cannot be limited to capital investment in physical projects but must involve a comprehensive approach addressing all inputs necessary to achieve the desired objective, including institutional and other socio-cultural factors (Wiener, 1972, pp. 136-38).

3. Current roles of water in socio-economic development

The foregoing overview of the various factors related to socio-economic development provides perspective for analyzing the roles of water in the development process. To some extent, water is a unique resource due to its biological functions and the fact that some water is required for essentially all development activities; the total absence of water would constitute an absolute impediment to development. But many applications of water are not based solely on absolute needs. Above some minimum requirement for domestic needs of workers and certain other essential uses, the amount of water used in many productive activities is a somewhat discretionary decision. As in the case of other inputs, an important consideration is the possible substitution of other inputs in response to relative costs. There are limits to substitution in activities such as agriculture, but substantial flexibility exists even here.

Another conclusion arising from general consideration of the factors in socio-economic development is that the role of water cannot be isolated and defined independently of other development factors. Water's role in development generally is closely associated with the roles of complementary factors, and the existence of favorable water resource conditions without the availability of complementary development factors may not be sufficient in itself to ensure development. For example, provision of irrigation water through construction of necessary facilities may fail to produce anticipated increases in crop production without corresponding attention to socio-cultural factors related to adoption of necessary changes in farming practices.

The specific roles of water in development vary among individual development situations. One determinant consists of initial resource endowments and other natural conditions of the country involved. For example, the extent to which water contributes to development through the irrigation process will vary as conditions of natural rainfall vary. Similarly, the significance of a negative role, such as contributions to the spread of disease, varies with the status of climatic and other factors related to the occurrence of the disease. The existing level of development will also influence the role of water. Expansion of agricultural and industrial water supply would be expected to receive relatively more emphasis in a developing nation while preservation of natural water environments may receive relatively greater attention in a nation having already achieved a relatively high level of material welfare. In addition to reliance on these tangible factors, the role of water will also depend on the range of value judgments regarding development objectives and strategies made through the applicable political processes. The role of water will be different, for example, in a basic needs strategy relative to a strategy for maximizing economic growth. In the former case, emphasis may be placed on improvement in the water supplies of rural communities while development of industrial water supply and hydropower may receive priority in the latter.

Although the specific roles of water in the development process are situationally determined for each nation on the basis of such factors as resource endowments and value judgments, history provides a basis for delineating a wide range of individual roles that potentially may be important to the development of a particular country. In an attempt to provide an overview, the following sections consider these hypothetical roles and relationships within four categories: (1) positive roles of water, (2) negative roles of water, (3) adverse effects of water resources development, and (4) adverse effects of socio-economic development on water.

3.1 Positive roles of water

To facilitate discussion, this category will be further subdivided into three classes: (1) water as a domestic commodity, (2) water as an input to productive processes, and (3) water as an element of psychological welfare. The first category includes domestic applications where water is a final consumer good, with drinking water supply the most important use. The second category consists of the various functions of water in relation to productive activities that produce goods and services of value to man. The third category encompasses amenity values provided by water that contribute to psychological welfare. Boundaries between these categories must be somewhat arbitrary. For example, domestic water supply facilities, in addition to providing a direct commodity, also frequently contribute to productive activities by serving as a component of socio-economic infrastructure. Nevertheless, the classification provides a useful framework for discussion although some overlap among categories exists.

3.1(a) Water as a domestic commodity

The most fundamental role of water in socio-economic development is its use for domestic purposes. Use for drinking, personal hygiene, and other domestic purposes constitutes a primary component of welfare that is inadequately provided in much of the developing world (Biswas (2), 1978, p. xiv). Improvement in water supply conditions is seen by some as the most important individual factor in controlling disease and improving living conditions, especially in the developing countries where the greatest portion of the population without adequate supplies lives (WHO, 1978, p. 972). The goal of the International Drinking Water Supply and Sanitation Decade, covering the 1981-1990 period, is to make safe water and sewage disposal available to as many people as possible.

Health benefits from improved water supply occur in several forms. The most direct occurs when safe water is substituted for a contaminated supply, thereby eliminating the ingestion of infective agents associated with waterborne diseases or other harmful pollutants. Availability of a greater quantity of water can improve health by allowing improved personal hygiene and general sanitation. A more convenient collection point can reduce exposure to disease through elimination of the need for contact with natural bodies of water containing parasitic organisms or supporting mosquito or other disease-spreading insect populations (Saunders and Warford, 1976, pp. 31-55).

Although some have concluded that improved water supply is the single most important factor in reducing disease, such improvement may not be a sufficient condition to significantly improve health in the absence of other actions. Health is a function of numerous environmental and cultural factors such as nutrition, human waste disposal, and personal hygiene. Due to complex causal relationships and interactions among these factors, prediction of the specific health gains likely to be achieved through a particular water supply improvement is difficult. The extent of health benefits is therefore likely to be increased when water supply improvements are combined with other programs, including public education designed to modify behavior in such areas as hygiene (Feachem, 1978, pp. 355-56; Saunders and Warford, 1976, pp. 33-55).

Although the provision of water supply to prevent disease and provide other benefits must be a component of any development program, the type of service provided will vary among individual situations. In developed countries, the accepted standard of service is an individual supply for each residence of water in essentially unlimited quantity, with a high level of quality and reliability. Considering limitations of resources, this standard is not universally appropriate within the developing countries. Application of such a standard would result in a high level of service for a few and no service for many. A more appropriate standard may be the extension of an acceptable minimum level of service to the greatest number. Such minimum service is not likely to involve individual connections in all cases but likely would be limited to common supply points within reasonable distance of all users.

Determination of the minimum level of service to be provided involves several factors. While the amount of water needed daily for human consumption is only a few liters per person, additional water for personal hygiene is important in the control of certain diseases. For some diseases, availability of water in adequate quantity apparently is more important than water quality. A ten-year study in Singapore concluded that a daily supply of 90 liters for each person was a minimum amount for control of diseases associated with water (Biswas (2), 1978, p. xv). Quantities of water for domestic use depend significantly on whether water-carried methods of domestic waste disposal are employed. In addition to expanding water needs, water-carried methods also create the need for wastewater treatment facilities to prevent possible health problems and environmental degradation.

Related to the question of minimum level of service to be provided is the more general issue of appropriate technology in the provision of domestic water supply. Many village water systems have fallen into disuse (WHO, 1978, p. 980), generally due to lack of compatibility with local needs and conditions. Since domestic water use is closely related to many other activities that form daily behavior patterns, water supply facilities must be compatible with values and traditions in order to be accepted and maintained. Maintenance must be considered during system design if water supply facilities are to function as a long range improvement. Adoption of equipment that cannot be serviced and repaired locally assures short-lived usefulness (ITDGL, 1978, pp. 1105-62).

Although domestic water supply serves as a basic component of welfare in its role as a direct consumer commodity, it also functions as an element of socio-economic infrastructure. Existence of an adequate domestic water supply is a factor in community stability that can affect the success of many of the other components of development. This dependence on water supply includes large urbanized areas and rural communities as well. The capability of a city to support its population and economic activity is related to adequacy of water supply. In rural areas, the success of agricultural and other projects is related to the existence of an adequate domestic water supply for the workers involved. The success of these economic activities depends on a variety of other factors as well, but water supply inadequacy can be a significant constraint.

3.1(b) Water as an input to productive processes

The role of water as an input to productive processes has a variety of dimensions since most productive activities involve water use. At a fundamental level, water contributes to a wide variety of natural productive processes. Water also plays a role in most of man's productive processes, including directly productive activities such as food production and manufacturing operations and as an element of basic economic infrastructure. This infrastructure role, in addition to including public water supply as considered previously, also encompasses such functions as power supply and transportation.

Natural productive processes

Water functions as part of the ecosystem to provide a wide range of beneficial services without the intervention of man. While many of these services take the form of intangible amenity values (to be considered later), significant tangible benefits are also provided. The tangible benefits primarily occur as fish, wildlife, and natural plants that provide useful products and services.

Fisheries provide an example. Fishing activities contribute to human welfare in several ways, most directly by providing a source of food. Although fish provide only about one percent of the world's total food energy and about 11 percent of all animal protein, the importance is much greater in some nations and regions. For example, 25 percent of the animal protein in Africa comes from fish, with the proportion exceeding 70 percent in some regions. While only ten to 15 percent of the total world catch is from freshwater, the freshwater catch constitutes an important source of food in some areas (Norse, 1979, pp. 32-24). In addition to fishing as a source of food, recreational fishing is a major activity at some locations. In addition to the direct welfare aspects of recreation, substantial economic activity is generated for suppliers of associated goods and services.

Although fisheries are an important natural productive process in many countries, both food and recreational fishing are subject to enhancement by management programs. Enhancement within relatively natural ecosystems may include such practices as maintenance of more desirable water temperatures through controlled reservoir releases and artificial propagation for release in natural water bodies. Aquaculture within controlled environments offers potential for increasing food output and has been identified as an activity that should be expanded in developing nations (FAO, 1978, pp. 920-22). However, unintentional disruption of fisheries and other natural productive processes can also result from development activities. A primary concern relative to these processes therefore is proper consideration in development planning to avoid unnecessary disruption.

Agricultural production

Increase in food supply is a primary socio-economic development objective since adequate nutrition is a basic element of welfare that currently is not available to a portion of the world's population. Increases in production in recent years have resulted in large surpluses of agricultural commodities in a variety of nations, but malnutrition continues as a major problem in other nations. Per capita food production in certain developing countries has decreased in recent years, often as a result of rapid population growth but in some cases because of actual decreases in production (Picard, 1986). The most severe cases of hunger have involved weather-related crop failures such as those occurring in the Sahel region of Africa. Better distribution of food commodities has potential to significantly reduce hunger, but increased production within areas of shortage will be necessary because of such factors as national desires for food self-sufficiency and obstacles to trade among nations.

Increased agricultural production within developing nations has potential to contribute to development in ways beyond the reduction of hunger due to the major role of the agricultural sector in the economies of many developing nations. Approximately two-thirds of the people in the developing world draw their livelihood from agriculture (World Bank, 1982, p. 90). In addition, there are many linkages between agriculture and the rest of a nation's economy (Zuvekas, 1979, pp. 203-241). Included are such diverse interrelations as linkages with suppliers of agricultural inputs and processers of agricultural products and creation of demand for manufactured products within the rural population. The history of many nations indicates that growth in agriculture usually parallels industrialization and general economic growth (World Bank, 1982, pp. 39-45; Biswas, 1979, p. 245). Thus, agricultural growth must be viewed as a key developmental objective.

Improvement and expansion of irrigation are generally seen as essential to increasing agricultural production (FAO, 1978; Falkenmark and Lindh, 1976, p. 27). Although other factors such as development of improved crop varieties have also contributed, much of the increase in agricultural output during the past

20 years is attributable to new or rehabilitated irrigation areas (World Bank, 1982, p. 62).

Irrigation can increase agricultural output in several ways. A primary means is by increasing crop yields from presently cultivated lands. Although the extent of increase in any particular case depends on several factors, yields from irrigated lands can be substantially higher than those from similar lands under dryland farming (Frederick, 1982, p. 27; UNECWA, 1980, p. 3). The relationship between water supply and crop yield is most obvious in arid or semi-arid areas, but irrigation can increase yields even in relatively humid climates. Brief periods of drought can inflict significant losses in crop production when they occur during certain stages of plant growth, creating a potential situation for beneficial use of supplemental irrigation (Raney, 1967). Expansion of agricultural productivity through such actions as increased use of fertilizers and improved seed varieties may be constrained by inadequate moisture. Thus, irrigation may be necessary to realize the potential benefits associated with these factors (Falkenmark and Lindh, 1976, p. 60). Irrigation can increase agricultural output in some areas by allowing multiple-cropping of lands now producing but one crop per year due to seasonal variations in precipitation, with one or more extended dry periods during the typical year. Where other climatic conditions are favorable, irrigation may remove this limitation on cropping and thereby substantially increase output (Norse, 1979, pp. 26-28).

A second basic means for irrigation to increase agricultural output is through expansion of the agricultural land base by permitting cultivation of arid and semi-arid areas not otherwise available. Substantial quantities of unused arable land exist where inadequate precipitation is the primary limitation on agriculture (World Bank, 1982, p. 59). However, not all of this unused land can be irrigated and cultivated due to lack of adequate irrigation water supplies or other constraints. Substantial amounts of unused arable land are not available in some nations or regions such as South Asia where cultivated areas are near their potential limits (World Bank, 1978, p. 38). In such areas, increased output must be achieved through increased productivity of existing cultivated lands.

In addition to the increased agricultural production from extension of irrigation to presently non-irrigated lands, improvement of existing irrigation operations is also a major potential means of increasing agricultural output. This potential results from the low levels of efficiency with which many existing irrigation projects are operated. Rehabilitation of existing projects may have a lower cost than development of new irrigation schemes (UNECWA, 1980, p. 16). A frequent problem with existing irrigation operations is lack of adequate drainage facilities (Donnan and Houston, 1967). Waterlogging and soil salinity problems associated with water management are significant limitations on agricultural productivity in many irrigated areas (FAO, 1978, pp. 913-14; Kovda, 1977). These considerations must be a central aspect of rehabilitation efforts and new irrigation programs.

21

Irrigation projects have produced mixed results, especially in developing countries (Zuvekas, 1979, p. 217; FAO, 1978, p. 924; Yotopoulos, 1980), indicating that investment in facilities does not guarantee achievement of desired improvements in agricultural output. A major reason for the disappointing results achieved by many projects has been lack of proper attention to the full range of interdependent factors affecting agricultural operations. Major problem areas have included inadequacies in irrigation project operation and maintenance; on-farm water management; farmer education; availability and financing of other inputs such as proper seed varieties and fertilizers; and transporting, storing, and marketing of agricultural output (Darnell, 1975; Economides, 1980). The failure of many irrigation projects to achieve intended objectives due to this range of problems emphasizes the importance of a comprehensive approach encompassing all the factors affecting agricultural production.

Although water can be the limiting factor without which other improvements will have little effect on agricultural output, the fundamental nature of water in agriculture does not imply complete lack of flexibility regarding quantities needed. In fact, determination of future irrigation water needs by extrapolation of historical experience is likely to overstate needed supplies due to widespread inefficiencies in water use (United Nations Water Conference Secretariat, 1978, p. 58). However, reduction of amounts of water used generally involve substitution of other inputs such as capital and managerial skills that may themselves be scarce, and minimum crop requirements are substantial in some cases. Relatively large quantities of water therefore may remain necessary, and water costs are likely to be a substantial portion of total production costs. This significance of water as a factor of production indicates the prominent role that irrigation must play in expansion of agricultural output.

Industrial production

Since industrialization is a principal mechanism of increasing the output of goods and services, factors relevant to industrialization are of special importance in development programs. Water is necessary for essentially all industrial activity, if only for the domestic needs of employees. Other applications are also common, including use as a raw material, for various transport and process purposes, and cooling. Due to these various functions, many industrial products traditionally have involved use of prodigious quantities of water for each unit of output (Linsley and Franzini, 1979, p. 407). Although generally not highly consumptive, industrial water use accounts for a significant percentage of water withdrawals in the developed countries. For example, 58 percent of all water withdrawn for offstream use in the United States during 1980 was for industrial use, with cooling at thermoelectric power installations the primary industrial use. Approximately four percent of all water withdrawn for self-supplied industrial use was consumed (Solley, Chase, and Mann, 1983, p. 23).

The large magnitude of industrial withdrawals in the developed countries suggests the need for large supplies of water as a necessary condition for industrialization in the developing countries. However, this assumption must be viewed with caution. While industrial operations generally will be precluded by the total absence of water, the definition of essential minimum supplies is difficult due to the flexibility that many industries possess to alter the amount of water used through process modifications and water reuse. Due to this flexibility, large variations in water withdrawals often exist among industries producing the same product (United Nations Water Conference Secretariat, 1978, p. 54). Minimum with-drawals are attained through use of complete recycling of cooling and process waters. Although complete elimination of withdrawals is not possible due to water consumption during use, withdrawals after adoption of recycling in many cases are a small proportion of withdrawals necessary without recycling (Goodman, 1984, p. 91). A tendency toward recycling, often encouraged by increasingly restrictive control over wastewater discharge, has been reflected in decreases in industrial water withdrawals in several countries (Parsons, 1978).

These considerations indicate that, while water supply is an essential industrial input, the assumption that industrial development requires the amounts of water historically used may not be warranted. Historical water-use data are especially likely to overstate essential requirements where it is derived from water-abundant locations or from other situations where institutions have allowed industry to view water as a free resource to be used without consideration of displaced uses. Evaluation of industrial water demand therefore must consider the potential reductions in use that physical water scarcity and/or higher water supply costs may encourage. Realization of these potential reductions may be limited by associated costs, however. Water reuse schemes or other special processes for reducing water demand generally involve additional capital investment. If capital is scarce, achieving potential reductions in water use may impose a burden on the industrialization process.

Electric power production

Electricity is an important input into most productive activities as well as a direct component of human welfare when used as a consumer good. Inadequate supply can serve as a significant obstacle to achieving industrialization, expansion in agricultural output, and other basic development objectives. The role of water in power production is most direct in hydroelectric power generation. Hydropower has declined as a proportion of total power produced in many countries, but increases in the costs of other sources of energy may tend to reduce or reverse this trend. Due to the ease with which the rate of electricity generation can be varied at hydropower facilities, this source remains significant in meeting demand during peak periods of electricity use, even in areas where other sources of power satisfy most of the base demand. Undeveloped hydropower with potential for use to meet either base or peak power needs is a significant potential resource in certain countries, especially some of the African nations (Pluzhnikov, 1978; United Nations Water Conference Secretariat, 1978, pp. 59-61).

Water also plays a significant role in steam-electric generation, primarily as a cooling medium. Cooling is a major purpose of water withdrawal in many developed countries. As in the case of other industrial water uses, quantities of water needed for cooling purposes can be dramatically reduced by recycling, a change involving substitution of other inputs, primarily capital investment, for the large quantities of water traditionally used (United Nations Water Conference Secretariat, 1978, p. 52).

Waterborne transportation

Transportation systems are a major component of economic infrastructure with potential to affect economic activities within individual nations and among nations. Transportation costs traditionally have been a significant component of total costs in many economic activities. These costs historically have declined in their relative importance due to such factors as improvement of transportation technology, greater efficiency in the use of material inputs that reduce the quantities of materials needed, increased substitution among material inputs, and growth in light industry (Norcliffe, 1975, pp. 20-24). Regardless of this trend, transportation costs continue to affect all industries, some to a significant extent.

Due primarily to major improvements in alternative transportation modes, waterborne transportation has declined in relative importance but still plays an important role. Marine navigation continues to provide the principal form of transporting raw materials and products in international commerce. Inland navigation continues to play an important although selective role in international and national transportation systems, especially in the case of major river systems such as the Rhine, Seine, Danube, Elbe, Nile, Volga-Don, Ganges-Brahmaputra, and Mississippi. Inland navigation remains the predominant form of transportation in some geographical areas. For example, river navigation accounts for as much as 70 to 80 percent of goods transported in certain remote northern regions of the Soviet Union (Voropaev, 1986, p. 25). In general, however, inland navigation currently accounts for a relatively small portion of total transport of raw materials and products. Transport on inland waterways is largely oriented toward commodities such as minerals and grains susceptible to bulk handling techniques and liquids suitable for tanker shipment (Ben-Zvi, 1981, pp. 27-28). Water also contributes to transportation through use as a suspension medium for transport of certain solids by pipelines.

Waste disposal

A further traditional role of water in support of productive processes has been the provision of waste disposal services. Since many water-using activities historically have been based on a flow-through approach in which water is discharged after a single passage through an industrial or other process, large quantities of wastewater have resulted from growth in population and economic activity. Use of natural bodies of water for discharge of wastewater has been accepted as a valid use of the water resource during much of history. Natural water bodies serve to dilute wastewater and, in the case of some contaminants, provide natural treatment through such processes as decomposition of organic substances. But increasing volumes of wastewater and development and use of chemical substances not subject to natural decomposition have resulted in major water quality problems that endanger human health, adversely affect aquatic organisms, and displace other water uses. The significance of this problem has resulted in actions in many countries to limit waste discharge to an extent necessary to reduce adverse effects to acceptable levels. Such programs have created the incentive for increased recycling of industrial process and cooling waters, a development that has substantially reduced water withdrawals in some countries.

The extent to which limits are imposed on use of natural waters for waste disposal purposes is likely to vary between developed and developing countries. In developing countries, environmental protection may be seen to be in conflict with the primary objective of improving living conditions for those experiencing nutrition, health, and other deficiencies associated with poverty. In this situation, restrictions on waste discharge may be viewed as an undesirable restraint on economic growth and general socio-economic development. However, water quality controls cannot be viewed strictly as a concern for the developed nations. Contamination can threaten health in developing and developed countries alike, and environmental degradation is adverse to many long-range development objectives in all nations. Thus, it is likely that controls over waste disposal and other forms of environmental degration will receive higher priority as any nation moves toward higher levels of development.

3.1(c) Water as an element of psychological welfare

Beyond its utilitarian functions as a commodity and an input to productive activities, water's beneficial roles also include intangible contributions to welfare. These intangible contributions may take the form of satisfaction of spiritual needs as in the case of religiously significant waters or through the provision of amenity values that add to psychological welfare.

A wide range of amenity values are associated with water in its natural state, and these values can serve as the basis of substantial opposition to water resources development projects that involve alteration of natural water bodies. In addition, amenity values arise in connection with manmade water bodies such as reservoirs. Whether intentionally developed for amenity value (as in the case of lakes within parks and recreational areas) or for other purposes, manmade lakes generally possess significant amenity value that can become a factor in economic growth and development of the surrounding area. These values can serve as the basis for development of a recreation and tourist industry, attract permanent residential development, and become a factor in industrial location decisions. The fact that amenity values can be significant with respect to both natural and developed water conditions indicates that water project construction will have both positive and negative effects on amenity values, although not necessarily of the same magnitude.

3.2 Negative roles of water under natural conditions

Water, as it naturally occurs and moves through the phases of the hydrologic cycle, has the potential to constrain socio-economic development in several ways. Significant constraints arise from natural fluctuations in water availability. First, naturally occurring periods of shortage can disrupt normal water-using activities. Second, periods of excess may lead to flooding and the disruptions associated with such events. A third constraint consists of the occurrence of water under conditions of poor drainage such that productive land use is restricted or prevented. A fourth constraint consists of water's role in disease transmission, a function that diminishes human welfare and can retard or prevent settlement of certain geographic regions.

3.2(a) Shortages caused by natural fluctuations in supply

The fact that water supply naturally occurs in a non-uniform pattern encompassing periods when supplies may be much below average substantially reduces the utility of the resource. Since most socio-economic activities require a supply of high dependability, only a relatively small portion of the total resource from a source such as a stream may be available for continuous use under natural conditions. As water use increases as a percentage of average flow, the frequency of the occurrence of shortages and associated disruptions increases until dependability becomes unacceptably low.

One of the basic objectives of water development projects traditionally has been to extend the utility of water supplies by increasing water availability during low flow periods, primarily by means of storing water during periods of excess flow in artificial impoundments. Such modification of flow characteristics increases the level of dependability of the supply involved since it increases the amount of time that a specified minimum flow rate can be expected to be available.

Programs for management of water supply shortages increasingly include controls on water demand to supplement efforts to expand dependable supply. Development of demand reduction strategies for temporary application during periods of water shortage can minimize disruptions resulting from shortage and thereby create potential for avoiding or postponing expansions in water supply facilities.

3.2(b) Flooding

Flooding is one of the major natural disasters affecting man. The adverse effects of flooding on human welfare occur in a variety of forms ranging from direct impacts such as loss of life and psychological costs associated with related fear and uncertainty to a variety of less direct but important socio-economic disruptions. Loss of life and property occur in catastrophic magnitude in relatively infrequent flood events but also occur on essentially a continuous basis as a result of more frequently occurring, smaller flood events.

Next to loss of life, the most significant impact of flooding is damage to property, including residential structures and personal belongings, productive facilities such as industrial establishments, agricultural lands and crops, and elements of infrastructure such as roads and communication networks. Economic output is also reduced due to resulting disruptions in productive activities. Such property and production losses are a burden on any nation, but the impact of such losses are likely to be greater in developing nations due to such factors as the greater number of people living near subsistence levels and lack of adequate programs and resources for relief activities.

A broad range of responses to flooding is possible, but certain approaches have seen more use than others. Modification of hydrologic processes to reduce flooding traditionally has received emphasis in many countries. This approach includes a variety of structural measures such as construction of impoundments to store floodwaters, channel improvements and levees to contain floodwaters, and various land treatment measures to reduce runoff. Programs of relief and rehabilitation for victims of flooding have usually accompanied structural control measures.

An attempt has been made in some countries to supplement these traditional measures with programs to modify behavior and susceptibility to flooding damage. Included have been land-use controls to prohibit or restrict use of flood-prone lands, floodproofing programs for reduction of the damage potential of structures located in flood-prone areas, and improved emergency warning systems to provide opportunities for evacuation or other protective actions. Flood insurance programs have been developed for financing flood losses. Not all of these potential measures will be feasible in every case. For example, the usefulness of prohibitions against development of flood-prone lands may be limited if most land suitable for development is subject to flooding. The appropriate mix of alternative measures in response to a particular flooding problem will depend on the circumstances of the individual situation (White, 1969, pp. 47-55).

3.2(c) Inadequate natural drainage

Excess water can serve as an obstacle to development by limiting necessary land-use activities. Excess water problems can range from a relatively permanent state where lands are covered or saturated with water during much of the year to situations involving runoff-related problems during brief periods following precipitation.

The short-lived runoff problem is of major concern where intensive land use is involved due to potential water-related damage to property. Thus stormwater management must be viewed as a basic component of urban development.

Relatively permanent conditions of excess water hinder use of land for most development purposes. While such lands may serve important functions as components of natural ecosystems, they generally must be artifically drained before being suitable for direct use by man. Development of land for agricultural use has constituted a major purpose of drainage. Excess water adversely affects crop production in several ways, including interference with needed air circulation in the soil, encouragement of certain diseases and parasites, creation of salt and alkali problems, and hindrance of farm operations. Agricultural land drainage has been conducted on a large scale in many countries (Falkenmark and Lindh, 1976, p. 49; Voropaev, 1986, p. 21). Agricultural drainage has been identified as an important water management need for increasing crop yields in certain developing regions (FAO, 1978, p. 914).

3.2(d) Transmission of disease

Previous attention has been given to the positive role of domestic water supply in preventing disease when provided in proper quality and adequate quantity for personal hygiene, but water's role in disease transmission can take several forms. White, Bradley, and White (1972, p. 163) have presented a classification of infective diseases associated with water containing four categories: (1) waterborne, consisting of diseases caused by ingestion of bacteria or other infective organisms carried by water (typhoid, cholera); (2) water-washed diseases, consisting of hygiene-related diseases associated with inadequate quantities of water (gastro-intestinal diseases, skin diseases); (3) water-based diseases, consisting of parasitic diseases involving aquatic organisms as part of the life cycle of the parasite (schistosomiasis); and (4) diseases associated with water-related insect vectors, consisting of diseases transmitted by insects that breed in water or prefer habitat near water (malaria, filariasis, onchocerciasis, Gambian sleeping sickness).

These contributions to the spread of disease can provide a major negative impact on human welfare and on socio-economic development. In addition to the direct impact in the form of loss of life and suffering, disease has an economic effect in the form of resulting production losses. In extreme cases, the threat of disease may prevent use of geographic regions otherwise suitable for agriculture or other productive activities related to the development process.

3.3 Contributions of water resources development

Consideration of the positive and negative roles of water in socio-economic development suggests a wide range of potential contributions of water resources development activities. Many of the positive attributes of the resource summarized above can be enhanced by alteration of natural conditions; some potential benefits may not be realized at all without development actions. In addition, most of the negative roles of water are amenable to reduction or elimination under certain conditions. Thus water development activities have potential to contribute to a variety of aspects of socio-economic development.

But the benefits of water resources development are not limited to those associated with narrowly defined water-use activities contributing to specific aspects of socio-economic development. This section considers two broader issues associated with water resources development: (1) the concept of integrated water resources development and (2) the role of water resources development as a mechanism to stimulate general economic growth of communities and/or geographic regions.

3.3(a) Integrated water resources development

The concept of water resources development has expanded as demands on water resources and technological capabilities have grown. Through much of history, the scope of water resources development was relatively narrow. A primary indication of this limited scope was the tendency of development projects to focus on individual water-use activities. This single-purpose development strategy traditionally has been followed for development undertaken by private parties or by local governments for such purposes as domestic water supply. This approach is generally dictated by the relatively narrow range of needs and water development capabilities of these parties, particularly where individuals are involved. But at an earlier period in history, the single purpose approach was a common water development strategy by national governments as well for such projects as navigation improvements or provision of irrigation water (White, 1969).

A major step toward a more comprehensive approach was the adoption of the multiple-purpose development strategy addressing two or more water management needs in a coordinated fashion. An important factor in the adoption of this approach was the advancement of technology in related areas of construction. For example, development of capability to build large dams has made possible the use of single large-scale projects to replace several smaller, single-purpose structures in many cases. Multiple-purpose construction creates the potential for economies of scale and complementarities among purposes not possible in the single purpose approach (Voropaev, 1986; White, 1969; Weber and Hufschmidt, 1962; White, 1957). However, the multiple-purpose approach tends to involve large projects, and significant opposition to such undertakings has developed in recent years due to such factors as concern for potential environmental impacts (Shumacher, 1973; Sale, 1980). Thus, the multiple-purpose concept, while offering substantial potential to enhance the benefits of water resources development, must now be evaluated in relation to these broader and somewhat contradictory considerations.

In addition to the multiple-purpose project concept, another aspect of the integrated development approach is coordinated management of water resources within a basin-wide framework (Wengert, 1981; White, 1969). Basin-wide management allows consideration of physical interactions within hydrologic systems, including the design and operation of individual water projects as components of systems such that total benefits exceed those attainable by independent projects. Advances in analytical capabilities for optimizing system operation under a variety of operational objectives and constraints have facilitated the integrated approach, both with respect to obtaining greater benefits from operation of individual multiple-purpose projects and coordinated operation of multiple projects.

The focus on basin-wide water development has drawn attention to the basin as a physiographic unit for water planning and management, sometimes including the creation of special basin-oriented institutional entities such as river basin authorities. The extent to which water management responsibilities have been successfully consolidated within river basins has varied substantially among nations and even among regions within nations. Institutional design is dependent on many factors, some of which may conflict with the basin approach. For example, institutions reflecting divisions of responsibility among economic sectors may be incompatible with the consolidated basin approach. Other factors affecting the feasibility of the basin approach include shape and size of the particular basin under consideration and the degree to which political and economic boundaries coincide with basin boundaries (Schramm, 1980).

Although the integrated approach to water management traditionally focused on development of water resources for a limited range of purposes, the scope of considerations has broadened to include an expanded range of societal needs and values. This expansion has resulted in adoption of new project purposes and acceptance of additional constraints on developmental activities. Greater consideration of natural environmental amenities is a primary example of constraints. Increased recognition of environmental values has tended to reduce support for multiple-purpose construction projects such as large reservoirs due to associated adverse environmental impacts. Thus, the original construction orientation of the integrated development approach has been somewhat deemphasized, and inclusion of a wider range of alternatives has become characteristic of water resources management (Wengert, 1981).

The integrated approach traditionally has been closely related to the view that water resources development is a central component of comprehensive regional development (Wengert, 1981). In this view, the benefits of water development exceed a simple summation of individual project outputs and include a synergistic combination of direct and indirect project effects of major significance in the realization of an area's economic potential. The following section evaluates the role of water development as a mechanism for achieving local or regional economic growth.

3.3(b) Water resources development as a factor in local or regional economic growth

The economic growth of particular localities or regions is often adopted as a specific socio-economic development objective since economic growth continues to be viewed as a central element of the broader concept of development. The focus of such attempts may be areas that lag behind general levels of national development. In other cases, attempts to stimulate local or regional economic growth may arise as a result of particular settlement objectives such as population dispersion.

General relationships between water development and economic growth

Consideration of water resources development as a mechanism for stimulating economic growth arises from the fact that all economic activities require at least a limited water supply, with many activities utilizing other water-related services as well. Historical evidence in-dicates that natural bodies of water and water development were major influences in establishing patterns of economic growth during earlier periods. For example, the importance of navigable waters and water power is reflected in the location of many major cities and concentrations of economic activities. In addition, many nations have employed water development as a primary mechanism to expand frontiers and stimulate economic growth in underdeveloped regions. Recognition of the historical role of water in development and the continuing role of water as a necessary factor in economic growth creates the incentive to continue to view water development as a primary mechanism to encourage economic growth.

Water resources development can contribute to economic growth during both construction and operational stages. Since many water projects are large public works undertakings, construction can create employment opportunities and therefore may be used to address conditions of high unemployment. In addition, project construction may generate significant economic activity among such firms as suppliers of materials. Of course, construction-related impacts are likely to be of limited duration and not as important to continued economic growth as are the impacts of project operation.

Project operation potentially can stimulate economic growth through a variety of direct effects that enhance water's positive attributes and/or control its negative effects. The nature and magnitude of direct growth impacts of water development vary with the type of water development and other characteristics of the individual situation.

For development that increases the dependable water supply and/or lowers the cost of water, the potential stimulating effect extends to all productive activities using water as an input. The impact will be greatest for water intensive activities where water constitutes a major input in terms of quantity and/or cost. For example, the fundamental importance of irrigation water as an input for agriculture in arid regions suggests that expansion of water supply in such areas would have substantial potential to produce growth in agricultural production and related economic activities. Similarly, expansion of water availability, particularly in the form of reservoirs, has substantial potential to stimulate growth in economic activity associated with recreation due to the significant role of water in many recreational activities.

Water supply enhancement also may stimulate a wide range of industrial activities, but the potential impact may be less than in the case of agriculture. Water supply is generally a more flexible requirement in the case of industry and constitutes a smaller proportion of total cost of industrial operations (Lewis et al., 1973, p. 80). Industrial location theory identifies a wide range of factors affecting the location decision, including the availability and cost of raw materials, labor, and energy; the occurrence of agglomeration economies associated with concentrations of economic activities; access to product markets; governmental influence exerted to achieve social objectives other than economic efficiency; and behavioral factors associated with individual decision makers (Smith, 1981; Miller, 1977; Hunker, 1974; Sener, 1972; Riley, 1973; Collins and Walker (eds.), 1975; Hamilton and Linge (eds.), 1981; Hoover, 1948).

The relative importance of water and these other factors varies among industries and with conditions such as the state of technology and applicable political institutions. Water supply is likely to to be of high significance in regions of general water scarcity and may be an important factor for certain water intensive industries even if not of major importance to industry in general. However, several of the other factors are likely to predominate over water supply as determinants of location in the typical case, and water supply, at least in non-arid areas, often tends to be viewed as a secondary factor in the industrial growth of regions (Hunker, 1974, p. 102; Sener, 1972, pp. 342-44).

Although often considered a secondary factor in regional industrial location, the availability of water generally is accorded substantial importance in relation to selection of a specific site within a general region that satisfies the range of locational requirements. A site with direct access to a body of water may be preferable to sites without access, or a site served by public supply, or suitable for such service, may be more desirable than those without existing or potential service. But even at the site selection stage, other factors remain important and may predominate over the water factor (Sener, 1972, p. 341; Hunker, 1974, p. 78).

Water resources development providing other services in addition to increased water supply also can have a direct effect on economic activity. As in the case of water supply enhancement, the potential impact of providing other water-related services varies among economic activities. Projects that improve navigation have the greatest potential to encourage growth in economic activities with high transportation costs relative to total costs, provided that the commodities involved are amenable to shipment by water. Similarly, hydroelectric power development has the highest potential to affect energy-intensive activities.

As in the case of water supply, the importance of these other water-related services is situationally determined and varies among nations. For example, the importance of navigation improvements depends directly on the status of alternative transportation systems; in the case of hydroelectric power facilities, significance depends on the general adequacy of power supplies. The potential economic growth impacts of any service provided by water development generally are greater where such service is in limited supply.

The potential impact of water resources development on economic growth is not limited to provision of direct inputs to productive processes but also includes indirect growth effects. These indirect impacts include multiplier effects operating through linkages with related areas of economic activity (Lewis et al. 1973, pp. 81-88). For example, increased agricultural activity and output resulting from an irrigation project will produce increased activity among suppliers of agricultural inputs and processors of agricultural products. While such effects may involve transfers of activity from other regions and therefore not constitute actual gains from a broad perspective, they are real benefits from the local perspective.

Water resources development also has the potential to stimulate economic growth indirectly by improvement of living conditions for the local population. While such effects contribute directly to the broader aspects of socio-economic development as well, improvement in living conditions can enhance prospects for economic growth by increasing the availability and productivity of labor. In an area lacking water supply necessary for community existence, water supply development to support the necessary population is essential to growth. In developing countries in particular, water supply development may contribute to increased labor productivity by improving health conditions that adversely affect work performance. Although caution has been urged against overestimating the growth impacts of community water supply development in developing countries (Feachem, 1978, pp. 3-4; Saunders and Warford, 1976, pp. 63-64), water supply development must be considered as one element of the total growth process. Within countries at a somewhat more advanced stage of development, water development may enhance the growth potential of an area already satisfying other requirements for growth by providing improved recreational opportunities and environmental amenities associated with water resources development such as reservoir construction.

Although the potential for water development to stimulate economic growth exists in all nations, the manner in which water resources considerations are incorporated into the growth process is fundamentally different among alternative political systems. In the case of centrally planned systems where natural resources and means of production are publicly owned, major decisions concerning economic growth are made by government. Both the construction of water projects and the establishment of industrial and other economic activities capable of utilizing project output are subject to governmental control in accordance with established plans and policies. These decisions generally could be expected to be guided by direct considerations of broad social goals as well as by considerations of economic efficiency. Examples of comprehensive economic growth programs including major water development activities have been documented in countries with centrally planned economies (Voropaev, 1986, pp. 19-32).

Within a market economy based on private enterprise, however, centralized control is limited. While the construction of major water projects is often a governmental function within market economies, decisions involving industrial location and other key factors in the economic growth process generally are not subject to direct governmental determination. Regulatory actions to control the negative effects of private economic activity, together with other government incentives designed to promote social goals, influence the location of economic activities, but location decisions are primarily within the control of private managers acting in response to the profit motive and subjective behavioral factors.

The extent to which water resources development attracts privately controlled economic activity is of special importance in market economies since public works projects are generally viewed as a principal means for governments to stimulate economic growth. In addition, public officials responsible for location decisions in centrally planned economies must consider, together with other relevant conditions, the same factors that influence private decision makers. The next two sections of this report review two types of information concerning the influence of water development on location of private economic activity: (1) empirical analyses of growth patterns in relation to water availability and water resource development and (2) results of surveys of private industry regarding factors that influence the location decision. After review of these studies, an attempt is made to determine if the results have potential applicability to nations beyond those where the data originated.

Empirical evidence concerning the relationship between water development and growth of private economic activity

Due to the complex nature of the economic growth process, isolating the influence of any one contributing factor is difficult. The problem is compounded by the general scarcity of ex-post evaluations of water development activities. Limited examples of such evaluation are provided by several studies investigating the role of water development in the economic growth of the United States in recent decades.

A preliminary indication of the potential for water resources development to stimulate economic growth is provided by examinations of the relationship between economic growth and existing availability of water and water services. In this approach, existing conditions are a function of both natural water resource availability and previous investments such as navigation improvements. An example of this type of

study is provided by Howe (1968) who investigated differences in employment growth during the 1950-1960 period among regions of the United States with differing availabilities of water and water services. Howe finds no statistically significant correlation between regional employment growth and water availability. The results of this study suggest that water availability, although possibly a more important growth factor at an earlier date (Lewis, et al., 1973, p. 96), was not a major determinant of regional patterns of economic growth in the United States during the study period.

In addition to analyses of the relationship between general water availability and economic growth, a second type of study of interest here is the attempt to identify growth impacts associated with individual water resource investment programs. Such studies have produced somewhat mixed results.

An indication of a positive correlation between water investment and economic growth is provided by several studies. A study (Cicchetti, Smith, and Carson, 1975) examining the effects of irrigation projects and other aspects of the public reclamation program in the southwestern United States during the 1930-70 period concludes that water resources investment has a positive effect on regional economic growth. Another study (Lewis, et al., 1973, p. 97) focusing on the eastern United States finds that water projects adding to an area's water availability will increase overall employment in water-oriented industries in that area.

A third indication of a positive correlation is given by growth in the Tennessee Valley Authority (TVA) service area within the eastern United States where substantial gains in per capita income have occurred since creation of TVA. However, this case illustrates the difficulty of attributing growth to individual causative factors. In the TVA case, isolation of the effect of water resources development is complicated by TVA involvement in programs to stimulate growth not related to water (such as improvement in agricultural practices). In addition, determination of growth that would have occurred in the absence of TVA is difficult. Critics of TVA have noted that other regions with similar socio-economic characteristics at the date TVA was initiated have experienced growth equal to that of the TVA region over substantial periods of time (Chandler, 1984, pp. 48-52).

The impact of water availability on location of economic activity within a specific geographic region is examined by Garrison and Paulson (1972) in a study focusing on the Tennessee River area of the United States. This study concludes that a significant relationship exists between minimum available stream flow and general employment levels in water intensive manufacturing firms and with growth of employment in such firms. These results indicate that water availability may be a significant factor in choice of a specific industrial site within a region.

In some cases, studies of economic growth in areas of water resources investment have failed to detect a positive correlation. One such study (Carson, Rivkin, and Rivkin, 1973) employs multiple regression analysis to investigate the possible correlation between water resources investment and economic growth in the United States during the 1960-1970 period. This study uses population growth and focuses on sample geographical areas consisting of four individual states chosen to be representative of the country. Water resources investment is measured as total costs incurred during the study period for projects completed by 1969 within a group of community-related water programs. The selected programs emphasize water supply and waste disposal but also include some multiple-purpose projects providing community-oriented services such as flood control and navigation improvements. The analysis shows no relationship between per capita water project expenditures and population growth (and, presumably, economic growth).

Results of surveys to identify determinants of private industrial location

The above empirical evidence regarding the influence of water development on location of private economic activity can be extended in the case of industrial location by consideration of results of surveys focusing on factors affecting private industrial location decisions. Although survey results are subjective, they provide an additional perspective on the importance of water as a factor in the economic growth of geographic regions.

The importance of water as a location factor is investigated in a 1969 survey of southeastern Great Britain (Rees, 1969). Of the approximately 250 responses (from 585 questionnaires), less than five percent of the respondents ranked water as the top priority factor in location decisions. Seventeen percent of the firms responding ranked water within the top three locational factors. The study notes that the results are consistent with findings of an earlier study and concludes that water is clearly not a critical location factor for a majority of firms within the scope of the study (Rees, 1969, p. 108).

A review of several industrial location surveys conducted in the Untied States (Lewis, et al., 1973) indicates general consistency with the findings from Great Britain. In a nationwide survey of 1000 of the nation's largest companies, water supply, cost of power and utilities, and water transportation are ranked as the seventh, eight, and ninth most important locational factors, respectively (Lewis, et al., 1973, p. 79). Although individual results vary in some aspects, other surveys are generally consistent with these findings and indicate water availability to be less important than several other factors influencing regional location decisions (Lewis, et al., 1973, p. 79).

A survey by the United States Economic Development Administration (United States EDA, 1970) provides evidence concerning the role of water supply in choice of an individual industrial site. Seventeen percent of all industries surveyed consider availability of raw water supply to be a "critical" factor in site location decisions while 22 percent consider availability of processed water to be a critical factor. Another 44 percent of the industries surveyed consider raw water availability to be "of significant to average value" as a site location factor, while 51 percent consider processed water availability to fall within this category.

The survey indicates that the importance attributed to water availability as a site selection factor varies significantly among types of industry. Those with greatest sensitivity to raw water availability include food and kindred products (64 percent ranked availability as a critical factor); chemicals and allied products (49 percent); petroleum and coal products (46 percent); wood products (37 percent); and pulp, paper, paperboard, and related products (32 percent). Thus, water availability is viewed as a major site location factor by significant proportions of the firms within certain industrial categories; nevertheless, the survey indicates that a substantial majority of United States industries view water as less than a critical factor in the site location decision.

These survey results appear to be a reflection of the fact that water costs generally constitute a small part of total costs of industrial operations, creating the likelihood that other factors accounting for greater portions of total costs will predominate in the location decision. The results also likely reflect the substantial flexibility that most industries possess with regard to quantities of water used.

Impact of varying national circumstances

Although the analysis of empirical evidence and survey results indicates some disagreement, the general conclusion that must be drawn from the studies is that the impact of water availability and water-project investment on private economic growth is not as significant as is often assumed, at least for the geographic areas and time periods considered. These findings therefore are of major importance if they have broad applicability among nations. However, caution must be exercised in any attempt to generalize. The studies considered represent a small range of national experiences, and the findings reflect specific national circumstances. Several factors limit the general applicability of findings to other national situations.

A major factor is the extent to which government controls the location of economic activity. The empirical evidence presented here is limited to the case where economic growth decisions are made by private entrepreneurs with limited governmental involvement. Although certain considerations (such as economic efficiency) will be important to public and private decision makers alike, the total range of considerations and the relative weight given to individual factors are likely to differ. A public manager may give more emphasis to non-economic objectives and less weight to profit maximizing considerations. Public managers also may be less affected by personal considerations such as the desire of a private manager to locate in close proximity to cultural or environmental amenities (although public sector managers to be personally affected by such decisions will not be immune from such considerations). In the case of public sector decisions concerning economic growth, water may attain greater importance as a factor. In fact, governmental encouragement of economic growth in accord with patterns of water and other natural resource availability could be adopted as an explicit policy.

A second consideration relating to governmental activity is variation among nations in commonly held views toward the responsibility and capability of government to undertake needed water development activities. In the United States, for example, the tendency to view water as a secondary factor relative to location of economic activity is influenced by the high level of commitment by local government to provide low-cost water for economic growth (Sener, 1972, p. 345). Although water shortages have occurred, adequate water supplies to accommodate economic expansion generally have been maintained as part of local efforts to compete for economic growth. This approach by local government has contributed to the widespread availability of water and strengthened the view that water is not a major locational factor. This view would be less valid in a nation where commonly held perceptions regarding the duty and capability of government to provide adequate water and water-related services are different.

A third factor that may cause differences among nations in the role of water in economic growth is variation in overall water availability. Although some of the data presented above cover areas of water scarcity, most of the individual studies originated in humid climates where water would be unlikely to be an important locational determinant due to its natural abundance. Findings associated with such areas may have limited applicability where water is less abundant. Since some amount of water is an essential requirement for all human activity, a general condition of scarcity increases the probability that water supply will serve as the limiting factor to economic growth. Falkenmark and Lindh (1976, p. 18) have indicated that water tends to become a limiting factor to economic growth when water use exceeds 20 percent of total runoff. While the point at which water use may become a limiting factor will vary with differing natural conditions and management strategies, a higher level of use relative to supplies implies the occurrence of more supply problems and greater sensitivity to water as a determinant of industrial location. This factor suggests that the importance of water in location decisions may increase over time within individual countries experiencing increasing water use, including those where water currently is considered to be a minor factor in economic growth.

A fourth reason why these findings may have limited applicability to other nations is the variation in composition of economic activity among nations at different stages of development. First, a developing country with higher dependence on agriculture is likely to exhibit a stronger relationship between water and economic growth than in the case of a developed country where the agricultural sector is less significant. Second, the composition of industrial activity varies between developed and developing countries. The greater proportion of primary and secondary industries likely to characterize the industrial sector of a developing country would generally involve greater dependence on water than would exist within a developed economy encompassing a higher proportion of service-oriented tertiary industries. Third, technological evolution within the development process may reduce the dependence on water. For example, industrial technological advances may in some cases reduce the demand for water (however, such advances may increase water demand in certain cases), and establishment of alternative transportation systems can reduce the need for use of water for navigation. A stronger relationship between water and economic activity therefore may have existed previously in the developed countries but have diminished during the development process.

These considerations suggest substantial limitations on the general applicability of conclusions concerning the role of water in economic growth drawn from limited national experiences; however, such conclusions are useful. The evidence suggesting that water currently plays a somewhat limited role in stimulating or deciding the location of economic growth in some countries at least indicates the need for caution in adopting water development as a generally applicable mechanism to stimulate economic growth.

This evidence emphasizes the complexity of the economic growth process and its dependence on many interacting factors. Although water in some minimum amount is a necessary condition for growth, its availability, even in abundant quantities, is not sufficient to guarantee growth. In the case of industrial growth, the flexibility and low cost of water as a factor of production means that other considerations such as labor and markets are likely to serve as more important constraints. Even where water is a major input such as in the case of agricultural operations in arid regions, complementary inputs such as fertilizers and a variety of institutional factors are important. No one factor in the economic growth process, including water, has such predominant status that it can produce growth without regard to other factors. The fact that the availability of abundant water supplies cannot ensure growth is illustrated by the existence of many water-rich areas without significant economic activity.

Regardless of these limitations on water's ability to stimulate private-sector economic growth, the fact that water availability is a necessary condition for growth indicates the potential importance of water resources development as part of the growth process. Any essential factor can become the limiting factor if given inadequate attention. Due to the essential nature of a minimum water supply and the potential importance of other water services, water resources development generally must be included as a component of the economic growth process. Development programs not recognizing the role of water are likely to encounter water-related constraints and may produce disappointing results. On the other hand, indiscriminate use of water resources development as a mechanism to achieve growth without attention to other factors is also likely to be unsatisfactory. Only within the context of a comprehensive assessment of the broad range of factors necessary for economic growth in a particular situation can the relative importance of water supply and other water services be determined.

3.4 Adverse effects of water resources development

Water resources development activities are generally undertaken to modify natural processes within the hydrologic cycle to enhance the ability of water to satisfy specific water-related needs or control undesirable effects resulting from water's natural characteristics; however, achievement of the intended results usually involves substantial costs. The most obvious form of costs consists of resources consumed in the construction and operation of necessary facilities. But, in addition to these direct expenditures, other adverse effects also may rise. These other effects may not be considered as costs in financial analyses since no requirement for compensation to those affected may exist, but they constitute losses in welfare of the affected population and therefore are real costs. After consideration is given to direct water project expenditures, these additional impacts will be discussed within the three categories of direct socio-cultural disruptions, economic disruptions, and environmental disruptions.

3.4(a) Resources consumed in project construction

Due to the nature of the construction involved, major water projects require large investments that often originate in the public sector, even in those countries where natural resources in general are privately owned and developed. Collectively, such projects may constitute a significant component of a national budget. No nation can afford to invest resources in the production of goods and services having less socio-economic value than the resources invested, indicating the need for thorough evaluation of investment decisions.

Careful scrutiny of water project investment decisions is also dictated by the need to obtain the greatest benefit from available public funds through proper choice of investment alternatives. Within a particular national budget, water projects are in competition with the whole range of alternative uses of public funds. Under conditions of limited funding, therefore, allocation of funds to a water resources investment program is likely to foreclose public expenditures in other areas. Similarly, the decision to fund a particular water project will likely displace other water projects. Benefits lost in connection with foregone alternative expenditures provide a standard for determining the appropriateness of a particular action. Application of this standard can help assure the best use of public funds, an important issue in all nations but especially significant in the developing countries.

3.4(b) Direct socio-cultural disruptions

Water resources development can produce a variety of adverse impacts on the socio-cultural characteristics of a given population. At the head of the list of socio-cultural disruptions is the displace-ment of human populations by the construction of large water development projects, particularly reservoirs. This impact is often significant and on occasion has been catastrophic. Among the most extreme examples of this type of impact have been the displacement of entire communities in tropical areas, sometimes without adequate provision for resettlement. For example, the Kariba Dam on the Zambesi River in Africa displaced approximately 57,000 people of the Tonga tribe. In addition to experiencing cultural shock, the displaced tribe members suffered from food shortages and disease due to inadequacies in the resettlement program. The Volta River project in Ghana required the movement of 78,000 people from over 700 towns and villages of generally small size. Considerable social disruption resulted from the consolidation of the diverse groups involved in 52 resettlement locations (Biswas, 1978, p. 294).

The adverse effects of resettlement are not limited to the developing nations or to any particular region but have been associated with most major water development activities. In an example from the United States, the Tennessee Valley Authority has had to relocate 12,000 families (Biswas, 1978, p. 295), primarily in connection with reservoir construction. Even in cases where relocation assistance is adequate to remove the primary physical problems associated with such operations, studies have shown that the affected population suffers substantial psychological stress and social disruption (Burdge and Johnson, 1973). These groups often are a basic source of opposition to water projects and have demonstrated an increasing effectiveness in organizing opposition and preventing project construction in some countries.

Adverse effects of dislocation can be substantially mitigated if properly incorporated into project planning. In order to control such effects, planning must consider the full range of potential socio-cultural impacts. In some situations, project-related relocation may provide opportunity for improving the condition of the population affected. For example, removal of a settlement from a high hazard area such as a flood plain may provide a net benefit if potentially offsetting adverse effects are controlled.

Related to the displacement of people is the inundation or forced relocation of culturally significant sites and objects. A prominent example is the forced relocation of some of the monuments of the Ancient Egyptian Civilization due to construction of the Aswan High Dam on the Nile (Biswas, 1978, p. 285). Many water projects disrupt cultural features such as archaeological and historical sites of local or sometimes broader significance.

In addition to displacement of residents and impact on cultural features, water project construction also frequently results in adverse socio-cultural impacts by producing changes in the size and composition of the population of the project area. These effects occur both during and after project construction. During construction, the primary effects relate to the influx of the work force. This population change can lead to social disruptions and adverse effects on public services in the affected area. Depending on the nature of the project, additional demographic changes may occur after project completion. For example, if a project expands an area's recreational potential and results in development of a recreational industry, an increase in the transient population would be expected, with resultant socio-cultural impacts.

Another major socio-cultural disruption associated with certain water resource developments, particularly irrigation projects in tropical areas, consists of the spread and intensification of water-related diseases. A major disease shown to be related to irrigation projects is schistosomiasis, a parasitic disease involving an aquatic snail as an intermediate host. Although a naturally occurring disease in tropical and semi-tropical areas, the introduction of perennial irrigation systems has extended snail habitats and provided more human contact with the parasites, thus significantly increasing infection rates in many areas. For example, infection rates in four selected areas of Egypt, within three years of introduction of perennial irrigation, rose from 10 to 44 percent, 7 to 50 percent, ll to 64 percent, and 2 to 75 percent. Availability of large quantities of water in reservoirs and canals is also associated with a variety of other diseases such as liver fluke infections, malaria, Bancroftian filariasis, and yellow fever. Water project operations that increase dissolved oxygen levels (such as spillway releases from reservoirs) can adversely affect health by improving breeding conditions for the insect carrier of onchocerciasis (Biswas, 1978, pp. 289-291).

Health impacts of water projects are sometimes made more severe by growth of aquatic weeds. Rapid weed growth can occur in tropical and semi-tropical areas and have caused significant problems in many impoundments and other water handling facilities. Weeds contribute to health problems by providing suitable environments for disease vectors (such as mosquitoes) and intermediate hosts (such as snails) for disease-causing agents. Aquatic weeds also cause a variety of other problems such as increased evapo-transpiration, interference with navigation, adverse effects on fisheries, and interference with operation of water management facilities (Biswas, 1978, pp. 291-293).

A further potential health-related impact of water development consists of reductions in quantity or degradation of the quality of drinking water at downstream locations. Reductions in quantity below the minimum needed for purposes of hygiene as well as addition of pollutants can adversely affect health and other dimensions of welfare.

3.4(c) Economic disruptions

Accompanying direct impacts on the affected population are impacts on production of goods and services. Of course the distinction between direct and economic impacts is somewhat artificial. Economic impacts have an ultimate effect on human well-being; similarly, direct impacts on man such as spread of infectious diseases have implications for productive processes. Although such interactions are acknowledged, this section focuses on impacts of water development that initially impact productive activities rather than man himself.

One class of adverse economic impacts associated with water resources development is displacement of other productive water uses. Although some water development purposes are complementary, significant conflicts also occur. For example, water consumed in an irrigation operation is not available for downstream use for industrial water supply. In addition to creation of adverse impacts by means of quantitative consumption of water, water development can also create adverse economic impacts on other water users through effects on natural flow patterns and water quality. Hydro-electric power generation projects provide an illustration of water resource development with significant potential to interfere with downstream uses through alteration of flow patterns. In many projects water is impounded for release during specific time periods, often the period of peak power demand. Even instream water uses such as navigation and fisheries enhancement can impact other potential water users since water that is reserved for such instream use is unavailable for application to consumptive use. Qualitative modifications can also have substantial economic impacts where downstream uses are precluded or made more costly due to increases in water treatment requirements. Although the impact varies among uses, most water uses tend to decrease water quality to some extent.

A second class of adverse impacts of water development on productive activities consists of productivity losses imposed with respect to the use of land and land-based facilities. For example, inundation of land by reservoir construction may force use of less productive land for agricultural purposes or use of industrial sites involving additional costs associated with access where equally advantageous agricultural land or industrial sites are not available. In addition, relocation of roads may result in greater transportation costs related to production of goods and services.

A special loss of productivity frequently associated with irrigation projects consists of decreases in crop yields resulting from waterlogging and/or increases in soil salinity. These problems, either individually or together, have affected irrigated lands in many areas of the world. These losses offset some of the anticipated benefits of irrigation and may in some cases include total destruction of agricultural production. Data compiled for the United Nations Conference on Desertification indicate that one-tenth of the world's total irrigated area is waterlogged, with an estimated productivity decrease of 20 percent. In addition, almost as much land has been made less productive by salinization (Brown, 1981, p. 10).

Economic disruptions can also occur as a result of productivity losses associated with modifications of sediment movements. An illustration is provided by the Aswan High Dam on the Nile. Downstream lands have been deprived of traditional annual depositions of fertile silt as a result of the dam, with resulting productivity losses. In addition, the removal of sediments by the reservoir has also had an adverse impact on fisheries in the Mediterranean (Hafez and Shenouda, 1978).

3.4(d) Environmental disruptions

Environmental disruptions potentially associated with water projects include a variety of adverse effects on natural ecosystems and aesthetic values. Such impacts often can be distinguished from those in the previous categories only in degree. An environmental impact can easily become a socio-cultural impact or an economic impact if it achieves an adequate level of significance. For example, a change in water quality would likely be viewed as an environmental impact if only aquatic organisms without known commercial value were affected, but such change would be viewed as an economic impact if commercial fisheries were affected.

The environmental effects of water resources development can occur in a myriad of forms. A single project can create a wide range of effects, and water projects encompass such diverse activities as dam construction, stream channelization, interbasin water transfer, dredging and filling, drainage, and waste disposal. These activities can alter the physical, chemical, and biological characteristics of water and, in some cases, totally transform an existing ecosystem into a different form. While some effects are direct and immediate, many are indirect and occur over a substantial period of time since they involve a series of biological responses as initial effects are transmitted by ecological processes.

The total environmental impact of a particular water project is the result of the interaction of the various changes produced by the project, and any attempt to consider the effects of individual changes creates the potential for neglect of the effects of such interactions. Nevertheless, consideration of changes by categories provides an orderly approach to analysis of the various environmental changes that can be related to water projects. Three categories of change will be employed here: (1) changes in discharge and/or levels of natural bodies of water, (2) alteration of water quality, and (3) total transformation of natural ecosystems.

Alteration in discharge and/or water levels

Many water resource development projects involve alterations in discharge where streams are involved or water levels where lakes are involved. In the case of streams, alterations may be produced by direct withdrawals without flow-regulating measures or may involve such flow-regulating measures as construction of impoundments. Projects that consist only of withdrawal of water from a stream reduce downstream flow by the amount of water consumed by the use involved where return flows are discharged back to their source. Flow is reduced by the total amount of withdrawal where use is totally consumptive or where return flows are discharged to a different body of water.

Different impacts occur where flow-regulating structures are used. Such development schemes generally involve storage of water during periods of high flow for release or use during low-flow periods, thereby creating potential mitigation of down-stream impacts during low-flow periods. Although storage

facilities can be operated
downstream impacts during n
or even to improve natura
storage is likely to result in
reaching downstream locan.
losses (reservoirs that replace cu.
tropical forest are not likely to increase .
atmosphere due to the high evapo-transpiratiu.
of such forests). Although losses by evaporation from reservoir surfaces may involve substantial quantities of water, such losses may have little downstream impact where they consist of stored floodwater that would not be available for use without the reservoir.

Streams most susceptible to environmental disruption from water withdrawal are perennial streams that support permanent populations of fish and other aquatic life. Parameters essential to the well-being of aquatic organisms such as stream width, depth, and velocity are dependent on discharge. Attempts have been made to correlate suitability of aquatic habitat with differing stream discharges as a percentage of average flow. Results of one such attempt (Tennant, 1976) indicate that 60 percent of average flow or higher provides excellent habitat for most aquatic life forms. Thirty percent is recommended as a minimum flow to sustain good habitat conditions for most aquatic life forms. The lower limits of suitability are reached when flow decreases to 10 percent of average flow. The 10 percent discharge is seen as a severe degradation in habitat involving such conditions as exposure of stream bottoms and destruction of riparian vegetation. This condition is viewed as being suitable only for short-term survival of aquatic organisms (Tennant, 1976, pp. 367-69). Although these indicators of habitat suitability have been shown to be applicable to a variety of stream types, variation among locations can be anticipated.

In addition to impact on aquatic organisms, other adverse environmental effects occur as a result of decreased stream flow. Wildlife can be affected, with impacts most significant with respect to waterfowl and other wildlife directly dependent on the aquatic environment. Wildlife dependent on riparian vegetation could also be affected substantially should flow reductions adversely affect such vegetation (Kadlec, 1976). Decreased flows produce adverse effects on aesthetic and recreational values as well, including such impacts as degradation of scenery in connection with exposed stream bottoms and interference with boating (Tennant, 1976, p. 368).

Although stream flow reduction during low-flow conditions is most likely to be considered as a potential source of environmental impact, other types of modifications can also be significant. Reduction in flood flows can, in certain situations, produce negative effects on fish and wildlife. For example, flood control may reduce beneficial flood scouring of fish spawning beds. In the case of wildlife, occurrence of flooding may be beneficial due to the role of flooding in maintaining essential habitat in the form of certain types of vegetation beyond stream channels (Kadlec, 1976, p. 362).

Other stream flow modifications with potential to produce impact include artificial fluctuations in flow and increases of natural flow. Fluctuations would

33

reservoir releases for such purposes as ~~j~~electric power generation during periods of peak ~~~and~~. Frequent variation in flow may produce such ~~~desirable~~ effects as interference with waterfowl nesting or degradation of aesthetic values (Kenyon, 1981). Increases in natural flow can arise where a stream is used for conveyance of water transported from another source. Some of the effects of such increase may be beneficial, but original conditions considered desirable may be disrupted by the increased flow.

Environmental impacts resulting from modification of lake levels are generally similar to those arising from streamflow modifications, but certain differences arise from physical distinctions between the two systems. Lake level decreases can result from such measures as direct withdrawal of water, increasing the capacity of natural outlets, or diversion of natural inflow. Increases in water levels can be accomplished by such means as artificially raising the elevation of natural outlets or by increasing inflow through diversion of water from sources outside natural drainage areas. Changes in water levels have the potential to modify the lake as an ecosystem since shore areas are important in the life cycle of many aquatic organisms (Ploskey, 1983). The aesthetic and recreational attributes of lakes are also sensitive to water level changes.

Withdrawal of groundwater generally does not directly produce environmental disruptions; direct impact is likely to be limited to effects on water use by others sharing the particular source of groundwater supply. However, hydraulic interconnection between surface and groundwater can result in environmental impacts where withdrawal of groundwater reduces streamflow or lake levels or eliminates wetlands. Surface water development can also affect groundwater levels. For example, the construction of reservoirs and other facilities such as canals, as well as the application of water to the land's surface for such purposes as irrigation, can increase local groundwater levels. Alternatively, diversion of water from a surface source can reduce groundwater levels under conditions where normal flow is from the surface source to the groundwater system.

Water quality alteration

Water quality alteration constitutes a major environmental impact of many water uses and water development activities. The most obvious source of quality alteration resulting from water use is the discharge of municipal and industrial wasterwater. Addition of toxic substances to natural waters is a change of special significance. Toxic substances have direct effects on aquatic organisms and other water consumers and, in some cases, can be biologically concentrated through food chains to affect a variety of aquatic and non-aquatic organisms, including man.

In addition to the effects of toxic substances, a wide range of other adverse effects can occur when waste products are introduced into water and produce changes in physical and chemical parameters such as the presence of infectious agents, temperature, turbidity, color, radioactivity, pH, salinity, and oxygen concentration. Changes in any of these parameters can

have direct environmental effects and can also produce impacts by modifying other parameters. For example, increase in temperature can affect aquatic organisms directly and also reduce the amount of dissolved oxygen available to such organisms. The extent of the effect of a given waste discharge depends on the environmental conditions under which the waste is discharged as well as on the characteristics of the waste itself. Thus, determination of the likely effect of waste discharge operations is a complex undertaking requiring site-specific analysis (Lamb, 1985, pp. 141-164).

Discharge of organic wastes containing substances that can be used in the metabolic processes of microorganisms can pose special environmental problems. The resulting increase in biochemical reactions utilizes dissolved oxygen and can substantially reduce or deplete supplies. Depletion of dissolved oxygen can produce severe ecosystem disruption and environmental problems such as odors associated with the anaerobic decomposition process that takes place in the absence of dissolved oxygen (Lamb, 1985, pp. 147-148).

Dissolved oxygen deficiencies are commonly associated with excessive algal growth resulting from discharge of certain nutrients that often serve as limitations on growth under natural conditions. Algal growth in many bodies of freshwater is limited by the availability of phosphorus. Nitrogen can also serve as the limiting nutrient, especially in estuarine areas. Where these nutrients are limiting algal growth, discharge of wastes providing a supply can produce major increases in growth with severe impacts such as creation of nuisance conditions, tastes and odors in water supplies, and dissolved oxygen problems when the algae decomposes (Lamb, 1985, p. 150).

Another basic mechanism of environmental disruption associated with waste discharge consists of alterations of natural stream bed conditions. Many aquatic organisms depend directly on the stream bed as permanent habitat while others have an indirect dependency in the form of food requirements, spawning sites, or other uses. Thus, any waste discharge resulting in the deposition of material on the bed of a stream has the potential to affect such aquatic life (Clark, Haverkamp, and Chapman, 1985, pp. 65-77). Formation of deposits also affects the aesthetic qualities of a body of water.

In addition to municipal and industrial waste discharge, another type of water use often having a major effect on water quality is irrigation. Return flows generally contain increased mineral content and may contain agricultural chemicals. This source of contamination is significant due to the large quantities of water used in irrigation and is a major factor in the quality of surface and ground waters in areas where irrigation is widely practiced. For example, salinity increases associated with irrigation in the United States' portion of the Colorado River Basin created the need for construction of a desalination plant to treat return flow from an irrigation project in order to restore the flow of the river to a level of quality compatible with terms of a treaty between the United States and Mexico (United States CEQ and Department of State, 1980, pp. 342-343).

rms of waste discharge are the
f water quality alteration related
activities, substantial quality
s the result of water development
ly considered to involve waste
le,impoundment and release of
il adverse effects on downstream
l problems are related to thermal
er in reservoirs during warmer
. During such periods, the upper
med, creating a density difference
lower layers that prevents mixing
stratification. While oxygen in the
pilimnion) can be replenished due
ie surface, the lack of mixing with
he hypolimnion) leads to oxygen
lower layer as normal oxygen
curs through such processes as
uatic organisms and decomposition
Other quality effects such as increases
and manganese also occur in the
izzle, 1981).
cted for hydroelectric power purposes
irge water from the hypolimnion,
ily creating downstream water quality
is low dissolved oxygen concentrations
ire reductions. For example, low
n concentration is a significant problem
lams in the Tennessee Valley Authority
United States (Chandler, 1984, pp. 156-
w dissolved oxygen concentrations are
and many other aquatic organisms, such
ute a significant environmental impact.
changes associated with reservoir releases
luce major environmental impacts. Such
produce fish kills when imposed suddenly
e of hydroelectric power releases. Where
lowered temperatures are produced in
waters, naturally occurring warm water
iy be replaced by cold water fisheries (an
may be viewed as desirable in some
While downstream temperature reductions
iently associated with releases from
er facilities, reservoir operations involving
releases can increase downstream water
ires and produce significant environmental
Smalley and Novak, 1978).
ition to these water quality changes associated
rmal stratification in reservoirs, other water
quality changes also can result from reservoir
operations. One of these additional effects is the
reduction in suspended solids in reservoir releases
resulting from sedimentation during impoundment.
This change may constitute a desirable improvement
in downstream water quality under some conditions
but may have adverse consequences such as decreased
fertility of the affected water, increased erosion
potential, or biological impacts associated with
increased light penetration into the clarified waters
(Petts, 1980; Taylor, 1978). Some of these problems
have been attributed to the Aswan High Dam (Hafez
and Shenouda, 1988). A further effect of reservoir
operation (and water diversion as well) is alteration
of salinity patterns in estuarine areas. Withholding or

increasing freshwater inflow can affect aquatic
organisms dependent on a special salinity range.

Reservoir operations can also adversely affect
downstream waters by means of aeration of the water
involved. Supersaturation of released water with the
gases contained in air can occur as a result of flow
over a spillway into a stilling basin when the water
and air mixture plunges to sufficient depth to force
the air into solution due to hydrostatic pressure. This
condition can lead to embolism in fish when gases from
the supersaturated water come out of solution and cause
formation of gas bubbles within the fish's body, which
can lead to death. Supersaturation was once viewed
as the most serious water quality problem in the United
States' Pacific Northwest due to the large number of
dams within the Columbia River Basin, but spillway
modifications and operational changes have reduced
the problem in this region (Legg, 1978; Boyer, 1973).

The relationship between impoundments and
downstream water quality is complex. Some of the
effects are beneficial in certain situations while others
are harmful, with the net effect dependent on the nature
and magnitudes of the various changes and the
activities impacted by the changes. Many of the adverse
effects can be eliminated or controlled through design
of facilities and operating practices. The potential
severity of several of the possible effects emphasizes
the importance of their inclusion in project planning.

Another water management activity with potentially
significant implications for water quality alteration is
dredging and disposal of dredged materials. Both the
dredging operation and the disposal of dredged
materials can produce significant environmental
changes. Dredging substantially disturbs bottom
habitat through removal of material and affects water
quality by increasing turbidity and possibly by release
of contaminants such as heavy metals that may be
contained in bottom sediments. Disposal of the dredged
material can cause further destruction of bottom
habitat and can produce water quality problems similar
to those associated with the dredging operation
(Johnston, 1981).

Total ecosystem transformation

The environmental impacts considered within the two
previous categories may result in substantial
modification of natural ecosystems, but such systems
retain their original identity, at least in part—for
example, streams remain streams even if substantial
changes in discharge and water quality occur. In
contrast, certain water development projects produce
such extensive environmental modifications that the
result is the substitution of a totally new ecosystem
for the original system. The primary example of such
transformation consists of major reservoir construction, which involves replacement of a riverine system
and the adjacent terrestrial system by a lacustrine
system. A second example of relatively complete
transformation consists of draining and filling of
wetland areas, which essentially involves conversion
of a system at least partly aquatic in nature to a
terrestrial system. A third example is channelization

of natural streams, a process that can radically alter the original stream ecosystem.

Inundation of a free-flowing stream with a large body of essentially still water fundamentally changes suitability for aquatic organisms (Fowler, 1978). Although some fish and other organisms may adapt to either environment, the significant differences in conditions between flowing streams and lakes generally mean that lake formation is accompanied by major shifts in population of aquatic organisms. This change may involve an increase in total biomass, including desirable fish, but destruction of the original fishery and associated ecosystem may in some cases be viewed as a significant loss (Hagen and Roberts, 1973, pp. 201-05).

Reservoir construction may create especially adverse effects on streams used for spawning by anadromous fish. In addition to downstream impacts in the form of stream flow and water quality alterations, a dam and reservoir have several additional impacts. First, a dam can form an impediment to upstream migration, which can be at least partially overcome by structural modifications. Second, a reservoir eliminates the inundated portion of the stream from use for spawning purposes. Third, the still waters of a reservoir, together with dams and associated equipment such as turbines, may impede downstream movement of young fish to the sea. These impacts collectively can result in substantial obstacles to population maintenance (Schwiebert (ed.), 1977; Raymond, 1979).

In addition to major changes in fisheries and aquatic ecosystems, substantial modification of aesthetic and recreational values occur as a result of stream impoundment. Although impounded bodies of water possess their own aesthetic and recreational attributes, loss of free-flowing streams is considered by many to constitute a major environmental disruption.

Inundation of terrestrial ecosystems by reservoir construction also constitutes a significant environmental disruption. Flooding of wetland areas, floodplains, and other lowland areas often will have significant impact on wildlife due to the general importance of such areas as habitat and the greater natural productivity of many stream valleys relative to other areas. The most significant effects occur where relatively unique terrestrial ecosystems, or specialized habitats of rare animal or plant life, exist in the area to be inundated.

Inundation of land adjacent to streams has important aesthetic implications due to the nature of landforms and geologic structures frequently occurring in such areas. Inundation of canyons, special rock formations, and other natural features associated with streams is likely to be viewed as a major loss of aesthetic values that amplifies losses associated with inundation of the stream itself.

A second example of water projects constituting an essentially complete transformation of natural environments is the draining and filling of wetland areas. While reservoir construction can result in replacement of wetlands by water areas, draining and filling result in replacement by dry land. Such replacement is accomplished for a variety of reasons such as the disposal of dredged materials or the creation of additional land for agricultural use or other development purposes. Destruction may also occur as a result of water development projects such as surface water diversions or ground water withdrawal.

While unrestrained draining and filling of wetlands once was generally considered to be in the public interest, the important ecosystem functions of such areas have been recognized in recent years. Marine wetlands have been acknowledged to be among the most productive of lands and play an important role in the life cycles of many marine organisms, including a variety of commercially valuable species. Plant material produced in such wetlands serves as a basic energy source for estuarine and marine food webs. Marine wetlands serve as habitat for a diverse group of organisms. In the case of some marine organisms, wetlands serve as nursery grounds and therefore have an essential role in the continuance of species not normally found in wetlands as adults (United States CEQ and Department of State, 1980, pp. 303-304).

Freshwater wetlands serve important habitat functions such as provision of cover, food, and breeding sites for a variety of wildlife. They are of major importance to waterfowl, especially in the provision of nesting sites. Other wildlife such as wading birds and aquatic mammals (e.g., muskrat and beaver) are also directly dependent on the aquatic environment offered by wetlands. Natural marsh areas may provide protective cover for wildlife such as deer not directly dependent on an aquatic environment. Drainage of such wetlands and the clearing of associated natural vegetation therefore have significant potential to adversely affect wildlife over a considerable surrounding area (Found, Hill, and Spence, 1974, pp. 52-59).

In addition to impact on wildlife dependent on the wetlands themselves, drainage of freshwater wetlands can produce environmental impact by means of altering the hydrologic characteristics of surface waters. Under conditions where wetlands gradually contribute water to a surface drainage system through either surface or subsurface flow, more rapid removal of such water by means of artificial drainage will tend to increase stream flow during certain periods but result in decreases at other times. Where drainage operations are extensive, this change in the timing of contributions to stream flow may result in increased flood flows and reduced low flows. These changes, together with other modifications such as water temperature increases associated with removal of sheltering vegetation, may lead to changes in stream ecosystems.

A third example of ecosystem transformation, which often accompanies drainage activities but is also used for other purposes such as flood control, is stream channelization. Channel modifications such as straightening, widening, deepening, and removal of obstructions designed to increase hydraulic efficiency are likely to have adverse effects on biological functions of the stream. The most extreme impact will occur when the natural channel is replaced by a concrete-lined or other totally artificial channel, but an altered natural channel also may have significantly decreased capacity to serve as habitat. This reduced capacity results from such factors as shortening of channel length due to straightening, creation of uniform bottom conditions, and removal of vegetation. The uniformity of channelized streams is a significant contrast to the variety of a natural stream where alternating riffles and pools produce variation in current velocity and patterns, light conditions, water depth, and bottom materials. Elimination of variety in habitat types reduces the diversity of organic organisms that can be supported. Removal of vegetation from a stream's channel and banks will affect both aquatic and non-aquatic organisms since riparian vegetation often serves as essential habitat for wildlife (Duvel et al., 1979; Found, Hill, and Spence, 1974).

4. Impact of socio-economic development on water resources

To be complete, an overview of the interactions between water and socio-economic development must consider the impacts of development on water resources. Attention has previously been given to some of the negative effects of water resource development projects on certain attributes of the resource, but a wide range of other development activities also produce negative effects on water. This section will focus on impacts of these other activities; however, the effects of water development activities often are closely related, creating the need for limited additional consideration of the impacts of water projects as an integral aspect of socio-economic development in general.

The impacts of socio-economic development on water resources will be discussed within three categories: (1) modification of climate, (2) modification of surface and groundwater movement, and (3) water quality modification.

4.1 Modification of climate

Climate modification is one of the potentially most significant means by which socio-economic development may affect the water resource. The availability of water in usable form within the terrestrial environment is determined by the amount and distribution of precipitation, a direct function of climate. In addition, climate controls the evaporation process through which water is lost from the earth's surface to the atmosphere. The water cycle is an integral component of broader climatic processes that involve the atmospheric conditions of heat, moisture, and air movement. Energy from the sun drives climatic processes. A basic component of these processes is mass transfer between the earth's surface and the atmosphere by means of the evaporation-condensation cycle. These interacting transfers of energy and mass occur within atmospheric and oceanic circulation patterns generated by unequal solar heating of the earth. These atmospheric moisture transport processes are essential to maintenance of water supplies for the earth's land areas since the force of gravity otherwise would tend to concentrate water in the oceans.

Significant climatic changes have occurred during the earth's history as a result of natural factors. While these natural factors will continue to operate, man's activities now have attained a previously nonexistent potential to join natural factors as a significant influence on climate. Man's activities are most likely to produce climate modifications through three mechanisms: (1) changes in composition of the atmosphere, (2) direct addition of heat to the atmosphere, and (3) land surface changes (Munn and Machta, 1979, p. 170).

4.1(a) Changing the composition of the atmosphere

A principal mechanism of climatic modification is the addition of gases and particulate matter to the atmosphere such that transmission of solar and terrestrial radiation is affected. Additions of these substances enhances the "greenhouse effect" whereby the atmosphere maintains earth temperatures at higher levels than possible in its absence. This effect results from the atmosphere's ability to transmit most of the short-wavelength radiation passing from the sun to earth while absorbing a large part of the long-wavelength radiation that normally would be emitted by the earth (Critchfield, 1974, p. 14; SMIC Report, 1971, pp. 84-85).

Although addition of a variety of gases may affect radiation processes, carbon dioxide and water vapor are of special interest in relation to the greenhouse effect. Much attention has been focused on the possible impacts of substantial increases in carbon dioxide in the atmosphere resulting primarily from the combustion of fossil fuels and perhaps from deforestation. In addition to potential effects such as melting of glaciers and ice caps, such warming could also change general atmospheric circulation as a result of changed temperature gradients between equatorial and polar regions (Fedorov, 1979, p. 18). Such changes would have major implications for water resources due to modified precipitation patterns (Gribbin, 1982).

Water vapor in the atmosphere, in addition to its contribution to the greenhouse effect, serves a variety of functions in earth's energy cycle. Water in the atmosphere, especially after it has condensed to form clouds, is an important determinant of the portion of incoming solar radiation reflected back to space without contributing to earth's heat budget (SMIC Report, 1971, pp. 78-79). Thus, activities leading to increased cloud cover (such as evaporation of water in industrial cooling operations and irrigation) have potential to decrease the amount of solar radiation reaching the earth's surface. Man's activities have been estimated to have increased annual evaporation by about 3.5 percent (Munn and Machta, 1979, p. 188). Another function of water vapor in heat transfer processes occurs during the evaporation-condensation cycle during which large quantities of latent heat are transferred from the earth's surface to the atmosphere (SMIC Report, 1971, pp. 65).

Particulate matter in the atmosphere affects climatic processes in several ways. Particles affect incoming solar radiation through scattering and absorbing sunlight and also modify the terrestrial radiation process by which heat is emitted from earth to space. A second effect consists of the role of particles in condensation since water vapor condenses on particles (SMIC Report, 1971, p. 188). Precipitation processes are therefore directly dependent on the concentration and size of atmospheric particles. Addition of particulate matter to the atmosphere may increase cloud cover or precipitation in the affected areas (SMIC Report, 1971, pp. 224-25). In some cases, particles are added to the atmosphere directly while in others gaseous substances are added that are later transformed to particles (SMIC Report, 1971, p. 51). Such addition occurs from a large number of sources, both natural and man-related. Significant sources of man-related increases in atmospheric particulate matter include the combustion of fossil fuels and agricultural practices that disturb natural ground cover and result in addition of dust to the atmosphere through wind action (Munn and Machta, 1979, pp. 173-77).

An unprecedented but potentially catastrophic addition of particulate matter to the atmosphere has been predicted to occur in the event of large-scale nuclear war. The resulting addition of large quantities of dust, soot, and smoke to the atmosphere has been seen as a threat to all life on earth not destroyed directly by such conflict. This material would block incoming sunlight and produce considerable cooling and darkness that would kill vegetation on which other life depends (Ehrlich, et al., 1984).

Special concerns have arisen in connection with modification of the composition of the stratosphere. Ozone contained in the stratosphere is important in shielding man from undesirable ultraviolet radiation, and modifications of ozone concentrations could have important biological consequences. Although, the processes through which such changes may occur are not fully understood, decreases in ozone concentrations have been associated with addition of certain substances such as chloroflururomethanes to the atmosphere (SMIC Report, 1971, pp. 258-75; Munn and Machta, 1979, pp. 180-82). Although of major potential importance from a broader perspective stratospheric ozone changes appear less significant in relation to water resources than some of the other impacts of development.

4.1(b) Direct addition of heat to the atmosphere

One of the consequences of many activities associated with socio-economic development is the addition of large quantities of heat to the atmosphere. In addition to transfers of latent heat that occur when water vapor is added to the atmosphere, direct transfers are also significant. A major source of heat releases is the generation of electricity. In the case of fossil fuel and nuclear generating facilities, a large portion of the total heat contained in fuels cannot be converted into electricity with currently available technology and must be discharged, either to water or directly to the atmosphere. Additional releases occur when the electricity is put to use. Direct use of fossil fuels in

transportation and other activities also contributes substantial heat to the environment.

The direct addition of heat to the atmosphere has the potential to disrupt naturally occurring energy balances and therefore to produce changes in climatic processes such as air circulation patterns; however, current heat generated by human activities is very small in relation to the heat provided by solar radiation. Significant impacts on climate therefore are likely to be limited to somewhat localized areas with concentrated heat releases. Within areas of up to a thousand square kilometers, heat generated by human activities can be of the same order of magnitude or even exceed net solar radiation (Munn and Machta, 1979, p. 182).

4.1(c) Land surface changes

Socio-economic development can substantially alter the earth's surface in ways with potential to modify climate. Some of these changes are likely to produce only local effects. For example, wind movements may be altered locally by construction of tall buildings and clearing of forests (Munn and Machta, 1979, p. 187).

Other changes have potential for more widespread effects, particularly by modifying heat transfer processes. One manner in which changes in heat transfer are effected involves modification in the reflectivity of the earth's surface. Changes that increase reflectivity include such activities as clearing of forests and desertification, while decreases in reflectivity would generally result from such activities as creation of man-made lakes and irrigation activities. According to one estimate of the net impact of reflectivity changes over the last 6000 years, a drop of 0.13 degrees Celsius in global surface equilibrium temperature would have occurred if other factors had remained constant. Since changes in reflectivity are not uniformly distributed but are concentrated in certain regions of the earth's surface, regional modifications in atmospheric circulation and other climatic changes may result from such changes (Munn and Machta, 1979, pp. 183-84).

Changes in heat transfer can also be produced by alterations of the thermal properties of the earth's surface. For example, concrete structures have different heat storage properties than the underlying land. Even greater alterations in heat storage capacity result from replacement of land areas by reservoirs (SMIC Report, 1971, p. 64).

4.1(d) Problems in determining net effects of socio-economic development on global climate

The ability of socio-economic development to produce local climatic alterations has been documented. For example, urbanization has been found to produce such changes as increases in local temperature, cloudiness, and precipitation (Landsberg, 1979, pp. 202-203). But prediction and measurement of impacts on global conditions pose greater difficulties. This difficulty extends even to the most commonly acknowledged alterations. For example, limited ability exists to estimate the magnitude and distribution of effects associated with increased atmospheric carbon dioxide although major impacts on such phenomena as oceanic circulation and precipitation patterns are anticipated (Munn and Machta, 1979, p. 201).

These difficulties in defining climatic changes and their impacts arise from several factors. A major obstacle to identification of impacts is the natural variability of climate. Man-made effects are likely to be obscured by natural changes that are not fully understood under the present state of knowledge (SMIC Report, 1971, pp. 2-3, 10). A second major obstacle is the existence of multiple impacts and interactions (Munn and Machta, 1979, p. 170). Change in a single climatic parameter may result in several effects, some of which may be complementary and amplify one another while others may produce opposing impacts that suppress one another. For example, evaporation of water at the earth's surface involves transfer of heat from the land to the atmosphere, but the addition of water vapor to the atmosphere also can affect climate by modifying incoming solar radiation and outgoing terrestrial radiation. Thus the net impact on climate is more difficult to determine than the impact of any of the individual effects considered alone.

The situation is made more complex by the fact that socio-economic development activities are likely to change several of the parameters of climate at the same time. An activity such as urbanization simultaneously produces such effects as changing the reflectivity and heat storage properties of the earth's surface, releasing heat to the atmosphere, and adding gaseous and particulate substances to the atmosphere (SMIC Report, 1971, pp. 114-122; Munn and Machta, 1979, p. 171).

4.2 Modification of surface and groundwater movement

The natural patterns of water movement, once initiated by the fall of precipitation to the earth's surface, are subject to modification by a variety of changes in the terrestrial environment occuring during development. In addition to the continuing influences of climate (especially temperature, which controls the physical state of the water), the major determinants of water movement in response to gravitational forces are physiographic factors (such as soil types, slopes, and condition of the land's surface) and land-use activities. These factors directly influence the proportion of precipitation that will infiltrate into the soil in relation to the proportion that becomes surface runoff; in addition, they control rates of movement of both subsurface and surface flows.

Developmental activities can substantially modify the behavior of water after it reaches the land's surface. Water development projects are the most obvious source of change, but other development activities are significant as well. A major change is produced when land is covered by impervious surfaces such as buildings and pavement. This change will increase the proportion of rainfall that becomes surface runoff due to reductions

in infiltration, surface depression storage, interception by vegetation, and evaporation. The increase will be most notable where the affected area has a high natural infiltration capacity but less significant where a low capacity naturally exists.

In addition to the increased volume of runoff, rate of movement will also be increased due to the lower resistance offered by smooth artificial surfaces. Important in this regard is the extent to which natural drainageways are improved or replaced with artificial conduits. These changes tend to result in higher peak discharges for a given occurrence of precipitation in relation to the unaltered condition. However, the impact of such changes will not be the same under all conditions. For example, peak flows may be decreased where an urbanized area is located in the lower portion of a drainage basin. In this case, the increase in flow rate may result in removal of runoff from the lower basin area before contributions from the remainder of the basin are received. Other factors such as the direction of storm movement also influence the impact that will be produced in a particular situation (Yu, 1982, pp. 6,7; Costin and Dooge, 1973; Brater and Stangal, 1969; SEUHE, 1974).

Where the urbanization process results in increased runoff, less groundwater recharge and reduced streamflow during normal low-flow periods would generally be expected. These effects may not occur in isolation but instead are likely to be accompanied by other impacts of urbanization that may either accentuate or offset such effects. For example, water consumption within the urban area may further reduce low flows, or, alternatively, disposal of wastewater effluents from an imported water supply may augment low flows. With respect to groundwater conditions, further reduction in supply may occur where groundwater is the principal source of individual or public supply; but development of an alternative supply for the urban area may allow an increase in groundwater levels or artesian pressures where previous levels of use are reduced (Waananen, 1969).

Other development activities in addition to urbanization affect hydrologic processes relating to surface and groundwater. Major alterations of natural environments such as removal of forests and development of new agricultural lands generally modify natural hydrologic processes even if unaccompanied by overt water management activities. Removal of forests generally increases runoff from the area involved. The water yield of forested areas is substantially less than similarly situated grasslands due to greater interception and evaporation by a forest's tree canopy and greater transpiration losses from forests (Binns, 1979, pp. 56-58; Clarke and McCulloch, 1979). At least part of the increased runoff resulting from forest removal occurs as increased peak discharges since deforestation generally reduces infiltration rates and surface detention (Douglass, 1975, pp. 33-35). In the case of development of new agricultural lands, impact on hydrologic processes is likely to be amplified by water management activities such as drainage, irrigation, or runoff control measures. Impacts of these practices can combine with those resulting from agricultural operations such as cultivation of the soil to produce significant hydrologic impacts.

4.3 Water quality modification

The quality of water is determined by the nature of its exposure to substances that can be held in solution or suspension and therefore will reflect a wide range of changes in the environment resulting from socio-economic development. Traditionally, the focus of water quality concern has been on bodies of surface water, with principal emphasis placed on discrete discharges of wastes from such sources as industries and municipalities. The range of concern has now undergone significant expansion, and general recognition has been given to the fact that water quality changes occur during all phases of the hydrologic cycle.

4.3(a) Contamination of atmospheric moisture

The impact of development on water quality begins while the water is contained in the atmosphere where water vapor is affected by atmospheric gases and particulate matter. Even under natural conditions, water quality is affected by atmospheric substances prior to its contact with the earth's surface. For example, contact with carbon dioxide results in formation of carbonic acid. Sulfur dioxide and hydrogen sulfide from natural sources such as volcanoes and forest fires can result in formation of sulfuric and nitric acids (van Lier, 1981, pp. 9-10).

But the concentration of potential water contaminants in the atmosphere can be substantially increased by developmental activities. A major result of human activities has been an increase in atmospheric gases with potential to increase precipitation acidity. Although some disagreement among scientists continues, many believe that "acid rain" problems have been caused by significant increases in sulfur dioxide and nitrogen oxides resulting from combustion of fossil fuels. The full spectrum of long range impacts of acid rain are unknown, but significant adverse effects on aquatic ecosystems have been identified, particularly in eastern North America and Europe (van Lier, 1981, pp. 5,23-28; Eisenreich (ed.), 1981).

Although other forms of water pollution also can have far-reaching impacts, the potential areal extent of contamination resulting from atmospheric processes is especially significant. Considerable distance may separate the source of the contaminants and the resulting effects on water at the earth's surface. This characteristic has important implications for management since transgression of political boundaries is likely to occur.

4.3(b) Contamination of runoff

The importance of quality changes occurring during overland flow prior to runoff's entry into a permanent body of surface water has also been recognized as indicated by broad usage in recent years of the term "nonpoint source pollution." A principal contaminant

of runoff consists of sediment resulting from erosion. Erosion and sedimentation processes occur naturally, but they can be substantially increased by development activities that disturb the land's surface such as agriculture, urban development, mining, and forestry operations. Although substantial increases in sediment yields relative to natural conditions can be caused by a wide variety of activities, construction activities associated with urban development are a particularly significant source. Areas subject to construction activities have been observed to produce sediment at rates from two to several hundred times the rate from undisturbed lands (Wolman and Schick, 1967, p. 457).

The transport of sediment into surface waters creates several undesirable consequences. Substantial impact on aquatic organisms is one effect. These impacts result from alteration of bottom conditions, changes in light penetration, and other habitat modifications. Sediment reduces the capacity of stream channels and reservoirs, thereby causing loss of water storage capacity, interference with navigation, and increased flooding. Water treatment costs rise with increasing sediment. Recreational and aesthetic values are diminished, both while the sediment is suspended and after its deposition (Clark, Haverkamp, and Chapman, 195, pp. 61-103).

A special water quality problem operating through natural runoff processes accompanies deforestation of relatively arid watersheds in certain areas. This phenomenon, which consists of increases in salinity, has occurred primarily, but not exclusively, on the Australian Continent where it exists on a regional scale and has necessitating adoption of extensive and costly control programs. The necessary precondition for development of this dryland salinity problem is an accumulation of salts in the soil profile. Such accumulation can occurs naturally where atmospheric deposition of ocean salts occur in areas of deep soils and high evapo-transpiration from native forests and other vegetation. Clearing of natural forests causes a significant fall in evapo-transpiration losses, which is accompanied by rising groundwater levels and leaching of accumulated salts into surface waters. The salinity problem will eventually rectify itself when leaching removes the accumulated salts, but a natural solution will not be acceptable in most circumstances since the equilibrium time may be hundreds or thousands of years (Sadler and Williams, 1981).

Runoff from areas affected by socio-economic development can also be contaminated by many other substances in addition to natural products. The nature of such contaminants is determined by the type of activities within the drainage area. In an agricultural area, principal contaminants in addition to sediments are nutrients from animal wastes, fertilizers, and pesticide products (Clark, Haverkamp, and Chapman, 1985, pp. 105-135). Urban runoff can contain a broad range of substances, with some of the more important being the nutrients of phosphorous and nitrogen; heavy metals such as zinc, lead, copper, and chromium; and hydrocarbons. Peak concentrations of pollutants in urban runoff generally occur shortly after the initiation of storm runoff and may extend over a short period of time only. Urban runoff has been found to have a significant impact on downstream water quality during wet weather conditions (United States EPA, 1983). Conveyance of urban runoff in a combined sewer system also used for transport of sewage and other municipal wastes creates the potential for water quality problems when flow rates exceed the capacity of municipal treatment and/or wastewater storage facilities and untreated releases occur (Yousef, et al. (eds.), 1980).

4.3(c) Contamination of groundwater

Contamination of groundwater has also become a major concern in areas affected by socio-economic development activity. Groundwater can become contaminated by many waste disposal practices involving burial of potential contaminants within the earth or placing them on the land's surface. Such sources include landfills, waste injection wells, waste lagoons, and various forms of land application of wastes. These land-based forms of waste disposal are often adopted to reduce waste discharge to surface waters but may simply transfer the problem to the subsurface. Due to hydrologic interconnection, however, contamination of groundwater by subsurface waste disposal may result in surface water pollution (just as disposal of wastes into surface waters can lead to groundwater pollution under certain conditions).

In addition to waste disposal as a potential source of groundwater contamination, many other activities not directly involving waste disposal can also alter groundwater quality. Natural resource extraction operations are one important source of contamination. In addition to associated waste disposal activities, mining and well drilling can serve as direct mechanisms of groundwater pollution. For example, drilling of deep oil and gas wells can establish paths of movement for naturally occurring mineralized water or waste products placed underground to move into freshwater aquifers (United States EPA, 1977, pp. 428-29). Pumping of groundwater itself can result in contamination of groundwater supplies where pressure or water level reductions from pumping cause intrusion of seawater or movement of other water of undesirable quality (Ballentine, Reznek, and Hall, 1972, pp. 16-21; United States EPA, 1977, p. 426). A wide range of other activities at or near the earth's surface can adversely affect groundwater quality, including such major sources of pollution as spills and leaks of chemicals, agricultural activities, and highway deicing (United States EPA, 1977, pp. 418-41).

Groundwater contamination is of special concern due to the long time cycle often involved in natural cleansing resulting from the slow rates of groundwater movement. Once contaminated, an aquifer may be unsuitable as a source of water supply for many years. On the other hand, the slow rate of spread of contamination tends to keep pollution problems confined to relatively small areas and may facilitate later remedial actions such as pumping of the water for treatment should such action become feasible.

4.3(d) Direct waste discharge to surface waters

Recognition of these new dimensions of the water quality problem does not diminish the importance of direct effluent discharges to surface waters as a source of contamination of the water resource. An inevitable consequence of the socio-economic development process is the production of waste products, many of which can be discharged to water as a means of disposal. To the extent that the applicable institutional framework allows such discharge without accountability for adverse consequences, a direct economic incentive exists to employ this means of disposal. This incentive applies not only to owners of private waste-producing facilities but can also extend to managers of public facilities such as municipal sewage works and other public enterprises if the perspective of the decision maker is limited to the interests of the particular enterprise or local geographic area.

5. References for section II

Ballentine, R. K., S. R. Reznek, and C. W. Hall. "Subsurface Pollution Problems in the United States" (TS-00-72-02). Washington: U. S. Environmental Protection Agency, 1972.

Ben-Zvi, Samuel. "Determining Industrial Comparative Advantages in Areas of Proposed Water Navigation Projects: An Industrial Location Analysis." Fort Belvoir, Va.: U. S. Army Corps of Engineers Institute for Water Resources, 1981.

Binns, W. O. "The Hydrological Impact of Afforestation in Great Britian." In *Man's Impact on the Hydrological Cycle in the United Kingdom*. Ed. G. E. Hollis. Norwich: Geo Abstracts (University of East Anglia), 1979, pp. 55-69.

Birdsall, Nancy. "Population and Poverty in the Developing World." *Population Bulletin*, 35 (1980), no. 5, pp. 3-41.

Biswas, Asit K. "Climate, Agriculture, and Economic Development." In *Food, Climate, and Man*. Eds. Margaret R. Biswas and Asit K. Biswas. New York: John Wiley and Sons, 1979, pp. 237-259.

Biswas, Asit K. "Environmental Implications of Water Development for Developing Countries." In *The Social and Ecological Effects of Water Development in Developing Countries*. Ed. Carl Widstrand. Part 1 of *Water and Society: Conflicts in Development*. Vol. 7 of *Water Development, Supply and Management*. Series ed. Asit K. Biswas. Oxford: Pergamon Press, 1978, pp. 279-297.

Biswas(2), Asit K. "Editor's Introduction." *United Nations Water Conference: Summary and Main Documents* (Ed. Asit K. Biswas). Vol. 2 of *Water Development, Supply, and Management* (Series ed. Asit K. Biswas). Oxford: Pergamon Press (for the United Nations), 1978, pp. ix-ivii.

Biswas, Margaret R. "United Nations Water Conference: A Perspective." *United Nations Water Conference: Summary and Main Documents*. Vol. 2 of *Water Development, Supply and Management*.

Series ed. Asit K. Biswas. Oxford: Pergamon Press (for the United Nations), 1978.

Boyer, Peter B. "Gas Supersaturation Problem in the Columbia River." In *Manmade Lakes: Their Problems and Environmental Effects.* Eds. William C. Ackerman, Gilbert F. White, and E. B. Worthington. Washington: American Geophysical Union, 1973, pp. 701-705.

Brater, E. F. and Suresh Sangal. "Effects of Urbanization on Peak Flows." In *Effects of Watershed Changes on Streamflow.* Eds. Walter L. Moore and Carl W. Morgan. Austin: University of Texas Press, 1969, pp. 209-214.

Brown, Lester R. "World Food Resources and Population: The Narrowing Margin." *Population Bulletin,* 36 (1981), no. 3, pp. 3-43.

Burdge, Rabel J. and K. Sue Johnson. "Social Costs and Benefits of Water Resources Construction." Lexington, Ky.: Kentucky Resources Research Institute, 1973.

Carson, John M., Goldie W. Rivkin, and Malcolm D. Rivkin. *Community Growth and Water Resources Policy.* New York: Praeger Publishers, 1973.

Chandler, William U. *The Myth of TVA: Conservation and Development in the Tennessee Valley, 1933-1983.* Cambridge, Mass.: Ballinger Publishing Company, 1984.

Cicchetti, Charles J., V. Kerry Smith, and John Carson. "An Economic Analysis of Water Resource Investments and Regional Economic Growth." *Water Resources Research,* 11 (1975), pp. 1-6.

Clark, II, Edwin H., Jennifer A. Haverkamp, and William Chapman. *Eroding Soils: The Off-Farm Impacts.* Washington: The Conservation Foundation, 1985.

Clarke, R. T. and J.S.G. McCulloch. "The Effect of Land Use on the Hydrology of Small Upland Catchments." In *Man's Impact on the Hydrological Cycle in the United Kingdom.* Ed. G. E. Hollis. Norwich: Geo Abstracts (University of East Anglia), 1979, pp. 71-78.

Collins, Lyndhurst and David F. Walker, eds. *Locational Dynamics of Manufacturing Activity.* London: John Wiley and Sons, 1975.

Costin, A. B. and James C. I. Dooge. "Balancing the Effects of Man's Actions on the Hydrological Cycle." In *Man's Influence on the Hydrological Cycle* (Irrigation and Drainage Paper Special Issue 17). Rome: Food and Agriculture Organization of the United Nations, 1973, pp. 19-51.

Critchfield, Howard J. *General Climatology.* 3rd ed. Englewood Cliffs: Prentice-Hall, Inc., 1974.

Currie, Lauchlin. *Accelerating Development: The Necessity and the Means.* New York: McGraw-Hill Book Co., 1966.

Currie, Lauchlin. *Obstacles to Development.* East Lansing, Mich.: Michigan State University Press, 1967.

Darnell, George Frederick. "World Bank Group Activities in the Field of Irrigation." In *Proceedings: Contribution of Irrigation and Drainage to the World Food Supply.* 14-16 August, 1974. Biloxi, Mississippi,: American Society of Civil Engineers, 1975, pp. 356-361.

Donnan, William W. and Clyde E. Houston. "Drainage Related to Irrigation Management." In *Irrigation of Agricultural Lands.* Eds. Robert M. Hagan, Howard R. Haise, and Talcott W. Edminster. Madison, Wis.: American Society of Agronomy, 1967, pp. 974-987.

Douglass, James E. "Southeastern Forests and the Problem of Non-Point Sources of Water Pollution." In *Non-Point Sources of Water Pollution: Proceedings of a Southeastern Regional Conference.* 1-2 May, 1975. Eds. Peter M. Ashton and Richard D. Underwood. Blacksburg, Va.: Virginia Water Resources Research Center, 1975, pp. 29-44.

Duvel, Jr., W.A., Robert D. Volkman, Winona L. Specht, and Fred W. Johnson. "Environmental Impact of Stream Channelization." *Water Resources Bulletin,* 12 (1979), pp. 799-812.

Economides, Paris. "World Bank Experience with Irrigation, Drainage and Land Reclamation Projects." In *Irrigation and Agricultural Development.* Ed. S. S. Johl. Oxford: Pergamon Press (for the United Nations), 1980, pp. 305-314.

Ehrlich, Paul R., Carl Sagan, Donald Kennedy, Walter Orr Roberts. *The Cold and the Dark: The World After Nuclear War.* New York: W.W. Norton, 1984.

Eisenreich, Steven J., ed. *Atmospheric Pollutants in Natural Waters.* Ann Arbor, Mich.: Ann Arbor Science Publishers, 1981.

FAO (Food and Agricultural Organization of the United Nations). "Water for Agriculture." In *Water Development and Management: Proceedings of the United Nations Water Conference.* Vol. 1 (in four parts) of *Water Development, Supply and Management.* Series ed. Asit K. Biswas. Oxford: Pergamon Press (for the United Nations), 1978, part 3, pp. 907-41. (prepared in draft by FAO and subsequently revised by a consultant panel convened jointly by the Director-General of FAO and the Secretary-General of the United Nations Water Conference).

Falkenmark, Malin and Gunnar Lindh. *Water for a Starving World.* Transl. Roger G. Tanner. Boulder, Colo.: Westview Press, 1976.

Feachem, Richard. "Domestic Water Supplies, Health and Poverty: A Brief Review." In *The Social and Ecological Effects of Water Development in Developing Countries.* Ed. Carl Widstrand. Part 1 of *Water and Society: Conflicts in Development.* Vol. 7 of *Water Development, Supply and Management.* Series ed. Asit K. Biswas, Oxford: Pergamon Press, 1978, pp. 351-362.

Fedorov, E. K. "Climatic Change and Human Strategy." In *Proceedings of the World Climate Conference: A Conference of Experts on Climate and Mankind* (WMO No. 537). 12-23 Feb., 1979. Geneva: World Meteorological Organization, 1979, pp. 15-26.

Frederick, Kenneth D. *Water for Western Agriculture.* Baltimore: The Johns Hopkins Press (for Resources for the Future), 1982.

Found, W. C., A. R. Hill, and E. S. Spence. *Economic and Environmental Impacts of Land Drainage in Ontario* (Geographical Monographs No. 6). Toronto: York University, 1974.

Fowler, Jennifer A. "Effects of a Reservoir upon Fish." In *Environmental Effects of Large Dams.* New York: American Society of Civil Engineers, 1978, pp. 51-64.

Garrison, Charles B. and Albert S. Paulson. "Effect of Water Availability on Manufacturing Employment in the Tennessee Valley Region." *Water Resources Research*, 8 (1972), pp. 301-316.

Goodman, Alvin S. *Principles of Water Resources Planning.* Englewood Cliffs, N.J.: Prentice-Hall, 1984.

Gribbin, John. *Future Weather and the Greenhouse Effect.* New York: Delacorte Press/Eleanor Freide, 1982.

Grizzle, J.M. "Effects of Hypolimnetic Discharge on Fish Health Below a Reservoir." *Transactions of the American Fisheries Society*, 110 (1981), pp. 29-43.

Gurley, John G. "Economic Development: A Marxist View." In *Directions in Economic Development.* Notre Dame: University of Notre Dame Press, 1979, pp. 183-251.

Hafez, M. and W.K. Shenouda. "The Environmental Impacts of the Aswan High Dam." In *Water Development and Management: Proceedings of the United Nations Water Conference.* Vol. I (in four parts) of *Water Development, Supply and Management.* Series ed. Asit K. Biswas. Oxford: Pergamon Press (for the United Nations), 1978, part 4) pp. 1777-1786.

Hagan, Robert M. and Edwin B. Roberts. "Ecological Impacts of Water Storage and Diversion Projects." In *Environmental Quality and Water Development.* Eds. Charles R. Goldman, James McEvoy III, and Peter J. Richerson. San Francisco: W. H. Freeman and Co., 1973, pp. 196-215.

Hamilton, F. E. Ian and G. J. R. Linge, Eds. *International Industrial Systems.* Vol. 2 of *Spatial Analysis, Industry and the Industrial Environment: Progress in Research and Applications.* Chichester: John Wiley and Sons, 1981.

Hamrin, Robert D. *Managing Growth in the 1980s: Toward a New Economics.* New York: Praeger Publishers, 1980.

Hayter, Teresa. *The Creation of World Poverty.* London: Pluto Press, 1981.

Hoover, Edgar M. *The Location of Economic Activity.* New York: McGraw Hill Book Co., 1948.

Howe, Charles W. "Water Resources and Regional Economic Growth in the United States, 1950-1960." *The Southern Economic Journal*, 34 (1968), pp. 477-489.

Hunker, Henry. *Industrial Development: Concepts and Principles.* Lexington, Mass.: Lexington Books, 1974.

ITDGL (Intermediate Technology Development Group Limited). "Water for the Thousand Millions." In *Water Development and Management: Proceedings of the United Nations Water Conference.* Vol. 1 (in four parts) of *Water Development, Supply and Management.* Series ed. Asit K. Biswas. Oxford: Pergamon Press (for the United Nations), 1978, part 3, pp. 1105-62.

Johnston, Jr., S.A. "Estuarine Dredge and Fill Activities: A Review of Impacts." *Environmental Management*, 5 (1981), pp. 427-440.

Kadlec, John A. "Methodologies for Assessing Instream Flows for Wildlife." *Proceedings of the Symposium and Specialty Conference on Instream Flow Needs.* Vol. 1., Bethesda, Md.: American Fisheries Society, 1976, pp. 355-63.

Kenyon, G.F. "The Environmental Effects of Hydroelectric Projects." *Canadian Water Resources Journal*, 6 (1981), pp. 309-314.

Kovda, V. A. "Arid Land Irrigation and Soil Fertility: Problems of Salinity, Alkalinity, Compaction." In *Arid Land Irrigation in Developing Countries: Environmental Problems and Effects.* Ed. E. Barton Worthington. Oxford: Pergamon Press, 1977, pp. 211-235.

Lamb, III, James C. *Water Quality and Its Control.* New York: John Wiley and Sons, 1985.

Landsberg, Helmut E. "The Effect of Man's Activities on Climate." *In Food, Climate, and Man.* Eds. Margaret R. Biswas and Asit K. Biswas. New York: John Wiley and Sons, 1979, pp. 187-236.

Legg, David L. "Gas Supersaturation Problem in the Columbia River Basin." In *Environmental Effects of Large Dams.* New York: American Society of Civil Engineers, 1978, pp. 149-164.

Lewis, W. Cris, Jay C. Anderson, Herbert H. Fullerton, and B. Dellworth Gardner. *Regional Growth and Water Resource Investment.* Toronto: Lexington Books, 1973.

Linsley, Ray K. and Joseph B. Franzini. *Water-Resources Engineering.* New York: McGraw Hill Book Co., 1979.

Meadows, Donella H., Dennis L. Meadows, Jorgen Randers, and William W. Behrens III. *The Limits to Growth: A Report for the Club of Rome's Project on the Predicament of Mankind*, 2nd ed. New York: New American Library, 1974.

Miller, E. Willard. *Manufacturing: A Study of Industrial Location.* University Park, PA: The Pennsylvania State University Press, 1977.

Mishan, Ezra J. *The Costs of Economic Growth.* New York: Praeger Publishers, 1967.

Munn, R. E. and L. Machta. "Human Activities that Affect Climate." In *Proceedings of the World Climate Conference: A Conference of Experts on Climate and Mankind* (WMO No. 537). 12-23 Feb., 1979. Geneva: World Meteorological Organization, 1979, pp. 170-209.

Myrdal, Gunnar. *Asian Drama: An Inquiry into the Poverty of Nations.* 3 Vols. New York: The Twentieth Century Fund, 1968.

Myrdal, Gunnar. *Value in Social Theory: A Selection of Essays on Methodology by Gunnar Myrdal.* Ed. Paul Streeten. New York: Harper and Brothers, 1958.

Norcliffe, G.B. "A Theory of Manufacturing Places." In *Locational Dynamics of Manufacturing Activity.* Ed. Lyndhurst Collins and David D. Walker. London: John Wiley and Sons, 1975, pp. 19-57.

43

Norse, David. "Natural Resources, Development Strategies, and the World Food Problem. In *Food, Climate, and Man*. Eds. Margaret R. Biswas and Asit K. Biswas. New York: John Wiley and Sons, 1979, pp. 12-51.

Parsons, P.J. "Methods of Projection of Water Use—Industrial and Public Water Demand." *Proceedings of the Seminar on Long-Term Planning of Water Management, Zlatni Piasatzi, Bulgaria 17-22 May 1976*. Included in *Water Development and Management: Proceedings of the United Nations Water Conference*. Vol. I (in four parts) of *Water Development, Supply and Management*. Series ed. Asit K. Biswas. Oxford: Pergamon Press (for the United Nations), 1978, part 3, pp. 1218-1224.

Petts, G.E. "Long-Term Consequences of Upstream Impoundment." *Environmental Conservation*, 7 (1980), pp. 325-332.

Picard, Louis A. "Self-Sufficiency, Delinkage, and Food Production: Limits on Agricultural Development in Africa." In *World Food Policies Toward Agricultural Interdependence*. Eds. William P. Browne and Don F. Hadwiger. Boulder, Colo.: Lynne Rienner Publishers, 1986, pp. 121-136.

Ploskey, G.R. "A Review of the Effects of Water-Level Changes on Reservoir Fisheries and Recommendations for Improved Management." (Tech Report E-83-3). Vicksburg, Mississippi: U.S. Army Engineer Waterways Experiment Station, 1983.

Pluzhnikov, V.N. "Methods of Projection of Water Use: Agriculture and Hydroelectric Power." *Proceedings of the Seminar on Long-Term Planning of Water Management, Zlatni Piasatzi, Bulgaria, 17-22 May 1976*. Included in *Water Development and Management: Proceedings of the United Nations Water Conference*. Vol. I (in four parts) of *Water Development, Supply and Management*. Series ed. Asit K. Biswas. Oxford: Pergamon Press (for the United Nations), 1978, part 3, pp. 1224-1234.

Raney, W. A. "Irrigation Problems of Humid-Temperature and Tropical Regions." In *Irrigation of Agricultural Lands*. Eds. Robert M. Hagan, Howard R. Harie, and Talcott W. Edminster. Madison, Wis.: American Society of Agronomy, 1967, pp. 1082-1086.

Raymond, H.L. "Effects of Dams and Impoundments on Migrations of Juvenile Chinook Salmon and Steelhead from the Snake River, 1966 to 1975." *Transactions of the American Fisheries Society*, 108 (1979), pp. 505-529.

Rees, Judith Ann. *Industrial Demand for Water: A Study of South East England*. London: London School of Economics and Political Science, 1969.

Riley, R. C. *Industrial Geography*. London: Chatto and Windus, 1973.

Ryan, Bryce F. *Social and Cultural Change*. New York: The Ronald Press Co., 1969.

SEUHE(Sub-group on the Effects of Urbanization on the Hydrological Environment of the Coordinating Council of the International Hydrological Decade). *Hydrological Effects of Urbanization*. Paris: The Unesco Press, 1974.

SMIC Report (*Inadvertent Climate Modification: Report of the Study of Man's Impact on Climate*). Cambridge, Mass.: Massachusetts Institute of Technology Press, 1971.

Sadler, B.S. and P.J. Williams. "The Evolution of a Regional Approach to Salinity Management in Western Australia." *Agricultural Water Management*, 4 (1981), pp. 353-381.

Sale, Kirkpatrick. *Human Scale*. New York: Coward, McCann and Geoghegan, 1980.

Saunders, Robert J. and Jeremy J. Warford. *Village Water Supply: Economics and Policy in the Developing World*. Baltimore: The Johns Hopkins University Press (for the World Bank), 1976.

Schwiebert, Ernest, ed. *Columbia River Salmon and Steelhead*. Washington, D. C.: American Fisheries Society, 1977.

Scheffler, Israel. *Science and Subjectivity*. Indianapolis: The Bobbs-Merrill Co., 1967.

Schramm, Gunter. "Integrated River Basin Planning in a Holistic Universe." *Natural Resources Journal*, 20 (1980), pp. 787-806.

Sener, Ismail. "Water as a Factor to Attract Industries." In *Guide to Industrial Development*. Ed. Dick Howard. Englewood Cliffs, N.J.: Prentice-Hall, 1972, pp. 335-48.

Shumacher, E. F. *Small is Beautiful: Economics as if People Mattered*. London: Blond and Briggs, 1973.

Smalley, Daniel H. and John K. Novak. "Natural Thermal Phenomena Associated with Reservoirs." In *Environmental Effects of Large Dams*. New York: American Society of Civil Engineers, 1978, pp. 29-49.

Smith, David M. *Industrial Location: An Economic Geographical Analysis*. New York: John Wiley and Sons, 1981.

Solley, Wayne B., Edith B. Chase, and William B. Mann, IV. "Estimated Use of Water in the United States in 1980" (Geological Survey Circular 1001). Alexandria, Va.: U. S. Geological Survey, 1983.

Stockwell, Edward G. and Karen A. Laidlaw. *Third World Development: Problems and Prospects*. Chicago: Nelson-Hall, 1981.

Streeten, Paul et al. *First Things First: Meeting Basic Human Needs in the Developing Countries*. New York: Oxford University Press (for the World Bank), 1981.

Taylor, Karl V. "Erosion Downstream of Dams." In *Environmental Effects of Large Dams*. New York: American Society of Civil Engineers, 1978, pp. 165-186.

Tennant, Donald Leroy. "Instream Flow Regimens for Fish, Wildlife, Recreation and Related Environmental Resources." *Proceedings of the Symposium and Specialty Conference on Instream Flow Needs*. Vol. II. Bethesda, Md.: American Fisheries Society, 1976, pp. 359-73.

UNECWA (United Nations Economic Commission for Western Asia). "Irrigated Agricultural Development in the ECWA Region." In *Irrigation and Agricultural Development*. Ed. S. S. Johl. Oxford: Pergamon Press (for the United Nations), 1980, pp. 1-30.

United Nations Water Conference Secretariat. "Resources and Needs: Assessment of the World Water Situation." *United Nations Water Conference: Summary and Main Documents.* Ed. Asit K. Biswas. Vol. 2 of *Water Development, Supply and Management.* Series ed. Asit K. Biswas. Oxford: Pergamon Press (for the United Nations), 1978, pp. 25-69.

United States CEQ (Council on Environmental Quality) and Department of State. *The Global 2000 Report to the President: Entering the Twenty-First Century.* 3 Vols. Washington: U.S. Government Printing Office, 1980.

United States EDA (Economic Development Administration, U. S. Department of Commerce). *Industrial Location Determinants 1971-1975.* Washington: U. S. Government Printing Office, 1973.

United States EPA (Environmental Protection Agency). "Results of the Nationwide Urban Runoff Program." Vol. 1 - Final Report. Washington: U.S. Environmental Protection Agency, 1983.

United States EPA (Environmental Protection Agency). "The Report to Congress: Waste Disposal Practices and Their Effects on Groundwater." Washington: U. S. Environmental Protection Agency, 1977.

van Lier, Irene H. *Acid Rain and International Law.* Toronto and Alphen Aan Den Rizn, The Netherlands: Bunsel Environmental Consultants and Sijthoff and Noordhoff, 1981.

Voropaev, G. V. "Socio-Economic Aspects of Water Resources Development in the USSR" (Unesco Technical Documents in Hydrology). Paris: Unesco, (1986).

WHO (World Health Organization). "Report on Community Water Supplies." In *Water Development and Management: Proceedings of the United Nations Water Conference.* Vol. 1 (in four parts) of *Water Development, Supply and Management.* Series ed. Asit K. Biswas. Oxford: Pergamon Press (for the United Nations), 1978, part 3, pp. 971-91. (prepared in draft by WHO in collaboration with the World Bank and subsequently revised by working group of experts convened by the Director-General of WHO and the Secretary-General of the United Nations Water Conference.)

Waananen, Arvi O. "Urban Effects on Water Yield." In *Effects of Watershed Changes on Streamflow.* Eds. Walter L. Moore and Carl W. Morgan. Austin: University of Texas Press, 1969, pp. 169-82.

Weber, Eugene W. and Maynard M. Hufschmit. "River Basin Planning in the United States." In *Natural Resources: Energy, Water, and River Basin Development.* Vol. 1 of *Science, Technology, and Development: United States Papers Prepared for the United Nations Conference on the Application of Science and Technology for the Benefit of the Less Developed Areas.* Washington: U. S. Government Printing Office, 1963, pp. 299-312.

Wengert, Norman. "A Critical Review of the River Basin as a Focus of Resources Planning, Development, and Management." *Unified River Basin Management: Proceedings of a Symposium.*

Eds. Ronald M. North, Leonard B. Dworsky, and David J. Allee. Minneapolis, Minn.: American Water Resources Assoc., 1981, pp. 9-27.

White, Gilbert F. *Strategies of American Water Management.* Ann Arbor, Mich.: University of Michigan Press, 1969.

White, G. F. "A Perspective of River Basin Development." *Law and Contemporary Problems,* 22 (1957), pp. 157-187.

White, Gilbert F., David J. Bradley, and Anne U. White. *Drawers of Water: Domestic Water Use in East Africa.* Chicago: The University of Chicago Press, 1972.

White, Leslie A. *The Concept of Culture.* Minneapolis: Burgess Publishing Co., 1973.

Widstrand, C. "Social and Economic Aspects of Water Exploitation." In *The Social and Ecological Effects of Water Development in Developing Countries.* Part 1 of *Water and Society: Conflicts in Development.* Ed. Carl Widstrand, Vol. 7, of *Water Development, Supply and Management.* Series ed. Asit K. Biswas. Oxford: Pergamon Press (for the United Nations), 1978, pp. 279-82.

Wiener, Aaron. *The Role of Water in Development: An Analysis of Principles of Comprehensive Planning.* New York: McGraw Hill Book Co., 1972.

Wilber, Charles K. and Kenneth P. Jameson, "Paradigms of Economic Development and Beyond." In *Directions in Economic Development.* Notre Dame: University of Notre Dame Press, 1979, pp. 1-41.

Wolman, M. Gordon and Asher P. Schick. "Effects of Construction on Fluvial Sediment, Urban and Suburban Areas of Maryland." *Water Resources Research,* 3 (1967), pp. 451-64.

The World Bank. *World Development Report 1982.* New York: Oxford University Press, 1982.

The World Bank. *World Development Report 1980.* New York: Oxford University Press, 1980.

The World Bank. *World Development Report 1978.* New York: Oxford University Press, 1978.

Yotopoulos, Pan A. "The Strategy of Irrigated Agricultural Development." In *Irrigation and Agricultural Development.* Ed. S. S. Johl. Oxford: Pergamon Press (for the United Nations), 1980, pp. 31-40.

Yousef, Yousef A., Martin P. Wanielista, Waldron M. McLellon, and James S. Taylor, eds. *Urban Stormwater and Combined Sewer Overflow Impact on Receiving Water Bodies: Proceedings of the National Conference.* Cincinnati, Oh.: U. S. Environmental Protection Agency, 1980.

Yu, Shaw L. "Changes in Stormwater Flow Dynamics Resulting from Urbanization." *Urbanization, Stormwater Runoff and the Aquatic Environment: Proceedings of an Interdisciplinary Symposium.* 27-28 Aug., 1981. Ed. Christian Jones, Garth W. Redfield, and Donald P. Kelso. Fairfax, Va.: George Mason University, 1982, pp. 2-15.

Zuvekas, Jr., Clarence. *Economic Development: An Introduction.* New York: St. Martin's Press, 1979.

III. Managing interactions between water and socio-economic development

Water management consists of all actions taken within a given society concerning the interface of that society with the water resource. These actions include adjustments in individual and social behavior in response to water resource conditions and, in all but the earliest stages of socio-economic development, involve attempts to improve the natural relationship between man and water by enhancing the positive attributes of water and controlling negative attributes. The nature and extent of these attempts vary with water resource conditions and national circumstances, but water management is a major activity in many nations or at least can be identified as an important national need. Many examples can be found where resolvable water problems continue to exist due to the inadequacy of the management response. As demands for water-related services continue to increase in relation to a resource that is relatively fixed in supply and subject to degradation from many sources, water management efforts will become even more significant.

The individual nation provides the appropriate perspective for analyzing water management systems due to general acceptance of the nation as the unit of social organization. Of course, water management involves problems and issues that extend beyond the boundaries of individual nations and also those that involve subnational units of government. Since institutions for water resource management generally do not exist above the national level, international management activities largely must be accomplished through voluntary cooperative actions of the individual nations involved. Subnational units of government often exercise significant water management responsibilities on the basis of divisions of authority among the national and other levels of government. Relations among nations and among levels of governments within a nation, while important aspects of water management, can best be considered within an approach that focuses on the national level as the primary organizational framework.

Water management involves a wide range of public and private activities. Within the public sector, the most obvious water management activity is the construction and operation of water projects, but management also involves many less visible activities. Project construction and operation requires a series of supporting activities such as data collection and analysis, planning, and financial management. In addition, other elements of water management include such diverse public sector activities as taxation, public assistance, regulation, and conflict resolution. In fact, a nation's water management system is an integral part of the overall political structure and cannot be considered in isolation of the general socio-cultural framework.

A major factor determining the structure of a nation's water management system is delineation of the boundary between public and private sectors of activity. The water management system of a nation where natural resources are publicly owned and developed will be substantially different from that of a capitalistic nation where natural resources are subject to private property rights and managed within the framework of a competitive market. In general, the former approach involves more direct management activity by public authorities.

Although the private sector plays a significant role in water development and use in capitalistic economic systems, governmental involvement is substantial. At a minimum, government must define property rights in water and establish procedures for enforcement and conflict resolution. Private rights are generally defined as subordinate to public rights such as navigation. In addition to constraints imposed through the process of property rights definition, governmental influence is also exerted through economic incentives in such forms as tax policies and through direct regulation. Regulation can take many forms but is generally intended to constrain the exercise of private rights to protect other holders of rights and the public interest from excessive adverse effects from private activities.

Significant governmental influence in water use and development decisions can be achieved through constraints and incentives applied to private property rights, but governmental involvement in water management in capitalistic systems generally goes beyond these measures to include direct governmental participation in water resource development. Such participation extends from collection and analysis of water resources data to construction of dams and other facilities for a variety of purposes.

Governmental regulation and direct participation in water resources development within capitalistic economic systems is based at least in part on the tendency of market failures to occur in association with the water resource. Significant market failures include occurrence of external effects that individual decision makers impose on other water users, the non-marketable nature of some of the services of water resources development, and the inherent tendency of certain water development activities to become monopolistic. These and other considerations often combine to result in substantial public sector involvement in water resources development.

The water management system of any nation consists of several interacting components. Although some of the components are widely shared among nations, variation occurs regarding their relative importance and the nature of the interactions among components. Such variation is an unavoidable consequence of differences among nations in socio-cultural characteristics and water resource conditions. In spite of such variation, however, the existence of certain universal requirements and issues allows construction of a generalized water management system with relatively broad applicability. The remainder of this section is a discussion of the basic components of such a generalized management system. Definition of the individual components is a somewhat arbitrary process since a water management system is an interacting whole rather than a collection of discrete elements. Nevertheless, separate consideration is given to the following components:

1. National water policy
2. Water legislation
3. Water planning
4. Data collection and analysis
5. Water allocation
6. Water quality protection
7. Preservation of selected natural water environments
8. Enhancing knowledge and awareness
9. Physical water management infrastructure
10. Financing water management
11. Administrative framework

The following sections address these components at a broad level that attempts to maintain a general relevance to the full range of socio-economic conditions existing among nations.

1. National water policy

A water management system provides a framework for a wide variety of water-related decisions: policy establishes principles to guide these decisions toward the attainment of national goals. One of the basic functions of policy is the establishment of objectives that set forth the aims of the water management program. These objectives then must be implemented through a set of principles that provide more specific guidance for individual water management activities. These statements of objectives and principles collectively define the role of water in socio-economic development and establish a basis for resolving the many potential conflicts that may occur within decision-making processes.

Water policy emanates from a variety of sources and exists in a variety of forms. Formal policy embodied in laws and official documents is the most visible. Formal policy is created through actions of legislative bodies, executive officials and agencies, and the courts. The relative importance of these sources varies among nations, but all the major components of government can be expected to contribute. Policymaking occurs at different levels of government. In addition to the national level, policy must be generated at subnational levels to the extent that these lower levels are involved in water management. The division of authority and responsibility among the different levels of government in a federal system is itself a primary policy concern.

Policy also originates from other sources and exists in less formal form. Policy is reflected in administrative organization, within the detailed provisions of administrative regulations, and in individual discretionary decisions of program administrators during day-to-day activities. Policy also originates outside government where it takes such form as attitudes and customs. A narrow definition of public policy may exclude these informal "policies," but they influence behavior in a systematic way and can significantly affect the implementation of more formal policy and therefore should be considered as elements of the policy framework.

In the ideal case, preparation of formal water policy logically should follow the articulation of policy for general socio-economic development. Water resources management is but one component of overall development and should be integrated into broader policy to ensure consistency and coordination among the various components of development. This integration includes fashioning of water policy to be consistent with broader policy and also the application of water policy to influence comprehensive development policy. In reality, however, a comprehensive statement of development policy is unlikely to exist since it continually evolves and rarely can be articulated in complete form. Water policy similarly will generally be incomplete and subject to continual evolution.

The potential content of water policy is as broad as water management itself; thus, any listing of policy issues must be incomplete. The following basic policy issues are discussed below:

1. Establishment of water management objectives
2. Establishment of management priorities
3. Promotion of integrated management
4. Facilitating public participation

1.1 Establishment of water management objectives

The ultimate objective of water resources management is to achieve from the resource the greatest enhancement of social welfare. But water management encompasses many individual activities focusing on narrowly defined components of welfare. In fact, management objectives generally must be limited to particular aspects of welfare in order to have operational meaning. The unbounded concept of welfare is too broad and difficult to measure to serve as an objective toward which progress can be measured.

The objective most commonly adopted as an indicator of increasing social welfare is economic growth. In the case of water management, this objective focuses on increase in the national production of goods and services by water-related activities. However, the general criticisms of economic growth as an indicator of socio-economic development are also applicable to its use as a water management objective. Economic growth may be an insensitive indicator of many dimensions of social welfare. When expressed in terms of national averages, economic growth may be a particularly inadequate indicator of welfare due to its neglect of distributional aspects of welfare. Increase in the national output of goods and services does not necessarily ensure improvement in living conditions for all segments of society and in fact may be accompanied by worsening conditions for some groups.

In addition to this lack of attention to distributional aspects of welfare, the economic growth objective tends to give inadequate attention to other dimensions of welfare traditionally not fully reflected through market transactions. Environmental quality is a primary example. Adverse environmental impacts associated with economic growth may significantly offset welfare improvements from increased output of goods and services.

Due to the potential deficiencies of economic growth as the sole water management objective, the economic growth objective may be constrained to ensure consideration of other dimensions of welfare, it may be supplemented by adoption of other objectives within a multi-objective framework, or it may be totally replaced by other objectives. Where constraints are imposed on the economic growth objective, they typically take the form of procedures to ensure consideration of the distributional aspects of management activities or the environmental consequences of such activities. Such constraints may specify performance criteria to be satisfied or, alternatively, may simply require evaluation and reporting of impacts within the planning process.

The multi-objective approach establishes two or more objectives to be considered simultaneously. National economic growth is likely to be retained as one of the objectives, with additional objectives taking such forms as regional economic growth or environmental quality protection. While separate objectives may be complementary in some situations, conflicts commonly occur. Resolution involves the evaluation of possible trade-offs among objectives to determine the socially optimum combination. To the extent that the objectives can be quantified and reduced to mathematical terms, evaluation can utilize mathematical optimization techniques. In other cases (which are likely to be more common), optimization will involve application of more subjective procedures such as debate within relevant political processes.

In situations where particular needs are urgent, more specific water management objectives may replace general objectives such as economic growth. For example, self sufficiency in food production or simply an increase in irrigated acreage may become the objective. While such specific aims may contribute to broader objectives such as economic growth, they may be pursued without explicit evaluation of the effect of individual management activities on broader objectives. This approach is based on the assumption that the relationship of certain activities to social welfare is self evident and therefore not in need of evaluation in terms of degree of contribution to general social objectives.

Determination of the objectives of water management, or assignment of weights among multi-objectives, depends on a variety of national circumstances. Socio-economic patterns and resulting water demands differ, as do water resource conditions. More fundamentally, objectives must be based on values that define what changes are viewed as improvements in well being. Because of their dependence on values and other unique national circumstances, objectives have limited transferability among nations. Decisions concerning objectives must be made through national political processes, the only appropriate forum for making the necessary value judgments and resolving other national societal issues (Bokhari, 1981; James, 1978).

1.2 Establishment of management priorities

Conflict resolution is a necessary aspect of water resources management, and a basic function of water policy is to establish priorities to guide such decisions. The need for conflict resolution can arise in several situations.

A variety of conflicts among multiple objectives is possible. For example, the economic growth objective is likely to conflict with an environmental protection objective due to inherent incompatibilities between development and preservation. Policy for resolving these and other potential conflicts may prescribe conditions under which one objective is to take precedence over others. In more typical cases, however, policy provides for compromise to achieve solutions contributing to each of the conflicting objectives. This approach is likely to be more politically acceptable in the absence of widespread agreement on the predominance of one of the objectives.

Conflicts among water uses and water-using sectors will involve water allocation law as a primary mechanism for resolution. The basic function of this law is to resolve conflicts and to establish principles to guide behavior for avoidance of conflict. Policy provisions of such law can incorporate appropriate preferences among general water-use categories. Preferences among categories of water-use and water-related sectors of an economy are also implemented through budgetary decisions for allocation of public funds for construction of related facilities.

Water-related conflict between urban and rural areas and between regions is also a frequent characteristic of water management. Policy to resolve such conflict may be explicitly designed to alleviate existing imbalances in socio-economic conditions between these areas. As in the case of conflict between water-using sectors, a basic resolution mechanism in this type of conflict is the budgetary process through which decisions are made concerning type and geographic location of publicly funded water management facilities. Resolution of such conflict involves policies broader than water management considerations alone, illustrating the subservient nature of water policy to national policy for socio-economic development.

1.3 Promotion of integrated management

The concept of integrated water management as used in this report refers to adoption of a broad perspective within all the associated areas of decision making. Use of the term here is similar to its use in the concept of "integrated river basin development" (United Nations, 1970), with the exception that the use here includes management activities beyond the traditional concept of development. In addition, its use does not necessarily imply acceptance of river basin boundaries as jurisdictional limits for administrative organization.

At a minimum, the concept of integrated management includes the following considerations:

1. Multiple-purpose project construction
2. Multiple means of achieving management objectives
3. Continuity of the hydrologic cycle
4. Water quantity and quality interactions
5. Water and land use interactions
6. Social aspects of water management
7. Environmental aspects of water management

1.3(a) Multiple-purpose project construction

The construction of projects to improve the utility of the water resource by altering its natural distribution or other conditions remains a basic water management tool; the concept of multiple purpose construction provides the potential for increasing total net benefits associated with such construction. The concept of multiple-purpose projects is well established, especially in the case of reservoir construction. The ability to use one facility to provide water supply for several purposes while simultaneously providing other services such as downstream flood protection often creates significant advantages in comparison to separate projects. Operation of reservoirs for multiple purposes involves potential conflicts, but operation can produce total net benefits in excess of those available collectively from single purpose construction. Mathematical optimization techniques have undergone substantial development in their application to multiple purpose projects and series of interrelated projects (Torno (ed.), 1985).

Although the concept of multiple-purpose construction is well established, such opportunities can be overlooked in individual cases. Such oversight is most likely to occur in projects under the control of private interests or governmental agencies with limited management perspective such as a power company or an agency responsible solely for irrigation development. To prevent opportunities for multiple-purpose projects from being lost due to lack of consideration, water policy should ensure consideration of such potential during the project planning process.

1.3(b) Multiple means of achieving management objectives

Failure of water managers to consider a reasonable range of alternatives frequently has been identified as a management problem. This failure has generally involved a bias favoring certain types of construction to modify natural hydrologic processes over other alternatives. A basic cause of this failure has been limited agency perspectives in managerial decision processes. Agencies limited in authority to implementation of certain types of alternatives tend to view those alternative means as ends. For example, dam construction can come to be viewed as a socially desirable end in itself by those agencies with a dam construction mission. Such views act as inherent limitations on range of alternatives considered by the agency. Integrated water management requires application of a broad perspective to ensure consideration of a full range of alternatives.

While dam construction and other manipulations of natural hydrologic processes remain an important means for achieving water management objectives, other means often exist and, in some cases, may be superior to water development projects. An expanded view of means has received substantial acceptance in several areas of water management. One of these areas is flood damage reduction. Control of exposure to flood damage has been accepted as an additional approach to supplement construction of facilities to control floodwater. Controlling exposure is achieved through such measures as restricting floodplain use, floodproofing of structures, and improved flood warning systems. The flood damage problem has also been addressed by measures focusing on the distribution of losses such as flood insurance programs (NSF, 1980).

A second area of water management where expanded means have been adopted for achieving water management objectives is water supply. Here the traditional approach has been to consider the single means of developing additional supply to meet continuing growth in water use as projected by extrapolation of past experience. This approach has been supplemented in recent years with the concept of controlling demand to achieve balance between supply and demand. Control of demand has been attempted both by regulatory means and by use of economic incentives. Adoption of realistic water prices and price structures designed to limit use have significant potential to encourage water recycling and other water-saving practices.

Consideration of both regulatory and economic-incentive approaches is itself an example of expanding available means for achieving management objectives. This issue is also relevant with respect to water quality protection where direct regulation of waste discharge has been the predominant means employed. Advocates of economic-incentive approaches such as imposition of effluent fees or taxes emphasize potential savings in attaining desirable water quality levels, but regulation remains the primary means employed in many nations.

One of the fundamental roles of policy is to create a water management climate that encourages consideration of a full range of means in these and other areas of management activity. This concept should be established as a general management policy and incorporated into specific guidelines for decision making within the water-related economic sectors.

1.3(c) Continuity of the hydrologic cycle

The concept of integrated water resources management is based on full recognition of the continuity of the hydrologic cycle and its many physical relationships. Recognition of quantitative interactions of water within a river basin is a basic factor in the traditional concept of integrated river basin development; projects are designed to operate in a coordinated fashion to maximize net benefits. The concept of integrated management adopted here requires that water management decisions, whether or not part of a river basin development scheme, include consideration of impacts transmitted by hydrologic processes. Thus, a proposal to divert water from one basin for use in another should involve an evaluation of the impact of the diversion on present and future water demands within the basin where the water originates.

The concept of integrated management also includes consideration of surface and groundwater interactions. The decision to develop one source should be made in view of likely impacts on the other source. Such impacts may take the form of reductions in available supply or may result in increased supply as in the situation where development of a surface water supply for irrigation purposes produces increased groundwater levels in the irrigated area. Both effects should be evaluated as part of the management process.

An important determinant of the extent to which hydrologic impacts are considered by the decision maker is the degree to which legal accountability is imposed. Where legal mechanisms for imposing accountability do not exist or are uncertain, such impacts become externalities from the perspective of the water developer and are likely to be ignored in the decision process. However, such impacts affect social welfare and should be evaluated independently of the compensation issue. Water policy therefore should mandate consideration of such impacts within water management decision processes.

1.3(d) Water quantity and quality interactions

Integrated water management requires application of a management perspective sufficiently broad to recognize physical interactions between water quantity and water quality. Major disruptions are possible in a management program that focuses on the quantity and quality dimensions independently. Water supply management efforts may be frustrated if available quantities of water, which otherwise are adequate for supply purposes, become unuseable due to contamination. The most severe impact involves long term contamination such as pollution of slow-moving groundwaters or the incorporation of toxic substances into stream sediments.

Similarly, achievement of water quality management objectives can be frustrated if inadequate attention is given to quantitative issues. Major qualitative impacts can be produced by any activity reducing water available for dilution and waste assimilation. Initiation of interbasin water transfers and water uses involving large amounts of consumption are therefore important in water quality management as well as in supply management. Groundwater pumping can create quality problems due to resulting movement of mineralized or other low quality water. In estuarine areas, qualitative impacts of flow-altering activities include possible shifts in salinity patterns resulting from changes in freshwater inflow. Even the addition of flow can be significant due to lowered salinity at certain points, which potentially can affect fish and shellfish. Water quality changes can result from the operation of flow-altering structures that have relatively minor effects on total streamflow reaching lower points. For example, a hydroelectric impoundment can adversely affect water quality due to different flow patterns or changes occurring in water quality as a result of impoundment. Such effects can also be beneficial under certain conditions.

The potential for interaction between water quantity and quality indicates that quantity management and quality management cannot be pursued independently but must be coordinated as components of a single management program. Such coordination may be difficult due to traditional divisions of managerial responsibility. Water quality management is often the responsibility of an independent agency while decision making relating to quantity is often divided among several agencies organized along sectoral lines. In addition, responsibilities for quantity and quality may be divided among different levels of government.

1.3(e) Water and land-use interactions

A natural body of water exists in an intimate relationship with its watershed. Many of its characteristics are determined by watershed conditions, and changes in these conditions through land-use activities can have far reaching effects on both the flow patterns and quality of the body of water. Land development often has the effect of increasing peak runoff and increasing the amount of sediment and other pollutants entering the body of water. These effects can have major water management impacts. For example, flooding can be increased, water supply may become less dependable, increased sedimentation rates can lead to significant loss of storage capacity in storage reservoirs, nutrient enrichment from nonpoint source pollution can produce excessive algal growth and substantial water quality problems, and clearing of forests in certain arid regions can lead to significant increases in salinity of the waters within a given catchment.

A special relationship exists between water resources and natural resources development within the watershed. Activities such as oil and gas development, mining, and forestry operations have potential for significant quantitative and qualitative impacts on surface and groundwaters. In addition, resource development activities can create substantial water demands, in both the resource development activity and in related socio-economic development. Proper consideration of these relationships requires coordination between water and other resource planning and management programs.

Exclusive focus of water management on the water resource system can be a major constraint to the solution of certain water problems. Water quality protection is one management area where land-use considerations are a fundamental factor in achieving water management objectives. Focus on treatment of wastes at the discharge point has been a partially successful approach, but realization has now been given to the fact that achievement of water quality objectives in many areas will require attention to land-use decisions. Choice of the type and density of land development activities may have overriding influence on future water quality that cannot practically be reversed by attempts to treat wastewater.

Flood damage reduction provides a second example where interaction between water management and land use is obvious. Governmental programs for controlling floodwater through such means as impoundments, channel improvements, and levees have produced beneficial effects but cannot reduce flood damages to an acceptable level if used alone. An approach including controls on use of flood plains along with traditional flood control methods has greater potential to produce acceptable results.

Efforts to integrate land-use considerations into water management is complicated by several factors. In some countries, public sector involvement in land-use decision making may be substantially less than in the case of traditional water management activities. Such public sector involvement in land-use control as does exist is likely to involve an organizational structure for administration independent of the water management framework. Regardless of these difficulties, however, water policy should recognize the interactions between water and land use and provide for their consideration in relevant decision processes. In addition, the water managment program must attempt to influence land-use decisions in pursuit of water management objectives.

1.3(f) Social aspects of water management

The deficiencies of much past water management activity have arisen in large part due to the assumption that water management is primarily a technical activity involving physical manipulation of physical systems. While the technical aspects of management are important, management has fundamental social dimensions that must be fully incorporated into decision-making processes.

The incorporation of social considerations into water management is necessary to establish and achieve management objectives and to avoid undesirable social impacts. Failure of many water management projects to achieve their objectives can be attributed to lack of attention to social aspects of activities essential to accomplishment of the objectives. Few technical operations affecting water resources are sufficient in themselves to accomplish their intended objectives. Provision of domestic water supply and improved

sanitation facilities does not ensure improvement in health. Provision of irrigation water does not guarantee desirable increases in agricultural output. Generation of electricity from a hydropower facility does not necessarily lead to industrial development. In each of these examples, achievement of the objective requires a variety of complementary actions, many of which are fundamentally related to socio-cultural factors. Consideration of such factors therefore must be a basic component of the water management process.

Consideration of social factors is also essential for avoidance of unintended adverse social consequences as a result of water management activities. The most obvious of such impacts is the dislocation of the population from land areas needed for projects such as reservoirs. But many more subtle impacts are possible. Water policy should provide for identification and evaluation of social impacts to allow water management decisions to be made in awareness of such consequences and with consideration of possible mitigation measures.

1.3(g) Environmental aspects of water management

Unanticipated environmental degradation has been a frequent consequence of water management activities, particularly where reservoirs and other large-scale facilities have been constructed. Environmental impacts often take the form of biological disruptions. Water in the natural state is an essential element of the ecosystems upon which living organisms depend, and all alterations of natural water conditions have potential to produce adverse effects. These adverse effects belatedly have been widely recognized as contributing negatively to social welfare, which water development is intended to advance.

One of the factors responsible for traditional lack of attention to such effects has been lack of knowledge. Although some human activities created noticeable environmental disruptions at an early date, the consequences of many activities were obscured by natural variation in environmental systems and the ability of such systems to absorb impacts and continue to function, although perhaps in a less than optimum manner. Understanding of the functioning of natural ecosystems has increased greatly in recent years, but much remains to be learned. What has been learned dictates caution in future water resources development and use due to the continuing discovery of new mechanisms of environmental injury.

A more basic reason for traditional lack of concern for environmental impact has been an overly narrow formulation of social welfare. Prevailing attitudes and values at an earlier period in some nations tended to equate all activities leading to economic growth and increase in material prosperity with increasing social welfare. To the extent that adverse environmental consequences were recognized, they were either explicitly or implicitly relegated to a position of little significance. Attitudes and values have undergone change in recent decades, and environmental values have significantly increased in standing as a component of welfare.

This increased standing has led to major efforts to minimize impacts of water development projects. In fact, efforts to protect environmental values associated with the water resource have gone beyond an attempt to limit the impact of water development to include concern for the total impact of socio-economic development. In addition to generating efforts to minimize adverse impacts, changed attitudes have also resulted in expansion of management objectives to include preservation and enhancement of selected water environments. For example, programs to set aside part of the resource to be preserved for its scenic and other natural characteristics have been adopted in some nations (Goodell, 1978).

Degree of recognition and status of environmental values continue to vary among nations, however. Attention to environmental protection has tended to lag in the developing countries. Protection of environmental values is likely to receive less attention where basic needs such as nutrition are not being met. Environmental management has become a political issue in many of these nations, but governmental programs may continue to be symbolic efforts only (Khator, 1984). But neglect of environmental conditions is a short term approach with possibly serious long term repercussions. Environmental quality must be viewed as a universal concern since environmental degradation can lead to health problems and a deterioration in the quality of life in both developed and developing countries. The desirable balance between economic growth and environmental quality may be different in the developing country as compared to the developed nation, but total neglect is not a reasonable approach. National policy must establish standards of environmental quality and principles to ensure consideration of environmental conditions within water resource management programs.

1.4 Facilitating public participation

Increased public participation in water management activity has been a major development in recent years. Although significant obstacles to effective public participation still exist in many situations, the traditional view that water management is the sole province of technical specialists and governmental officials has been modified substantially.

The importance of public participation to water management effectiveness arises due to the extensive social dimension of water management. Realization of water management objectives requires integration of water management technology into daily practices governed by the socio-cultural framework. Failure of water managers to thoroughly consider this framework has been an important factor in the frequently disappointing results of management efforts. Participation of those to be affected by and responsible for implementation is the most direct approach for incorporating the socio-cultural factor into decision making.

2. Water legislation

Water legislation is the principal formal expression of policies and procedures that define a water management system. While form and content of legislation will vary with national circumstances, the need for such legislation is universal since a well-defined framework is essential to rational and consistent decision making.

A major function of water legislation is the definition of the individual components of the management system, delineation of their respective responsibilities, and provision of necessary coordination mechanisms. Because of the many interactions between water and human activities, water management activities necessarily have a broad scope. This situation creates substantial potential for conflicting actions among individual governmental agencies but may also result in neglect of certain management functions not specifically assigned within the management framework. While a degree of flexibility must be maintained, legislation should define basic responsibilities to an extent necessary to ensure the operation of the management system as a whole.

Since water management involves the individual actions of a large number of water users, water legislation also must define the rights and appropriate constraints relative to such activities. The absence of well defined rights can lead to conflict and may result in a reduction in the contribution of water to socio-economic development.

2.1 Evolution of water legislation

The extent of the need for water management activities to be defined by legislation varies with national conditions. The need generally increases as demands for water and related services rise and therefore is likely to be greater at higher levels of development. Under favorable water resource conditions where few problems exist, complex legislation is not likely to be necessary; however, the need to define a basic management framework arises at an early stage of development. Interactions between water and socio-economic processes are important at all levels of development and require consideration within appropriate decision processes. Formalizaton of procedures for such consideration through incorporation into law is an important step in the development of an effective water management system and the overall insitutional framework for social governance.

Water legislation is not static but must evolve in response to changes occurring during the socio-economic development process. While a trend toward greater amounts of legislation generally accompanies increasing development, change also involves modification of existing law to ensure continuing consistency with changed conditions. Law appropriate under one set of conditions may become inadequate and even become an impediment to effective management under new conditions. An important function of the water management system therefore is to assess continually the adequacy of existing legislation and to identify necessary changes for addressing newly emerging management needs.

3. Water planning

Planning is a pervasive activity within socio-economic development processes since it is the means by which present conditions, trends, constraints, and opportunities are analyzed to provide information to guide future action. Because of variety among the applications and contexts of planning, general agreement concerning the nature and role of planning is lacking. Comparisons of planning among nations indicate basic differences in philosophical views. Nations with "centrally planned" economies generally will view governmental planning as a more fundamental activity than will those nations placing greater reliance on markets for economic decision making. Nations in the latter category engage in planning, but the absence of direct mechanisms for implementation results in diminished standing for planning.

Somewhat related to these differing views of the role of planning are differences in views regarding the appropriate scope and comprehensiveness of planning (Faludi, 1973). At one end of the spectrum is the "rational-comprehensive" model, which generally can be described as a systems approach to planning. Basic characteristics of this approach are its attempt to encompass a comprehensive range of factors and its long-range perspective. The rational-comprehensive approach tends to view planning as a process of objective analysis of alternative means of achieving predetermined ends that reflect a socially desirable view of future conditions (Meyerson and Banfield, 1955). Because of the broad scope of considerations and the long-term perspective adopted in this approach, the product of rational-comprehensive planning tends to be a planning document intended as a guide to future action. Such documents tend to focus on facility needs and identify projects to be constructed over the planning period.

In an opposing view, known as the "incremental" approach, the rational-comprehensive concept is seen as too idealistic in its underlying assumptions regarding political decision-making processes and the ability of planners to make accurate long-range forecasts, particularly in societies with relatively decentralized decision processes. The incremental approach focuses on short-range adjustments from current conditions. In this approach, policy making, planning, and implementation of decisions are seen as iterative processes without distinct boundaries of separation (Lindblom, 1959). Less emphasis is placed on preparation of a "plan" while more attention is given to policy analysis and mediation of interest group conflict.

Since these models represent extreme views, neither is a totally acceptable approach without modification. The comprehensive approach can become too utopian if preoccupied with the distant future and unmanageable if applied to increasing levels of detail. The incremental approach is inadequate if taken to mean that the narrow, short-range perspective is always to be adopted to the total exclusion of consideration of interactions among issues and the long-range perspective. A realistic strategy must combine elements of both approaches. The broad, long-range view can be exercised at a relatively high level of generalization without attention to detail while the more pragmatic incremental approach can be employed to address immediate problems within the context of actual political processes (Etzioni, 1967).

Planning has both a predictive and a declarative role. It is predictive when it attempts to forecast future conditions resulting from forces outside the influences of the planning organization. In this situation, the planner is a disinterested analyst not attempting to promote change. A completely detached status is difficult to maintain because of the many opportunities for the planner to interject value judgments into the analysis. But planning is not always conducted from a premise of neutrality; it often is conducted as an agent of change, and the planner becomes an advocate of a particular course of action. The posture of the planner is largely determined by the location of the planning organization within the management structure and the nature of the authority conveyed by laws and other relevant institutional factors (Beckman, 1964; Davidoff, 1965; Dyckman, 1961).

Water resources planning is a specialized application of planning theory and practice that focuses on water management problems and opportunities within the context of general socio-economic conditions. Water planning cannot be conducted in isolation but must recognize the pervasive nature of interactions between water and human activities. Planning is the means by which water-related demands and impacts of the various sectors of an economy can be analyzed and appropriate water management actions formulated. Water planning is also a mechanism for increasing awareness of water management issues within other sectors and the general public and exerting influence within other decision-making processes. The ability to increase awareness is important to the development of public support for water management activities. The capability to influence action by those who use and otherwise impact the water resource has increased in importance as the range of water management options has increased to include strategies based on modification of water use and land use in addition to strategies based on hydrologic modification

3.1 Levels of planning

In order to accomplish its diverse functions, water resources planning is generally conducted at several levels (Petersen, 1984, pp. 10-11). The term "strategic planning" or "framework planning" is often applied to the broadest level of planning. Such planning generally includes assessment of resource conditions and analysis of trends in water-use practices and other activities affecting the water resource. The need to consider many factors and their interactions requires a relatively comprehensive scope, but the process is kept manageable by maintenance of a general level of analysis. This broad analysis provides a basis for identification of future water problems and general management actions necessary for addressing such problems.

Strategic planning examines the overall role of water in socio-economic development and establishes a general framework for action within water management programs. It provides a basis for allocation of resources among competing interests, identification of needs for actions to protect environmental quality, identification of the potential for flooding or other damage and possible needs for avoidance measures, and identification of needs for storage for water supply or other purposes. Where water problems and the need for management activities are indicated, strategic planning provides a framework within which more detailed but more narrowly focused planning can be conducted. Strategic planning also has impacts external to the water management program by articulating policies and strategies that inform others of future directions and increase awareness of water problems and management issues.

Strategic planning is often supplemented by more intensive levels of planning. Regional planning and river basin planning are common examples of an intermediate level of planning between the strategic level and detailed project planning. Planning at the intermediate level generally studies the preliminary feasibility of a series of management actions for addressing water problems within a river basin or other area. At this level, problems resulting from cumulative impacts of socio-economic development can be assessed and interactions among individual water management activities evaluated.

At an even more detailed level, project-implementation planning evaluates the relative feasibilities of specific water management alternatives and recommends a preferred option based on forecasts of conditions with and without each of the alternatives. This investigation typically includes such components as preliminary design studies, economic analysis, environmental impact assessment, social impact assessment, and financial analysis. The following sections review basic issues associated primarily with the project planning process although they have some applicability to other levels of planning.

3.2 Forecasting

A central feature of planning is the estimation of future conditions to provide a basis for assessing potential problems or evaluating the effects of alternative means of addressing potential problems. In the case of water planning, a basic application of forecasting is the prediction of levels and types of future activities that affect demand for water services. Forecasting must also predict future water resource conditions. Water conditions change not only in response to specific management activities such as project implementation but also in response to development activities that modify natural hydrologic processes and to broader potential influences such as climatic change. Thus forecasting involves estimating conditions that will exist both in the absence of management activities as well as conditions that would result from implementation of such activities.

3.2(a) Forecasting future demand for water services

Forecasts of future water demand must be undertaken within a variety of water-use categories that correspond generally to the major sectors of an economy. Demand in each category has some relation to population level but also depends on a wide range of other factors, including a variety of policy decisions. For example, such demands depend on relative emphasis to be placed on alternative transportation modes, choice of power production technology, decisions regarding food self-sufficiency and primary food sources, decisions concerning the mix and level of industrial output, and policies concerning levels of water-supply and sanitation services. Forecasting water demands therefore must be undertaken within individual sectors and must be coordinated with more general social and economic planning at a national level and within sectors.

Approaches to water-demand forecasting differ considerably. At its simplest level, forecasting involves extrapolation of historical patterns within the particular water-use category. While such practice has often been used with adequate results, it is prone to significant error due to its reliance on a continuance of past causative factors. An improved approach involves the additional steps of identifying the causative factors, estimating future conditions for these factors, and calculation of projected demand from the factors as estimated for the future (Sewell, 1968). The more detailed approach can produce results significantly different from those produced by extrapolation where substantial changes in such factors as prices or regulatory policies are predicted to occur. For example, future water use per unit of product in many categories such as agricultural and industrial use may be substantially lower than traditional quantities if water prices increase.

3.2(b) Forecasting future water resource conditions

The effects of human activity on the quantity and quality of water available for future use must be projected in order to determine future water resource conditions and the capability of the resource to satisfy future demands.

Potential impacts of human activity on hydrologic patterns range from relatively small scale effects such as increase in rate and quantity of surface runoff in urbanized areas to large scale effects such as change in climate. Forecasts identifying the likelihood of occurrence and potential magnitudes of such effects may in some cases provide the opportunity for avoiding or reducing the impact through modification of development practices. For example, increases in surface runoff from urbanized areas can be controlled to some extent through special measures for detaining runoff and facilitating infiltration. Where the effects of development appear unavoidable, forecasting provides information necessary in adjusting to the changed conditions. If, for example, rise in sea level is seen as a consequence of temperature increases caused by the greenhouse effect, impacts on drainage in coastal areas can be assessed and alternative management strategies evaluated.

Forecasting must also include the quality dimension since adequacy of water to satisfy demand depends not only on sufficient quantity but also on reasonable freedom from contaminants. Most human activity has potential to adversely affect water quality either directly or indirectly, creating the need for an accounting of the individual and cumulative impacts on future water supplies. Water quality planning is a difficult undertaking due to the diversity of potential pollutants and pollutant sources and the complex nature of the many physical, chemical, and biological processes involved (Lamb, 1985). As in the case of forecasting development-induced changes in quantitative water resource conditions, forecasting of qualitative changes provides the opportunity for avoidance of certain adverse effects and development of necessary adjustments where impacts are unavoidable.

3.2(c) Limitations of forecasting

As necessary and desirable as accurate forecasting of future conditions is, forecasting is at best an inexact science. Forecasting is based to a large extent on the assumption that the future will have many similarities to the past and present and that deviations from past practices are predictable. Without such assumptions for defining the context of water-use decisions, prediction of future water demands becomes impossible. Part of the environmental, social, and technological context of water use does remain relatively constant during substantial time periods, but predictions are often upset by unanticipated changes such as technological breakthroughs and major modifications in socio-cultural conditions.

Due to the potential for unanticipated change in underlying assumptions, forecasting should involve analysis of the sensitivity of projections to changes in various factors. Such analysis allows special attention to be given to the predominant sources of variation, including analysis of alternative assumptions regarding the major factors. The likelihood of unanticipated change means that long range forecasts, and plans of action based on such forecasts, cannot be viewed as final determinations. They must remain under continual review and adjusted as dictated by changing circumstances, including the impacts of actions undertaken in response to the forecast.

Recognition of the limitations of long-range forecasting does not mean that it is without value. On the contrary, long-range trends need to be understood to the extent possible as a basis for establishing and refining management objectives and preventing oversights and mismanagement that can result from excessive concentration on more immediate issues. But recognition of the limitations of long-range forecasting emphasizes the importance of placing adequate attention on more predictable short-range events and maintaining flexibility to make necessary adjustments in response to unanticipated changes.

3.3 Identification of alternative management strategies

Several management responses are often possible for a projected water problem, but certain courses of action are likely to be superior in terms of their ability to address the given problem with the least consumption of resources and production of the least amount of other adverse effects. A critical step in the process of identifying the best alternative is the initial identification of a full range of alternatives for consideration. The most favorable option cannot be selected if it is excluded from consideration. The planning process therefore must be free of systematic bias that leads to identification of an incomplete range of alternatives.

Eliminating bias from the process of identifying alternatives may require development of generally applicable planning guidelines. Such guidelines should be developed by an entity with a perspective unrestricted by limitations of authority or historical practice, perhaps consisting of representatives of all the components of the water management system. Guidelines can take many forms, ranging from mandatory lists of types of alternatives to be included in a checklist of options merely to be considered. Another means of limiting bias in the identification of alternatives is involvement of the public from an early point in plan formulation.

3.4 Evaluation of alternatives

After a proper range of alternative measures for addressing a water problem has been identified, the planning process must subject each alternative to analysis to determine its relative suitability for approval as the preferred course of action. In the case of public projects, the ultimate criterion for approval is political feasibility, which in large measure depends on perceptions of public officials and the general citizenry regarding the significance of the problem and need for the proposed response.

A basic function of the water planning process is selection of a recommended alternative for submission to the political process. The results of such analyses generally are not binding on the ultimate decision makers but increase the information available for making a final decision. Such recommendations are based on comparative analysis of the alternatives by application of consistent evaluative criteria. These criteria must measure the contributions of each alternative to water management objectives and assess impacts in other areas of concern as identified within water management policy. These other areas of concern, if not reflected as objectives, serve as constraints on the stated objectives.

Since management objectives and constraints are not universal but must be selected to be compatible with particular national circumstances, criteria for evaluating alternatives will vary. In spite of this variation, however, certain considerations have broad applicability. Issues of broad relevance include physical and technical feasibility, technological appropriateness, economic feasibility, financial feasibility, environmental acceptability, and social acceptability. In addition, the planning process cannot ignore the broader aspects of political feasibility that must be satisfied for final approval.

3.4(a) Physical feasibility

A fundamental criterion for the acceptability of an alternative is its physical capability to perform a desired service over a specified time period. This largely technical evaluation involves preliminary design of facilities and programs in accord with predetermined performance standards and criteria. Where structures are to be built, engineering analysis determines the characteristics of the necessary construction in view of desired project output and initial resource conditions.

Hydrologic conditions are a primary determinant of water project feasibility. Information concerning average flows and the magnitude and distribution of low flows is critical to analysis of water supply alternatives. Information on the magnitude and distribution of high flows is essential to design of flood control facilities and other facilities that must safely withstand flood events. Another important hydrologic variable is sediment load since the long term operation of reservoirs and other structures can be significantly affected by sedimentation. In the case of groundwater development projects, information is necessary regarding aquifer recharge rate and other characteristics that establish limits on pumping.

Geological conditions are also important where structures are proposed. Analysis of foundation conditions is a critical aspect of the construction of dams and other large facilities. In addition to information about such factors as bearing capacity and permeability, information concerning the location of faults and the susceptibility of the area to earthquakes is needed.

Some of the factors involved in feasibility studies may change during the life of a project. Water quality may be affected by upstream agricultural or urban development. Flow patterns and sedimentation rates may be modified by a variety of developments within the watershed. The potential for such change should be considered in feasibility studies to allow adoption of necessary remedial or compensatory measures.

Feasibility studies require adoption of standards of reliability because of the probabilistic nature of hydrologic and other events. Water supply projects must be designed to provide at least a certain minimum amount of water for a specified percentage of time. Flood control projects are designed to eliminate flooding up to a flow of specified recurrence interval. Total reliability generally is not a feasible design criterion. Costs rise with increasing reliability, requiring selection of a level of dependability that can be afforded. Higher levels of reliability are generally incorporated into elements of project design affecting structural integrity of facilities such as dams. For example, spillways may be designed on the basis of an estimated maximum probable flood while flood protection provided may involve a much lesser design flood. The determination of these required reliabilites

and the degree of acceptable risk on which they are based is a basic policy issue.

Evaluation of physical feasibility involves personnel with a range of analytical skills in areas such as hydrology, geology, and structural engineering. Analysis of major projects, especially those including a series of reservoirs or other structures whose operations must be coordinated, can be greatly facilitated by analysis based on computer modeling, creating further demands for specialized staff.

3.4(b) Technology assessment

Closely related to the determination of physical feasibility is the assessment of alternative technology and its appropriateness within the particular physical and socio-cultural environment where water management activities are proposed. The issue of appropriate technology is generally discussed in relation to the developing countries, but it has application in the developed nations as well. The basic concern in both cases is whether the technology chosen for a particular application can be expected to perform its function adequately without producing an unacceptable level of adverse impacts.

In the developing nations, emphasis has tended to focus on the ability of specific technology to accomplish a specific objective. The issue goes beyond concern for the inherent capabilities of a given technology and includes interaction between the technology and the socio-cultural dimension of the problem to be solved. Since incompatibility between technology and socio-cultural characteristics generally leads to lack of success in achieving management objectives, such interactions should be considered during the process of evaluating alternatives. Within the developing nations, consideration of personnel needs, maintenance requirements, and other factors may in some cases lead to choice of less advanced technology. In other cases, adoption of advanced technology may be determined to be the appropriate approach. The planning process should provide an analysis of the consequences of the alternatives to allow informed decision making.

The problem of undesirable impacts of technology is an issue in both developing and developed societies. Technological development has always been a major force in social development. While many of these effects undeniably have been beneficial, negative effects are not difficult to identify. Recent increases in the rate of technological development has significantly raised the level of concern that technology is becoming master rather than servant (Unger, 1982; OECD, 1979).

The potential for technology to produce social impacts depends both on the technology and the socio-cultural context of its application. Nations differ both in the current state of technology and in their socio-cultural characteristics that may be impacted. Technology assessment therefore is a relatively broad activity that must involve both the physical and social sciences.

3.4(c) Economic analysis

The importance of economic analysis (generally referred to as benefit-cost analysis in the conventional form of application to water resources and other public works projects) in the evaluation of alternatives is directly related to the importance of economic growth as a management objective. Benefit-cost analysis provides a means to determine the contribution of each alternative to economic growth and thereby allows direct comparison of relative performance. Benefit-cost analysis is distinguishable from financial analysis. While the latter is concerned with actual cash flows involved in an undertaking, the broader concept of economic analysis is concerned with values created or consumed by the undertaking without regard to actual cash flows.

As a general concept, benefit-cost analysis includes any systematic comparison of positive and negative effects associated with the activity being evaluated. In this broad approach, all impacts of a given activity can be considered, including impacts that can be quantified and other effects that can be described in qualitative terms only. In practice, however, benefit-cost analysis tends to be limited to comparison of monetizable values, with other impacts left for separate evaluation.

While this approach makes benefit-cost analysis a convenient analytical tool, it also results in substantial controversy. Use of benefit-cost analysis in the public sector is opposed on at least two grounds. First, placing emphasis on quantifiable values is seen as relegating other values to positions of secondary importance. A tendency exists to view the results of benefit-cost analysis as a complete evaluation of merit rather than an evaluation having limited scope that neglects potentially important considerations. Second, objections are based on the potential for the analysis to obscure the incorporation of value judgments into results having the appearance of objectively determined facts. This potential exists whenever the analyst makes decisions regarding such items as what effects to include in the analysis and what values to assign to the effects (Bowie (ed.), 1981; Scherer and Attig (eds.), 1983; Baram, 1980).

If these potential weaknesses can be overcome by including appropriate safeguards in evaluation procedures, benefit-cost analysis has potential to contribute to evaluation of alternative proposals. Identification of the alternative with potential to make the greatest contribution to economic growth provides a useful standard of comparison. Whenever two or more alternatives make equal contributions to other objectives, the superior alternative generally will be the one making the greatest contribution to economic growth. Where contributions to other objectives are unequal and an alternative is selected due to its enhancement of another objective, the results of the economic analysis provide a measure of the economic-growth costs associated with advancing the other objective and therefore contribute to informed decision making.

Handling the time dimension

Application of benefit-cost analysis to activities extending over a period of time involves several issues relating to treatment of the time dimension in the analysis. One such issue is determination of the period of time during which benefits and costs will be considered. In some cases, this period will be determined by the life of the project as determined by physical and economic conditions. Where long-lived projects are involved, imposition of an upper limit on the period of analysis may be desirable due to the degree of uncertainty associated with benefits and costs occurring at distant future dates. If adopted, such limits should be applied consistently to all alternatives to maintain comparability.

Another general issue related to the time dimension is treatment of price changes occurring during the period of analysis. Since price changes will affect future cash flows involving benefit and cost payments, one approach is to estimate prices expected to exist at relevant future dates for use in calculations dependent on prices. Alternatively, general price changes can be ignored, provided that benefits and costs are treated in the same manner. However, differential changes in relevant prices must be reflected in the analysis. A differing rate of change among categories of prices will nullify the offsetting effect and produce distortions in the analysis if adequate consideration is not given (Riggs, 1982, pp. 307-319).

A third time-related issue that arises during benefit-cost analysis is the approach to be taken when summing benefits or costs that occur at different dates. Acceptance of the concept that value is time dependent means that a series of monetary values (e.g., a series of project benefits) expected to occur at different dates cannot be summed until converted to comparable terms at a common point in time, a conversion accomplished by standard discounting techniques.

Use of discounting within public investment decision processes involves special considerations. A major issue is choice of discount rate to reflect the appropriate time preference. Where borrowed money is to be invested, use of the interest rate imposed by the lender has a certain appeal but may not be a true reflection of the appropriate time preference. Interest rates employed in private financial markets may be viewed as too high due to differences between the public and private sectors. Lower risk associated with public ventures and the existence of a longer time perspective in the public sector are often seen as reasons for adoption of a discount rate lower than private sector rates (Eckstein, 1958, pp. 94-104). Inclusion of an inflationary component in private sector interest rates is another potential reason for use of a lower discount rate. However, treatment of the inflationary component of the interest rate should be consistent with treatment of inflation in the estimation of future prices used to determine benefits and costs. If the effects of inflation are included in prices, the inflationary component of the interest rate should be retained for discounting purposes.

Application of any discount rate greater than zero to public investments is opposed by some on the basis of the view that the underlying concept of time preference is inappropriate to societies in general due to their continuing nature. In this view, no basis exists for valuing a positive or negative effect less because it occurs in the future rather than at present. Particular objection is often taken to discounting intergenerational effects (McAllister, 1980, p. 111). But to ignore the concept of time preference can have clearly undesirable effects. For example, use of a zero discount rate would result in no preference being shown for an investment with potential to correct a problem and produce benefits at an early date relative to an equal investment producing the same benefits at a later date. This situation appears inconsistent with the best use of limited resources available at any given date, especially in view of generally increasing standards of living over time (UNIDO, 1972, pp. 154-155). As a result of such considerations, economic analysis of public investments generally employs a discount rate greater than zero in recognition of the time preference concept (Samuelson, 1973, p. 604).

Choice of discount rate can have a significant effect on the apparent contribution of a given investment to economic growth. Benefits of water development projects tend to be affected more by discounting than are costs because of the greater concentration of costs near the beginning of many projects. Due to the tendency for later occurring benefits to undergo a greater reduction in value during discounting, an increase in discount rate is likely to reduce the present worth of benefits more than it reduces the present worth of costs. Thus, projects are likely to be more difficult to justify economically at relatively high discount rates (James and Lee, 1971, p. 130). Change in discount rate can also affect the type of project that can be justified economically. For example, an increase in interest rate will increase the standing of an alternative with a higher proportion of its costs in the form of operation and maintenance costs relative to an alternative with a greater portion of its costs in the form of initial investment if other aspects of the two alternatives are the same.

Choice of discount rate therefore is an important policy decision. Due to the potential for the discount rate to affect the relative standing of alternatives, a central authority should specify the rate to be used in all economic analyses involving projects to be compared. Otherwise, differences in apparent economic worth among alternatives may be due to use of different discount rates rather than to differences inherent in the alternatives themselves.

Determination of benefits

Benefits associated with a water management alternative are its total positive contributions, subject to the limitation that the contribution be reasonably monetizable if benefits and cost are to be analyzed in monetary terms (with nonmonetizable benefits taken into account as information supplemental to the benefit-cost analysis). The limits of monetization cannot be defined completely. The range of potential

benefits include such diverse items as direct consumer products and services, inputs to productive processes, aesthetic enjoyment, health improvements, and greater security for human life. All of these categories of benefits can be subjected to attempts at monetization. For example, the value of a human life can be approximated as the potential earnings of the individual over an average lifetime.

This approach involving estimates of monetary values for all impacts of an activity is an attempt to make benefit-cost analysis an all-inclusive evaluation procedure that largely eliminates the need for other evaluation. Significant opposition has been raised to this approach on moral and other grounds (Baram, 1980). Aside from moral implications, attempts to assign values to many categories of effects face significant difficulties and provide opportunity for incorporation of individual biases due to their subjective nature. Benefit-cost procedures therefore often define monetized benefit categories to exclude project impacts posing special problems, leaving such benefits for separate evaluation.

Monetizable benefit categories generally include the increased production of goods and services in a substantial range of activities affected by water management. Productivity increases can result from expansion in production, as in the case of increased agricultural output resulting from provision of irrigation water, and from decreased costs of production, as in the case of transportation savings resulting from a navigation project.

Since large scale water management projects can produce hydrologic impacts over significant distances, certain benefits may be realized by parties other than the entity responsible for the project. For example, a community may enjoy flood protection benefits as a result of an upstream hydroelectric impoundment project. Such effects are real benefits from the perspective of total social welfare even if the effect is not a specific project purpose and produces no compensation to the project owner. If the uncompensated effect occurs across a national boundary, however, it will not likely be viewed as a benefit from the perspective of the upstream nation since water management is typically viewed from the national perspective. Such international effects would be viewed as project benefits if the project were a joint undertaking such that a broader management perspective existed.

Just as other parties can receive positive effects from a water project due to hydrologic processes, other parties can also benefit due to economic linkages with water project activities. Such effects take a variety of forms. They involve so-called "backward" production linkages such as increased purchase of material and equipment associated with direct project activities (e.g., purchases of farm equipment by the user of project irrigation water). They also include "forward" production linkages such as processing of project output (e.g., operations that process crops grown with project irrigation water).

The issue of whether these effects resulting from economic linkages (usually called "secondary" benefits) should be counted as project benefits has been controversial. A key factor is the accounting perspective taken. From the local or regional perspective, such effects clearly constitute economic benefits. From a national perspective, however, such increased activity may not be a net benefit if it displaces other economic activity that would be undertaken in its absence (Mishan, 1976, p. 75). If such displacements involve international relocation of economic activity, they would constitute a real benefit from the perspective of the new host nation but not from a broader perspective since they would be offset by the loss elsewhere.

Determining the value of benefits can pose special difficulties. A generally accepted standard for determining value is the willingness of consumers to pay for the given product or service. While prevailing prices for the good or service in question may constitute a valid indication of value under appropriate circumstances, prices may not reflect value in certain situations (UNIDO, 1972, pp. 39-51). For example, prices may be considered invalid indications of value where they are maintained at artificially high or low levels due to governmental policies or other factors. Prices also may be considered to be invalid indicators of value where distribution of income precludes participation of a significant portion of a population in economic activities. Under such circumstances, adjustments in prevailing prices may be necessary for purposes of economic analysis (Mishan, 1976, p. 81).

Even where benefit-cost analysis is limited to reasonably monetizable project effects, certain benefit categories may be included where the product or service does not involve a significant level of transactions based on payment of a price. For example, recreational benefits may be included in project analysis even though no fee is imposed for such activity. In such cases, benefits must be estimated without direct reliance on an existing price. In situations where the product or service provided by a water project is not a final consumer good but rather is an input to a productive process, a standard approach is to determine value on the basis of increased production in the affected activity. In the case of irrigation water, for instance, benefits can be measured as the value of increase in crop output resulting from use of the irrigation water supply (James and Lee, 1971).

A technique for estimating value that may be useful in special circumstances is the alternative cost concept. In this approach, the cost of the best alternative is adopted as the benefit of the alternative under consideration. Due to the potential for abuse, this technique must be applied with care. It generally is appropriate only in situations where some project is sure to be implemented and the alternative used for benefit estimation is a reasonable candidate for implementation in the absence of the one under consideration (James and Lee, 1971, p. 170). The alternative cost technique can be viewed as a form of cost-effectiveness analysis wherein the primary objective is to implement a predetermined course of action at the least cost.

Determination of costs

Since economic analysis is not limited to accounting of cash flows, costs, like benefits, potentially include a wide range of impacts without regard to the issue of actual payments made. Guidelines for determining costs are partially fixed by decisions regarding the determination of benefits since parallel treatment is desirable. For example, if the positive effects on a particular activity are included as benefits, associated negative effects should be included as costs to allow a determination of the net effect. The same principles for treating price changes and discounting adopted for benefit analysis should be applied to analysis of costs as well.

The proper standard for determining the costs of a water project is the value of the opportunities foregone as a result of its implementation (UNIDO, 1972, pp. 58-61). The most obvious category of costs are direct expenditures by the party responsible for the project for planning, design, land acquisition, materials and labor used in construction, operation and maintenance, and other costs incurred during the period of analysis as determined for purposes of benefit estimation. These items typically are included as costs since their use in a particular water management activity precludes their use in an alternative activity.

Special considerations become necessary when a particular category of resources used in a project have no alternative use. A primary example is labor employed by a project that otherwise would be unemployed (or underemployed). If value is measured by the opportunities foregone, the value of the resource consumed is zero in the case of the use of otherwise unemployed labor (or some portion of the wages paid where labor would be otherwise underemployed) (UNIDO, 1972, pp. 58-61). As an alternative to adjusting costs downward to account for this consideration, costs of unemployed or underemployed labor can be included as project costs while an equal category of "employment" benefits are added as an offsetting measure (Mishan, 1976, p. 65).

A category of potential costs related to direct project expenditures includes expenditures necessary for achieving project benefits incurred by parties other than the project owner. For example, the party responsible for managing an irrigation operation to receive project water may invest in improvements in water handling facilities. If the value of the increased output in such activity is included as a benefit, the costs of these related improvements should be included as a cost although they are not paid by the project owner.

Another category of costs includes uncompensated adverse impacts in the form of external diseconomies. Water projects have the potential to produce a wide range of adverse impacts, and failure to consider such effects has been a relatively common water management deficiency in the past. Although the party responsible for water resources management may not be required to make compensation for such effects, they represent opportunities foregone as a result of project implementation (Mishan, 1976, p. 109). They therefore affect welfare and should be included in the analysis to determine the overall desirability of the activity in question. From the perspective of an individual nation, adverse effects occurring outside national boundaries may be viewed differently from those within the nation depending on broader considerations of international relations.

Many of the adverse impacts of water development projects are difficult to monetize. Included in this class are many socio-cultural effects and disruptions of natural environmental systems. Where determination of monetary values for certain displacements is not possible, procedures independent of benefit-cost analysis are required to ensure adequate consideration. Special procedures for assessing environmental and socio-cultural impacts are discussed later in this report.

Decision criteria for determining economic feasibility, project scale, and ranking of alternatives

Economic analysis can assist in several decisions within the planning process, including a determination of overall feasibility of each alternative, the scale to which each alternative should be developed, and the ranking of competing alternatives.

Several methods of comparing benefits and costs can be used to determine economic feasibility of water management alternatives. A widely used form of comparison is the ratio of benefits to costs, with the requirement that the ratio equal or exceed 1.0 serving as the criterion of economic feasibility. A second measure is net benefits, found by subtracting costs from benefits. A result greater than zero indicates feasibility. The internal rate of return method uses as the indication of merit the interest rate that must be applied in discounting to make the present worth of benefits equal the present worth of costs. The resulting rate can be compared to a target value to determine the desirability of the proposed investment. The annual rate of return on investment is defined as the ratio of annual net benefits (annual benefits minus annual costs) to investment, expressed as a percentage. The inverse of this rate indicates the time necessary for the project to repay the investment and therefore can be used as an additional indication of project merit (ECAFE Secretariat, 1969; Riggs, 1982).

Measures of the economic merit of individual alternative can also be used to determine the scale of development at which an individual alternative makes the greatest contribution to economic growth (the economically efficient scale). At scales of development below the efficient scale, increasing the size of the alternative will produce additional benefits in excess of additional costs; beyond the efficient scale, increases in size require additional costs in excess of additional benefits. Locating the point where total net benefits are maximized is perhaps the most direct means of determining efficient scale.

Determination of the efficient scale of development is more complex where limited funding is to be allocated among several competing investment options. If the scale of development of each alternative is optimized independently, the returns associated with the last increments of investment in those alternatives selected

may be less than returns attainable through use of those last increments to implement one or more of the unfunded alternatives. The existence of interdependent alternatives therefore requires that scaling decisions be based on consideration of total returns from a given level of investment rather than on acceptance of scaling decisions that independently optimize the scale of development for individual alternatives (Eckstein, 1958, pp. 65-69).

Since projects are not designed on the basis of economic growth alone, scales of development other than the efficient one may be selected in some situations in consideration of other objectives. Scales lower than the efficient one may be selected in order to minimize environmental or social disruption, for example. On the other hand, scales greater than the efficient one may be selected for such reasons as maximizing flood protection or production of food. But determination of the efficient scale of development provides a basis for comparison and allows calculation of the economic growth costs associated with achieving other objectives.

A third use of benefit-cost comparisons is to determine the relative ranking of alternatives competing for limited resources. This application poses potential problems. Since the forms of comparison emphasize different characteristics of the benefit-cost relationship, they may not result in the same ranking if applied to a list of physically dissimilar projects (e.g., projects that vary significantly with respect to the relationship between initial costs and operation and maintenance costs). The fact that relative standing among alternatives can be affected by choice of the ranking mechanism as well as by the merits of individual alternatives indicates the limitations of economic analysis for comparing dissimilar alternatives and emphasizes the need for caution (Eckstein, 958, p. 53).

3.4(d) Financial analysis

While the theoretical economic merit of a proposed water management activity can be determined independently of cash-flow considerations, successful implementation and operation is directly dependent on funding. Many management activities require construction of facilities involving large initial investments. Implementation of such projects often involves use of borrowed funds to be repaid over an extended period of time. The financial analysis in this case must explore potential means of meeting repayment obligations such as tax revenues and user charges imposed on project beneficiaries. In addition to consideration of repayment of borrowed funds and associated interest, the financial analysis must also project operating and maintenance costs and identify sources of necessary funds.

Financial analysis is of substantially narrower scope than economic analysis. Since the focus is on meeting payment schedules, broader considerations of uncompensated benefits and costs are irrelevant. Debate over choice of discount rate reflecting the appropriate time preference is not an issue since only actual interest rates such as those applied to borrowed funds are needed. Problems of assigning values to project services without established prices do not exist since actual cash flows are the focus. But financial analysis is a basic component of the planning process because of the direct relationship between funding and the feasibility of water management activities.

3.4(e) Environmental impact assessment

Assessment of the environmental effects of water management activities has received substantial acceptance as a fundamental component of water planning in recent years (Goodman, 1984, pp. 453-487). This development is the result of increased awareness of potential impacts, a shift in values calling for greater protection of the environment, and increased recognition that such values are likely to receive inadequate attention in traditional benefit-cost analysis procedures. Although certain environmental effects can be monetized and included in benefit-cost analysis, many relevant values remain outside such analysis and traditionally have been neglected in decision making. Environmental impact assessment is a mechanism to remedy this deficiency by supplementing benefit-cost analysis.

One of the first phases of environmental impact assessment is the identification and description of the environment to be affected by a proposed activity. Not all environments are of equal value or of equal susceptibility to damage. Identification of environments to be given special attention is a policy decision generally requiring political action. Candidates for special protection include wetlands and other areas of exceptional biological productivity, habitats of rare species of fish and animal life, rivers with exceptional scenic characteristics, and other unique ecosystems and areas of special interest.

The actual evaluation of environmental conditions and the significance of potential effects of the proposed activity requires an expansion in scope of the traditional analytical capabilities of the organization responsible for planning. Water planning traditionally has largely been the domain of engineers and economists due to the predominance of technical and economic analyses. Environmental assessment requires broader disciplinary involvement, with representation of the biological sciences a special need.

An important issue in evaluating potential environmental impacts is the completeness of the range of alternatives considered. Non-traditional management strategies are sometimes more compatible with maintenance of natural environmental systems than are the traditional approaches. For example, non-structural approaches to flood damage reduction may involve less environmental impact than construction of impoundments, levees, or channel improvments. A key function of the environmental impact assessment process therefore is to ensure consideration of alternatives with potential to accomplish the management objective in a manner compatible with environmental protection.

The product of environmental impact assessment is the identification of consequences of the proposed action. Although impact assessment is more commonly associated with identification of negative effects, such assessments also provide a mechanism for including positive environmental effects in project evaluation. Water development activities can generate a range of positive environmental impacts such as water quality improvements, ecosystem enhancement through low-flow augmentation, and aesthetic improvements. These positive effects enhance social welfare and should be included in the assessment.

Nevertheless, identification of potential negative consequences of proposed actions is the primary thrust of environmental impact assessment. The major intent of such assessment is to improve the information upon which decision making depends. Negative consequences of activities that alter natural environments take many forms, including both direct and indirect effects. Potential indirect effects go beyond physical impacts of the proposed activity under study and include environmental effects generated by independent development activity undertaken in response to implementation of the proposed activity. For example, a comprehensive assessment of the environmental effects of an irrigation project would include such impacts as possible water quality degradation resulting from farming. Consideration of the full range of potential environmental impacts is difficult due to complex interactions and cumulative effects that may occur.

Environmental impact assessment requires special attention to problems of measurement and analysis due to the nature of the effects involved. The absence of generally recognized methods for objectively determining the value of many environmental amenities creates the danger that evaluation will be limited to subjective judgments. In this case, the results of the assessment would be dependent on the values of the individual and generally would not be reproducible by other individuals. Due to these problems, environmental assessment must be guided by standard procedures that minimize the impact of individual values and enhance objectivity and reproducibility (Ortolano, 1984; Rau and Wooten, 1980; Whitlatch, 1976).

To ensure that environmental considerations are included in the information base for water management, the results of environmental impact assessment must be available at all points where significant decisions concerning the proposed action are made. Such availability requires that the assessment be conducted at an early stage in the formulation of plans for management activities. Availability also requires that assessment results be made a part of the proposal for the management activity to ensure that decisions at different stages of the evaluation and review process are not made prior to receipt of the assessment. Without full incorporation of assessment results into relevant decision processes, establishment of environmental assessment procedures will have little effect on water management.

3.4(f). Social impact assessment

Social effects of water management activities are similar to environmental effects in their frequent neglect in traditional evaluation procedures focusing on

.nonetizable impacts. Greater awareness of the occurrence and significance of such effects has led to attempts to ensure systematic evaluation in the water planning process and incorporation of relevant considerations into management decisions (Daneke and Priscoli, 1979).

Although social impact assessment generally is at a lower level of development than is environmental impact assessment, many parallels exist between the two processes. One point of similarity is the need for expanded analytical capability within the planning process. Analysis of social impacts moves planning into such disciplines as sociology, psychology, anthropology, geography, and political science. These specialty areas traditionally have seen little involvement in water resources planning, but a serious effort to improve consideration of social impacts requires modification of traditional personnel policies.

Social impact assessment, like environmental impact assessment, must begin with preparation of a data base. Although a variety of socio-cultural data may exist or be attainable through collection programs, a key factor to the success of subsequent impact analysis is the identification of the key indicators of socio-cultural conditions and an understanding of the processes that define relationships among indicators and through which socio-cultural change occurs (Love, 1977). Once an organizing framework that provides a basis for interpreting individual variables is developed, conditions with and without each alternative under consideration can be projected and resulting impacts determined.

Data gathering and impact assessment can be organized around a variety of social units. Individuals and households are the appropriate unit for certain components of impact analysis. For example, changes in income, health, and security from natural catastrophies can be evaluated from this perspective. Individuals and households can be aggregated into larger units for a variety of considerations. Different income groups can be considered as units, with the distribution of benefits among such groups frequently a special concern in the analysis. Communities are another commonly used unit. Water development activities can produce a range of community impacts such as modification of the size and characteristics of population, effects on economic stability, and impacts on services and facilities. Even larger aggregations focusing on broad geographic regions or even an entire nation may be the appropriate unit of analysis for some purposes. For example, attainment of self-sufficiency in food production or other areas may be a relevant social impact from the national perspective.

Social impacts of water projects can be either positive or negative, and both types should be included since they affect public welfare. The tendency of water projects to produce unintended socio-cultural disruptions leads to emphasis on negative impacts, but unintended positive impacts can be significant. In addition, potential negative effects can be transformed into social benefits under some circumstances. For example, forced relocation of communities can provide opportunities for improvements in living conditions where the relocation site is subject to lower natural hazards, more healthful surroundings, or improved facilities for drinking water and sanitation.

3.4(g) Assessment of political feasibility

The ultimate formal test of a proposed project or program in the public sector is the process of approval and funding through political action (the informal test of social feasibility is applied after implementation of the action in the form of general public response). Political feasibility is an unbounded concept broader than the analyses conducted by planners. Since recommendations by planners are but one of a variety of inputs to the final decision, acceptance of such recommendations can never be assumed. Recommendations firmly supported by technical analysis generally have an inherent attractiveness encouraging their approval, but the planner's recommendation is advisory only and therefore subject to potential rejection (Beckman, 1964).

The primary reason for discrepancy between recommendations based on technical analysis and the final political decision on an issue is the exercise of discretionary judgment in the political process for resolving value conflicts within society. The political process is also subject to negative factors such as inadequate information, personal biases of individuals, and partisan considerations, but various checks and balances in the system limit their effect although they are not eliminated.

Should the water resources planner include the broader elements of political feasibility in the evaluation of alternatives? In one view, the planner performs a relatively objective function that is distinct from political considerations. But in perhaps a more practical view, the planner must consider all elements of feasibility if the planning exercise is to provide meaningful input to the final decision process. Water resources management activities in the public sector are social as well as physical processes, and all factors relevant to social processes should be considered. Recognition of the need for social impact assessment is itself a step toward acknowledgement of this position.

In this view of planning, an interactive relationship between planning and the political process is recognized, and the planner assesses the political feasibility of alternatives as an integral part of the evaluation process. A basic feature of this approach is more explicit acknowledgement and clarification of the value judgments incorporated into alternative courses of action. Achieving this purpose requires more emphasis on such factors as the distribution of impacts of proposed actions and an expanded scope for social impact assessment in general. Recognition that planning is a socio-political process as well as a technical process increases the potential of planning to influence public sector activities toward greater contributions to the public welfare.

4. Data collection and analysis

An essential foundation for scientific water resources management is adequate information for understanding the hydrologic systems upon which a society depends and the nature of the interactions between these natural systems and the socio-economic system. Satisfaction of this need requires programs of data collection and management in support of water management activities. Due to the universal need for water resource information in all elements of management, collection and management of data relating to hydrologic systems often exists as an independent component of the water management system. On the other hand, primary responsibility for demographic and other socio-economic data is likely to lie with other governmental programs outside the water management program, creating the need for coordination to ensure the availability of necessary information for water management purposes.

Although certain types of data can be collected during short-term planning studies, the nature of hydrologic processes, and to some extent the nature of socio-economic processes as well, requires long-term assessment. Ideally, this assessment should be initiated considerably in advance of specific water management activities such as construction of facilities for alteration of natural hydrologic patterns. This need arises primarily from the inherent variability of natural hydrologic processes. The characteristics of such processes generally can be understood only on the basis of statistical or other analyses of relatively long-term observations. Continuous assessment of socio-economic conditions is also necessary because of the need to understand complex causative relationships that affect demands for water services and the need to determine long-range trends in such demands.

In addition to collection, a data program must provide for conversion into useful information and use for a variety of purposes. A basic requirement of the program is analytical capability to conduct the necessary statistical or other analyses necessary to give operational meaning to the data. Another basic program requirement is capability to store data such that it can be conveniently retrieved for a variety of uses that may arise. The storage and retrieval system ideally should include all data collected by various components of the water management system. Such additional data should be coordinated with that collected by the data management agency to provide the broadest availability for management needs (ESCAP Secretariat, 1981).

A comprehensive data collection and management program to support water management activities must encompass several categories of data, including climatic data, surface water data, groundwater data, and data on water use and other interactions between the water resource and socio-economic systems.

4.1 Climatic data

For most large geographical areas, the most important determinant of water resource conditions is climatic factors controlling moisture input in the form of precipitation. The total amount and distribution of precipitation determine the availability of water for direct use in such purposes as agricultural production, for runoff that serves as the source of surface waters (except that which travels from other areas by means of river or groundwater flow); and for groundwater recharge. Where snow and ice are important sources of stream flow or groundwater recharge, special data collection to define the status of this resource may be necessary. Another major influence on water availability is exerted by those factors such as temperature and wind that affect loss of moisture through evaporation.

Data concerning precipitation and evaporation must be collected at a network of stations designed to reflect geographic variability. Data collected over a substantial period of time provide a basis for calculation of average values and indicators of the distribution of individual values around the averages. Variability of observed values around an average value is important both in terms of such measures as range and standard deviation and as an indication of cyclic patterns during annual or other time periods.

Reliance on statistical indicators of climatic factors such as precipitation is based on the assumption that climate is basically stable even if individual climatic elements are capable of significant variation. The potential for climatic change involving not just variation within given patterns but transition to new patterns of variation introduces a new dimension to climatic analysis. At present, divergence of opinion exists as to whether disruptive climatic events such as recent African droughts are reflections of extreme variation within established climatic patterns or indications of changing patterns. The possibility that climatic change is occurring increases interest in the potential for such change to be induced by man's activities. Some have argued that recent African droughts are related to the increased carbon dioxide and dust content of the atmosphere (Bryson, 1974).

Better understanding of current climatic patterns and possible trends of change is of basic importance to water resources management as well as in a variety of other activities. An important step toward improved understanding is expanded collection of climatological data. Data deficiencies cannot be quickly remedied, but continuation and expansion of data collection and analysis are essential to long term improvement. Conventional program activities should be supplemented with expanded research on global climatic processes and changes that may be occurring at present or may occur in the future. Such research will require international cooperation and a significant commitment of resources.

4.2 Surface water data

The collection of data on hydrologic phenomena associated with surface waters has long been recognized as an essential aspect of water resources management. The fundamental component of the traditional data collection system is a network of gaging stations for determining stream flow. Since both total available stream flow and variation of stream flow with time are important determinants of a stream's potential role in socio-economic development, flow gaging stations, like meteorological stations, must be designed to provide a record over a substantial period of time. At a minimum, such stations collect data regarding water level elevations that can be converted to flow rates by use of a stage-discharge relationship derived from simultaneous observations of water levels and velocities at sites of known stream dimensions.

From the perspective of the party responsible for water resources development activity, location of a gaging station at each development site would be desirable, but such location generally is not feasible due to the long lead times that would be necessary. Gaging stations are usually designed as a network to produce an acceptable level of data at lowest cost. Guidelines for network design have been developed for different climatic and physiographic conditions (WMO, 1972; WMO, 1976). Improvement in gaging station networks remains a basic water management need in many nations. Even if a generally adequate network exists, data will be needed at ungaged locations, resulting in the need to estimate flows based on data from other sites.

The usefulness of stream flow data depends in large measure on application of statistical analysis to the sample data to estimate potential extreme values and to determine probabilities of various levels of flow. Average stream flow provides an indication of the upper limit of resource availability, but water supply and most other water-related activities depend on the extent of variation of flow from the mean and the frequency distribution of various flows. In the analysis of flooding potential, a determination of the probable recurrence interval of flood flows of various magnitudes is a standard analysis. The dependability of different flows for water supply and other activities disrupted by low flows can be determined by such means as flow duration analysis, which indicates the percentage of time that various flows are exceeded. The capability to conduct these and other analyses of stream flow data is an important determinant of the adequacy of the data collection and analysis program. Such analyses are essential to transformation of the original data into information usable in the planning and design of water management activities.

In addition to stream flow rates, other data on surface water characteristics are necessary for accomplishing water management objectives. Since quality is an important determinant of the potential of the water resource for use, water quality monitoring is an important component of data collection. Quality monitoring traditionally has focused on a limited number of indicators for determining the suitability of water for various uses. Due to concern over the role of water as a vehicle for transmission of infectious diseases, an indicator of the presence of human or other animal wastes traditionally has been a major focus. Coliform bacteria, while generally not pathogenic themselves, are widely used as an indicator of bacterial contamination since they are contained in the wastes of humans and other warm-blooded animals.

As disinfection of wastewater has reduced the threat from bacterial diseases, greater attention in recent years has focused on other aspects of quality. A special concern has been the presence of an ever-increasing list of substances in water that have been shown to be carcinogenic or directly toxic to living organisms, sometimes at very low concentrations. Also of concern are the presence of radioactivity and substances that alter water's pH, a measure of the hydrogen ion concentration that indicates the existence of acidic or basic conditions. Dissolved oxygen concentration is an important indicator of the suitability of a given body of water as habitat for fish or other quatic organisms. A common measure of the potential of wastewater containing organic matter to consume oxygen is biochemical oxygen demand (BOD). The concentration of nitrogen and phosphorus compounds is important due to their potential to serve as plant nutrients and lead to excessive growth of algae. Presence of suspended solids, often the result of soil erosion, is reflected by turbidity measurements. Temperature is an important quality indicator due to the sensitivity of aquatic organisms to this parameter (Lamb, 1985, p. 105-119).

Water quality monitoring is a more complex undertaking than is quantitative measurement. Water quality at a particular point is a function of many factors. The amount of various contaminants entering the body of water is one determinant, but quality parameters are also affected by stream conditions such as the amount of stream flow and physical conditions of flow. These conditions change along the course of a stream and can also change with time. Point source waste discharges can vary with time, rainfall can affect the quantity of water available for dilution of contaminants and increase the inflow of contaminants from nonpoint sources, and quality changes occur relatively continuously as a result of natural processes and interactions among contaminants. Thus the ability to draw general conclusions from any given water quality sample is limited, and monitoring programs must be carefully designed if general water quality conditions are to be accurately determined.

Because of the increased attention now given to environmental quality in water management, surface water data collection and analysis must encompass a broader range of environmental conditions than just water quality alone. Information concerning existence and nature of biological resources and related habitat conditions is a necessary basis for environmental impact assessment. Short-term project-implementation studies can collect data on environmental conditions to some extent, but expanding the on-going data collection and management progam to include this dimension of the water resource has greater potential effectiveness.

Surface water data collection programs cannot be limited to hydrologic data but must also include other factors that influence surface water characteristics. Data on conditions such as topography, geology, soils, and vegetative cover are necessary to understanding of relationships between climatic and hydrologic events. Understanding of these relationships provides a basis for such activities as more accurate transposition of streamflow data to ungaged locations and estimating hydrologic impacts of changes in drainage basin conditions.

4.3 Groundwater data

The current importance of groundwater as a source of supply and its potential for expanded development indicate the need to give attention to groundwater in programs of water resource data collection and analysis. Knowledge of groundwater conditions in many locations is inadequate due to the difficulties that its assessment poses.

Estimation of groundwater potential requires data on aquifer dimensions and characteristics, including such measures as depth to the water table or top of an artesian aquifer and the thickness, areal extent, porosity, transmissivity, and type of water-bearing strata. These characteristics can be used to determine dimensions of the groundwater resource such as total volume in storage and potential withdrawal rates. Assessment of resource potential also requires determination of recharge rates. Recharge may depend on infiltration of precipitation and therefore be a function of precipitation rates and characteristics of the soil materials overlying the aquifer in question. In some areas, infiltration is essentially non-existent. In the case of aquifers overlain by relatively impermeable materials, recharge areas may be at considerable distance from potential points of water withdrawal. Some aquifers have substantial hydraulic interaction with surface water sources that must be considered during analysis of potential yield.

Determination of aquifer yield requires adoption of policy regarding desired aquifer life. Where recharge rates are substantial, a "sustained yield" or "safe yield" can be determined, which is the maximum withdrawal rate that can be continued indefinitely without aquifer depletion. This yield is ultimately dependent on recharge rate and may vary somewhat with changes in withdrawal due to effects of withdrawal on recharge rate and on natural discharge. Sustained yield may also be somewhat dependent on other factors such as location of withdrawals. Where recharge is insignificant, withdrawal of water results in aquifer depletion, which is generally called groundwater mining. Determinations of yield under mining conditions requires explicit assignment of an aquifer life during which aquifer storage will be depleted or pumping lifts increased to uneconomical levels.

Groundwater quality is also a significant factor in assessing potential of the resource. Quality is a function both of natural conditions and the activities of man within recharge areas. Groundwater development itself can adversely affect quality if contaminants gain access to aquifers by means of wells or if movements of mineralized or other waters of undesirable quality enter an aquifer being used for supply in response to withdrawal.

While certain information concerning groundwater conditions can be obtained from investigations at the land's surface or even by remote sensing, detailed investigation of the quantity and quality of supply requires collection of data from wells. Much data can be obtained from construction and operation of wells for groundwater production purposes. Reliance on this approach requires enforcement of a reporting requirement on all parties involved in well construction and operation and development of a program for management of the data generated in this manner. The organization responsible for groundwater data will need capability to drill test wells and special monitoring wells to supplement data generated as a by-product of well construction and operation by others. This activity is costly but is necessary for exploring groundwater conditions in areas without previous groundwater development activity and for conducting special studies not compatible with the operations of wells used for water production purposes.

4.4 Data on interactions between water and socio-economic systems

Water resources management activities are intended to improve the relationship between the water resource and socio-economic systems; therefore, data requirements include not only the characteristics of the resource but also the state of water-related activities resulting from the socio-economic characteristics of the particular society in question.

Data on water withdrawal for offstream use are an important component of the water resources data program. Such data should include the amounts and schedules of water withdrawals, location of withdrawals, the purposes of withdrawals, the amount and quality of water returned to the source, and the location of returns. Such data permit better understanding of the behavior of natural hydrologic systems and provide a basis for predicting future water demands and impacts of such demands on the resource. Of special value in planning are historical amounts of water withdrawn and consumed per unit of activity for various applications of water such as industrial use, crop irrigation, and satisfaction of domestic needs. Although continuance of historic patterns of use may not always be desirable, knowledge of such practices provides a starting point for quantifying future demands and assessing the adequacy of water resources in meeting those demands.

In addition to offstream uses, data on instream water-use activities should be included. Examples of potentially significant uses include waterborne transport; commercial and subsistence fishing operations; recreational activities such as fishing, boating, and swimming; watering of livestock; aesthetic enjoyment; power production; and wastewater dilution. Data concerning the extent of such activities, together with data concerning offstream water use and environmental conditions, are necessary in order to evaluate the impact and desirability of proposed water resource developments that would produce flow alterations (ESCAP Secretariat(2), 1980).

Land-use data indicate potential interaction between the socio-economic and water resource systems since land use affects both quantitative and qualitative aspects of water. Major changes in land use such as clearing of forests and urbanization can significantly alter surface and groundwater characteristics in an area; land-use data therefore must be updated periodically as a means of predicting potential changes in hydrological characteristics as socio-economic development occurs.

Data on certain negative interactions between water resources and socio-economic conditions are of special importance in water management decision making. The extent of flooding of occupied areas is a component of social welfare that should be assessed, including data on property damage and risk to human life. Another major negative interaction in some locations involves human health problems. Data on health problems such as those resulting from lack of adequate water for drinking and sanitation and other interactions with water are important to formulation of strategies for addressing such problems.

4.5 Water management with inadequate data

Water management decisions generally are no better than information on which they are based; yet decisions frequently have to be made with inadequate information because of pervasive deficiencies in past data collection and analysis. While the importance of reducing the occurrence of this situation by improvement in data collection and analysis programs cannot be overemphasized, realism requires acknowledgement that many decisions will continue to be made under conditions of inadequate information for the foreseeable future. A primary need therefore is an approach to such decisions that minimizes the impact of information inadequacies.

A major approach to accommodating information deficiencies in decision making is to adopt alternatives that are divisible into stages, with the first stage having relatively low information requirements. For example, a water supply alternative consisting of groundwater development generally can be more readily subdivided into components than construction of surface water impoundments and therefore may be a preferable alternative under conditions of limited hydrologic data. Among major surface water development proposals, some may be more susceptible to staged construction and therefore would be more suitable under conditions of uncertainty. Staged implementation provides a basis for progress toward achieving management objectives while additional information is being generated that allows improved analysis of the next stage of implementation. The possibility of cancelling later stages is retained should information gained during early stages so indicate (Wiener, 1972, p. 157).

A similar approach with more emphasis on information generation and less on actual project implementation is use of pilot projects. Such projects are essentially small scale demonstration projects to determine feasibility experimentally where lack of experience and other information creates a high level of uncertainty. They differ from the staged approach to implementation of management actions largely in their greater emphasis on experimentation.

The primary response to uncertainty resulting from inadequate data is to avoid commitments to long term courses of action to the extent compatible with the urgency of the need to make progress toward management objectives. Maintenance of flexibility allows compensating adjustments in response to unforeseeable developments. Such an approach is likely to be more costly than the one that would have been chosen if adequate data had been available initially; but an action-oriented approach that maximizes flexibility may ultimately be less costly than delaying action until data inadequacies are remedied or moving ahead rapidly while ignoring data deficiencies.

5. Water allocation

A basic component of the institutional framework for water resources management is the water allocation system that defines ownership of water or rights to use the resource. The importance of the allocation process arises from a combination of the large number of water-using interests possible and the ease with which the impacts of each individual water-use activity can be transmitted through hydrologic processes to other water uses. This high potential for conflict creates a need for a system of rules that provides guidance for the avoidance of conflict and principles for resolving conflicts that occur.

A major purpose of a water allocation system is to assist in achievement of water management objectives by facilitating water uses making the greatest contribution to those objectives. Because of the need for certainty of water availability in planning and implementing investments in water-use activities, the water allocation system must provide a legally secure right to the use of water under clearly defined conditions. Because of the tendency for each water use to displace other uses and produce environmental harm under conditions of scarcity, the allocation system must attempt to prevent use of water in excess of that reasonably necessary for each application and otherwise seek to control undesirable adverse effects. Because of the need for shifts in water use from less to more beneficial applications, the allocation system must make provision for termination of existing rights under certain conditions, for establishment of new rights, and for modification and transfer of existing rights to allow water-use changes. A water allocation system therefore must represent a careful balance between the concurrent needs for security and flexibility in water-use practices. The inherent conflict between these two dictates is a primary source of the complexity often exhibited by water allocation systems (Trelease, 1976).

The importance of water allocation law increases as water demands increase. Under conditions of water abundance where all demands can be satisfied without conflict, such law is relatively unimportant. But the potential for conflict even under conditions of general abundance results in development of at least simple water allocation procedures at an early stage of socio-economic development. Law governing allocation procedures generally evolves toward more sophisticated forms as water-use conflicts increase in frequency with increasing demands for the services of water.

While modernization of water allocation systems is a basic part of the growth of national water management capabilities, such modernization can be controversial. Water-use customs are a fundamental part of the socio-cultural framework, and attempts to modify customary allocation procedures are likely to be met with resistance. However, customary practices may be incompatible with intensive management programs and activities, and modernization of the allocation system is likely to become essential at some level of socio-economic development. The tendency to allow customary practices and alternative allocation systems to continue to exist in parallel with newly adopted controls should be resisted and existing rights integrated into a single allocation program (Teclaff, 1979, p. 887).

The form of water allocation law varies substantially among nations (Cano, 1977, p. 3.4) due to variation in such basic factors as ownership of natural resources. In the case of public ownership and development of resources, the water allocation system must apportion available supplies among various public enterprises competing for a limited supply. Conflicts may occur between alternative offstream uses such as irrigation and industrial use and may involve competition between offstream uses and instream uses such as maintenance of fisheries. The balance to be achieved between offstream and instream uses in a basic water policy issue, with the water allocation system a primary policy implementation mechanism.

The same types of conflicts among water uses are possible in nations where water is subject to private property interests. In this case, the water allocation system functions by defining the nature of the property interests in water and establishing limitations on the exercise of private rights recognized. The nature of the property interest recognized in water (and in land to a significant extent as well) is a basic component of the institutional framework within which water management takes place. Due to the nature of water, associated property rights generally are less absolute than in the case of fixed-location resources. Such rights are unlikely to extend to the ownership of water while part of a natural hydrologic system but are usually limited to use of the resource under prescribed conditions. In fact, water tends to be classified as a public resource subject to limited private rights even in those nations with a tradition of private resource ownership.

Beyond considerations of national political structure, water allocation systems also vary with respect to other factors, including hydrologic scope, administrative approach, and the basis and scope of individual water rights.

5.1 Hydrologic scope of the allocation system

The primary question concerning the hydrologic scope of a water allocation system is the extent to which it encompasses all interrelated phases of the hydrologic cycle. While some allocation systems apply relatively comprehensively to all water without regard to source, application of separate allocation systems to different phases of the hydrologic cycle, often embodying significantly different allocation principles, is a common approach. Frequently used legal classes include streams and lakes, unconfined surface runoff, and groundwater.

The physical unity imposed by interactions of the hydrologic cycle suggests that a water allocation system most logically should be based on a comprehensive view of the water resource (Cano, 1977; Trelease, 1977, p. 396). This approach provides a basis for recognition of interactions between water in different sources and is compatible with the concept of integrated water management.

An especially useful application of the comprehensive approach is conjunctive management of surface and groundwater. At a minimum, hydrologic interactions between surface and groundwater should be considered in all management decisions because of the potential for unintended adverse impacts. In addition, coordinated use of surface and groundwater supplies may provide a least-cost water supply option in some situations. Groundwater can be used to supplement surface water supplies during periods of low stream flow, thereby reducing or eliminating the need for costly surface reservoirs. Under appropriate conditions, groundwater could be deliberately overdrawn during dry periods and allowed to recover (or perhaps be artificially recharged) during periods of high surface water availability (Teclaff, 1979, p. 906). The comprehensive approach, while providing for such coordination among water sources, can also provide flexibility for consideration of special issues unique to a particular source of water. For example, special allocation rules different from those generally applicable could be applied to a hydrologically isolated groundwater basin where special management needs exist.

The approach to water allocation based on separate treatment of water from different sources poses inherent obstacles to integrated water management. Consideration of hydrologic impacts of use from one source on another source (e.g., groundwater pumping that affects a surface water body) is impeded by a jurisdictional boundary. Similarly, a tendency will exist for other water-use considerations to be affected by limits placed on the perspective of decision makers. Overcoming the potential distortions in management decisions resulting from limited management perspectives requires a significant coordination effort. Nevertheless, the tendency to isolate problems and address them within limited boundaries is a strong influence toward compartmentalization of the water resource, and allocation by water source is a frequently used approach under current institutional arrangements.

5.2 Administrative approach

The administration of a water allocation program can take several forms. Three basic issues define the approach taken: (l) the level of government responsible for the water allocation function, (2) whether the allocation function should be judicial or administrative in nature, and (3) if the administrative approach is adopted, the selection of the particular agency to exercise allocation responsibilities.

The issue of assigning the allocation function among levels of government is important in a federal political system and cannot be resolved independently of general legal principles for division of governmental responsibilities. The need for a broad perspective and coordination with other elements of the national water management program may suggest a need for the allocation function to be exercised at the national level. The need for sensitivity to water resource conditions and water demands that vary with geographic location suggest allocation at a lower level. The importance of flexibility to respond to local or regional conditions increases with increasing variability of conditions relating to water use within national boundaries. Should the allocation function be assigned to a lower level, however, coordination mechanisms for considering relationships between water allocation and other components of the water management program exercised by the national government are necessary. Constraints generally have to be imposed on the allocation authority of the lower level of government to accommodate exercise of national powers with direct impact on water allocation decisions.

The question of whether the allocation function should be performed through judicial proceedings or by an administrative body often becomes a primary issue in attempts to modernize traditional water allocation systems. At lower levels of socio-economic development, water allocation decisions tend to be made within general-purpose adjudicatory procedures rather than by specialized allocation processes. Customary practice tends to be adopted as a set of formal rules that continue to evolve within the context of individual conflicts. This approach operates effectively and at low cost as long as the combination of available water supply and demand is such that relatively little conflict occurs.

Traditional approaches based on general adjudicatory procedures may become inadequate with socio-economic growth and increased water-use conflict. The need for improved conflict resolution, especially the need to incorporate principles of scientific management into the allocation process, and the need to coordinate allocation with other aspects of management produce an incentive for conversion to an administrative approach. Such conversion generally requires adoption of legislation that establishes procedures for inventory of existing water use, quantification of water rights, and establishment of procedures for continued recognition of existing rights within the administrative allocation program. A substantial trend toward adoption of water allocation legislation and creation of administrative allocation procedures exists (Teclaff, 1979).

The decision to adopt the administrative approach requires resolution of the issue of appropriate location of the allocation function within the overall water management program. Several existing departments of government with water management responsibilities may be appropriate choices. However, the existence of other management responsibilities can create conflicts of interest if the other responsibilities involve water resource use and development activities. Avoidance of such conflicts requires location of the allocation responsibility with an agency not committed to a narrow water resources development mission.

Although avoidance of conflict of interest may suggest that administration of the water allocation program be separated from water development programs, the allocation program must be closely coordinated with other component s of management. Since the allocation function is a primary mechanism for achieving the entire range of water management objectives, linkages must exist with all components of the management program. Close ties with the water quality protection program are especially important because of interactions between the quantity and quality aspects of water.

5.3 Nature and scope of individual water rights

Water rights represent an assignment of specific legal interests to individual persons or organizations (either public or private) for use of water under prescribed conditions. Such rights define relationships among individual water users by establishing limits on the activities of each that may have adverse effects on the others. Water rights also define the relationship between the individual water user and the elements of the public interest in the water resource extending beyond those reflected in individual water rights. These broad elements of the public interest consist generally of instream water-use activities and natural environmental conditions now widely recognized as important components of welfare. Water allocation is an important mechanism for protecting these interests since it provides an opportunity for prohibiting or restricting adverse water use.

In order for proper consideration to be given to relationships among water-use activities, an allocation system should apply to all major water uses. Exemption of small uses without substantial hydrologic effect is justified on the basis of reducing administrative burdens, but exemption of significant uses undermines the ability of the allocation program to control conflict. Exemption is sometimes employed as a means of showing preference for particular categories of water use, but such preferences should be recognized within the allocation program rather than through exemption of the preferred use.

Preferences can produce difficulties even when employed within the allocation system. For example, preferences for domestic use (generally the highest preference use) can cause problems when the domestic class is interpreted to mean all public supplies since public supplies in urban areas encompass many types of use and attain large magnitudes. Because of iversity of use within the public supply category, blanket application of the domestic preference can result in distortions in the original purpose of establishing preferences. Categorical preferences of this type tend to reduce allocation flexibility and should be employed with care (Teclaff, 1979, p. 890).

Individual water rights established through an allocation system vary in form among nations. Under some political systems, water rights will be held as private property rights; in other cases, they will be held primarily by public organizations. But aside from differences in program details resulting from such distinctions among nations, all water allocation programs confront the same general issues concerning creation of water rights, definition of the scope of such rights, and continuing supervision of such rights over time.

5.3(a) Creation of water rights

All water allocation programs must establish a criterion to serve as the basis for legal recognition of the right to use water. Under administrative allocation programs, a water right is based on explicit permission from the allocation authority for a given use of water. Creation of the water right under this system is a somewhat discretionary decision of the administering agency as guided by provisions of law defining elements of the public interest to be protected. Legal recognition of the water right in this approach is generally acknowledged by issuance of a permit or license to the water-rights holder.

Some water allocation systems define water rights without explicit recognition by an allocation authority on a case-by-case basis. An example is the definition of water rights as a component of legal rights in certain types of property such as land adjacent to bodies of surface water or land overlying groundwater. Water rights defined in terms of associated land may be vested in individuals where land is under private ownership (e.g., under the riparian doctrine) or recognized as a collective right of groups such as the inhabitants of a community. Another general basis for legal recognition of water rights is temporal priority of use. This approach is based on the concept that water is a free public good to be taken by the first party with opportunity to make productive use. Recognition of the rights associated with an earlier use as superior to those associated with a use established at a later date protects prior investments and therefore encourages water resources development.

5.3(b) Scope of the individual water right

A water right must be defined in terms of the various parameters associated with the particular water-use activity. Relevant dimensions of the use may include purpose of use, place of use, total quantity of water involved, time pattern of use, and conditions of effluent return. These definitional elements collectively must provide security that a particular water-use activity can be accomplished without legal challenge while imposing limitations to prevent undesirable impacts on others due to excessive water use or other actions by the rights holder.

One approach to controlling excessive use is imposition of specific legal limits for use of water in various activities (e.g., the maximum amount of water to be applied to a unit of irrigated land during one growing season). This approach appears to be the most direct but is confronted by difficulties of establishing and enforcing meaningful limits in view of the variability among individual water-use operations, even those involving the same activity.

An alternative approach to regulation is imposition of a water withdrawal fee under which excessive use places an additional economic burden on the user, thereby creating an inherent incentive for more efficient water use while avoiding the rigidities of fixed limits on use. Although user charges are a common feature of water supply operations where a central supplier provides water to individual customers, user charges have seen more limited application for control of water withdrawal from natural sources of supply. Total reliance on user charges as an allocation mechanism may be undesirable due to the inability of certain socially desirable uses to compete on the basis of price, but significantly greater use of user charges would be feasible in many situations (Teclaff, 1979, p. 899).

Place of water use is another important factor in defining the scope of a particular water right. While some allocation systems impose few restrictions on place of use, others significantly restrict movement. Constraints can be imposed at a number of boundaries, including the limits of individual property in contact with a source of supply, the boundaries of a watershed or groundwater basin, and a variety of political boundaries. Such constraints generally are intended to protect interests within an area enclosed by a particular boundary from transfer of water for the benefit of parties outside those boundaries.

While decisions concerning water transfer should give full consideration to socio-economic and environmental impacts within a transfer's area of origin, categorical prohibitions of transfer across specified boundaries are likely to produce inefficiencies in water use. The benefits of transfer from a broad perspective may be substantial and more than offset adverse local effects. Equity considerations suggest that the beneficiaries of transfer provide compensation to the area of origin in an amount at least equal to associated adverse impacts.

5.3(c) Continuing supervision of water rights

Water allocation is not simply a process for creating new water rights but also involves continuing supervision of rights. While unallocated water remains available, new water rights can be created for initiation of new water uses; however, changes in existing water uses become an increasingly important means of adjusting to changes in water demand as overall demand increases.

A key factor regarding the maintenance of water rights over time is the duration established at the time of creation. Water rights can be created in perpetuity, with continuance conditioned only on compliance with any conditions inherent in the right. Water rights based on non-administrative approaches generally take this form. Administratively created rights also can exist in perpetuity, but such rights can be established for prescribed terms. Adoption of the time-limited approach has the advantage of providing greater governmental control over water use because of the opportunity to re-allocate water periodically. The primary disadvantage is the loss of certainty from the perspective of the water user (Trelease, 1977, p. 405). Uncertainty is a disincentive to investment in related facilities and therefore is an obstacle to maximizing beneficial water use. This problem can be mitigated through selection of permit terms compatible with the amortization periods of various water-use activities.

During the period of time a water right is in effect, an important issue is its status when water shortages occur. Whenever available supplies are below the amount needed to satisfy total allocations, conflict between rights holders may occur. In the absence of established procedures for managing such conflict, water users in hydrologically superior positions will obtain the greatest portion of available supply. Under conditions of conflict among offstream users, instream water-use activities and natural environmental conditions may suffer substantial harm.

The water allocation system can reduce such problems by incorporation of procedures for imposing restrictions on water rights holders during water shortages. Several principles can be used for imposing restrictions, including proportionate reductions in all water rights, reduction or curtailment in reverse order of priority of the date each right was established, and reduction by class defined on the basis of type of use. Environmental considerations can be incorporated into decisions regarding necessary reductions in use. The alternative approaches for imposing shortage-related restrictions have different impacts and different implications for water-use efficiency. Choice of approach is a policy decision.

Implementation of any of the approaches for imposing restrictions requires that adequate powers be contained in the legislative authority for the water allocation agency and that necessary limitations be included in all rights created to guide formation of appropriate expectations on the part of water users. Necessary procedures for imposing restrictions should be developed prior to occurrence of a shortage. Minimum flows necessary for environmental protection also should be determined prior to implementation of restrictions during a shortage.

The need for modification of a water right during its effective period can also arise from the perspective of the right holder. Potential modifications include changes in type of water use, place of use, point of withdrawal, or point of return and transfer of the water right to a second party. The need to facilitate increased water productivity mandates that such changes be allowed, subject to constraints for protecting other water-rights holders and broader aspects of the public interest. A potential impact of changes is the reduction in water available to other users when change in use involves greater consumptiveness or modification of established return flow patterns. While control of such impacts is necessary, constraints imposed to control

such impacts tend to become major obstacles to water-use changes and water-rights transfers (Trelease and Lee, 1966).

Continuing governmental supervision of water rights may involve termination of rights during their effective period under some conditions. While termination of a right being exercised according to its provisions would likely constitute a violation of the legal rights of the water user (except perhaps through exercise of condemnation proceedings and payment of compensation), termination for violation of conditions imposed on the right or because of failure to exercise the right is commonly practiced. Forfeiture provisions based on nonuse are a mechanism for avoiding invalid or exaggerated claims for water and facilitating maximum use of water. However, precautions may be necessary to prevent rights holders from wasting water as a means of avoiding forfeiture.

Another mechanism for termination of a water right is exercise of a legal preference by a preferred water use. An example is eminent domain condemnation of a water right for a preferred use such as public supply. Although condemnation may result in loss of a water right against the will of the holder, such action generally involves payment of compensation. In an alternative approach, absolute preferences can be included in water allocation law such that a preferred use may displace a use of lower preference without compensation.

6. Water quality protection

Water quality degradation is not likely to be a major problem during the early stages of development as long as population densitites remain low, but growth in population will ultimately produce water quality problems even if the level of development remains low. The diversity of potential pollutants tends to increase with increasing socio-economic development. Thus, water quality protection is an increasingly important component of water resources management in a large number of nations representing the entire spectrum of socio-economic development conditions.

Water quality problems result from institutional arrangements that allow waste disposal and other activities associated with development to be conducted without accountability for water resource impacts. Such institutional arrangements have been the rule until recent years. Private property rights traditionally have allowed development of land with little regard for offsite impacts, including until relatively recently the discharge of wastes into an adjacent stream. Rules governing operation of public enterprises within socialist political systems generally have allowed the same behavior by governmental organizations created to perform specific water-use or land-use activities. As a result, water quality problems have occurred on a world-wide basis.

The question of what level of quality to attempt to protect is a basic management issue. Quality varies with time and location in the absence of human intervention and therefore must be defined with regard to these factors. The natural state of the various parameters of quality at a certain location and time may represent a desirable condition to maintain, but some degree of deterioration in certain parameters may be viewed as acceptable, or improvement in certain parameters to a condition better than their natural status may be desirable. Although improvement of quality in relation to natural conditions may have limited feasibility in most situations, the range of choice in water quality goals is considerable.

A level of quality that may be useful as a goal or as a standard of comparison is the level that minimizes the total combined value of pollution damages and pollution-control costs (including waste treatment and other actions to reduce pollution such as process modifications) (Seneca and Taussig, 1974, p. 15). Reaching this economically efficient level requires that expenditures for pollution-control measures be added only as long as the additional increment is less than the additional benefits from resulting water quality improvements. Since incremental costs of removing an additional unit of most pollutants generally rise rapidly at higher levels of control, complete elimination of many pollutants will not be consistent with the efficiency criterion. An exception may occur in the case of pollutants that cause substantial damages at low concentrations.

Determination of the efficient level of water quality is complicated by uncertainties in determining damages caused by pollution. Certain impacts such as immediate fish kills are relatively easy to assess, but low level, diffused impacts of pollution, some of which may not become evident for long time periods, are difficult to measure or to estimate (Freeman, 1982). Many newly developed chemical substances have potential for long term human health or other effects not presently understood. The concept of efficient levels of pollution, while potentially a useful consideration in formulating certain aspects of pollution control policy, therefore must be applied with caution.

Efforts to improve water quality can take several forms, including instream activities such as aeration and low flow augmentation. But primary emphasis generally is placed on control of activities that result in the entry of contaminants into natural bodies of water.

6.1 Strategies for controlling entry of pollutants into water

In the attempt to control unacceptable water quality degradation, several strategies for controlling the entry of pollutants into water have been employed at different times and locations. These strategies have incorporated differing concepts of acceptable water quality and have employed a variety of approaches to achieving the desired level of quality. Regulatory approaches that invoke legal sanctions against parties responsible for excessive water quality alterations have seen most frequent use. Common regulatory approaches have included enforcement of ambient water quality standards, enforcement of effluent standards, and direct intervention in the design and operation of potential sources of pollution. Approaches based on economic incentives in the form of charges imposed

on waste dischargers or compensation to parties installing water quality protection measures have also seen substantial use. Approaches limited to education and persuasion have been applied in some cases. Control strategies often employ elements of several approaches simultaneously.

6.1(a) Enforcement of ambient water quality standards

A basic approach to controlling entry of pollutants into natural waters is to define as unlawful any water quality alteration that violates specific criteria established to protect certain beneficial uses of the body of water in question. This approach allows some degree of waste discharge to co-exist with other uses of water, provided the discharge does not cause modification of quality criteria beyond limits established by law. Water quality standards generally include such criteria as minimum dissolved oxygen concentration, an upper and lower value for pH, a maximum rise in temperature from ambient conditions, and maximum concentrations for other substances known to have harmful effects. Since water quality standards theoretically can be adjusted to protect any combination of water uses, or perhaps even to obtain the efficient level of water quality, for each individual stream, this approach appears to be inherently logical.

The water-quality-standards approach suffers from weaknesses, however. A primary weakness is enforcement, which requires the establishment of a cause-and-effect relationship between water quality at the point of standard violation and individual activities responsible for the violation. This case-by-case analysis creates a substantial administrative burden. In view of complex physical, chemical, and biological processes within natural bodies of water, establishing the necessary linkage between pollution and its source may not always be possible, especially where multiple potential sources exist (Ortolano, 1984, p. 116).

6.1(b) Enforcement of effluent standards

Effluent standards specify limits on the characteristics of wastes that may lawfully be discharged to natural waters. Such standards can be established in several ways. They can be established individually for each discharger based on conditions in the receiving water. This approach involves considerations similar to those arising in the enforcement of water quality standards and therefore is subject to the same general weaknesses. Alternatively, uniform effluent standards can be established for categories of similar waste dischargers, thereby reducing the associated administrative burden.

Uniform standards can be applied under several approaches. They can be developed for each receiving water, thereby allowing general consideration of the specific conditions and needs of each water body, or they can be applied more generally such as on a national basis. Implementation of uniform standards on a broad geographical basis minimizes administrative difficulties but ignores efficiency considerations since it does not attempt to match the level of control to receiving water conditions and does not consider differences in treatment costs among discharges (Downing, 1984, pp.162-164). To eliminate special hardships or extreme cases of excessive waste treatment under a uniform approach, special provisions for relaxation of standards under prescribed conditions may be necessary. Similarly, special procedures for imposing effluent standards more stringent than the uniform standards may be necessary where the generally applicable standards do not produce desired levels of water quality.

Effluent standards generally apply to point-source waste discharges, but potential exists for at least limited application to nonpoint sources as well. An example is the imposition of soil-loss limits for various categories of land-use activity. This measure is designed to address the dual objectives of soil conservation and water quality protection. Since soil loss through erosion processes is the major source of sediment as well as an important source of other contaminants transported with soil, imposition of limits on allowable losses may serve as a useful water quality control measure.

Since uniform effluent standards are not based on specific water quality considerations, they must have an alternative basis that generally will be politically determined. Such standards can be based on considerations of results attainable with use of state-of-the-art technology or some less stringent criteria. The effluent-standards approach provides the option for total prohibition of the discharge of specified substances. This extreme application is generally reserved for unusually hazardous substances whose entry into the environment poses unacceptable risks.

6.1(c) Direct intervention in the design and operation of potential sources of pollution

This approach is distinguishable from use of water quality or effluent standards in terms of the directness of the regulatory intervention involved. While use of standards requires modifications in the operations of regulated activities, the operator maintains flexibility in choice of appropriate response, which may include such diverse alternatives as process changes or addition of specialized waste treatment equipment. In the more direct approach, the pollution control authority specifies actions to be taken rather than results to be obtained.

Direct intervention can take several forms. Specification that a certain type of pollution control equipment be installed is one approach. In the case of nonpoint sources of pollution, a requirement that a particular runoff control practice such as maintenance of a grassed buffer zone near property boundaries be incorporated into a land-use activity may be imposed. A further example is the imposition of limits on the manufacture of certain hazardous products, including in some cases the total prohibition of production. Regulatory measures for restricting manufacture of products may include provisions for mandatory testing to assess hazards prior to manufacture of new chemical products.

Imposition of rigid requirements on potential sources of contamination rather than application of performance standards is usually reserved for cases involving unusual hazards or situations where actual performance is difficult to monitor. Because of the lack of flexibility associated with this approach, widespread application creates considerable risk of inefficient investment in pollution control facilities (Downing, 1984, p. 159).

6.1(d) Imposition of effluent fees on waste dischargers

The primary alternative to the various regulatory approaches to water quality protection is the imposition of a fee or tax for the right to discharge wastes. Under this approach, the waste discharger generally is not subjected to legally enforceable limits on the amount of waste that can be discharged but is required to pay a fee per unit of waste discharged (regulatory limits or prohibitions may apply to discharge of certain substances due to special problems or hazards). If the fee could be set for each discharger on the basis of full information concerning costs of available waste treatment strategies and costs of environmental damages associated with differing levels of waste discharge, an incentive would be created for movement toward an economically efficient solution to the waste management problem. An incentive would be created to treat wastes up to the point just prior to that where the cost of treating another unit of wastes would first exceed the effluent fee for discharging that unit. Thus, the fee system would create the incentive for each discharger to adopt that combination of treatment and waste discharge that minimizes total waste management costs. However, all the necessary information generally will not be available, and determination of the fee schedule to optimize waste management decisions will not be possible (Bower et al., 1981, p. 15).

Even if the inability to determine actual damages associated with waste discharge limits the potential for achieving a socially desirable optimum, the effluent-fee approach can provide a basis for achieving a least-cost combination of actions for achieving an arbitrarily chosen level of quality; however, information must be available on costs of alternative waste treatment strategies for all dischargers (Bower et al., 1981, p. 16). The key to the cost effectiveness of this approach is the flexibility allowed the individual discharger to achieve the least-cost balance between waste treatment and paying the effluent fee associated with discharge. The effluent-fee approach is unique in that it encourages more intensive treatment by those who can do so at lower costs while permitting those operating under relatively high treatment costs to treat at a lower intensity. The result of these individual adjustments will be a cost effective solution to attaining the particular level of water quality desired.

Where the fee for dischargers must be set arbitrarily without adequate information on either the damages produced or the costs of waste treatment confronting various waste dischargers, the fee-approach can no longer ensure a cost effective solution; however, even under these conditions, the fee approach continues to offer a significant advantage — a continuing incentive for application of the most efficient pollution control technology available (Bower et al., 1981, p. 17). The opportunity to lower total costs creates a constant inducement for the discharger to seek better waste treatment technology, thereby facilitating the early adoption of technological advances and stimulating further progress.

The effluent-fee approach has seen substantial application, but the regulatory approach continues to be the preferred approach in some nations. Even where effluent fees are being employed, they are normally supplemented by the traditional regulatory approach. The lack of more widespread acceptance of the fee approach is likely the result of a combination of the entrenched nature of the regulatory approach, public distaste for "selling the right to pollute," and at least partly the legitimate concerns over problems associated with implementation of the effluent-fee approach. One of the potential problems often raised is the amount of information needed to establish and implement the fee approach. Proponents counter that the regulatory approach requires even more information and indicate that the proper fee can be determined by estimation and subsequent adjustment until a desirable level of waste discharge is achieved (Kneese and Bower, 1968, p. 136). However, the trial-and-error approach may not be politically acceptable, and frequent or large changes in discharge fees may hinder investment decisions by dischargers (OECD, 1980, p. 9).

6.1(e) Payment of subsidies

A second approach to water quality protection based on economic incentives is payment of compensation to generators of pollution as an inducement for implementing controls. Subsidies can take several forms. Tax concessions in association with expenditures for pollution control equipment is a common example. Direct payments to assist in installation of control measures can also be employed.

Unlike the effluent-fee approach, the subsidy approach is based on the assumption that the generator of pollution has a right to degrade water quality and that injured parties or society in general should pay at least part of the costs of controlling pollution to a desirable level.

Adoption of this approach therefore requires an assumption concerning ownership of the rights to the natural environment that is fundamentally different from that accepted under the effluent fee or regulatory approach (Seneca and Taussig, 1974, pp. 222-223). As a result, the distribution of the costs of pollution control will be significantly different under the subsidy approach. If public funds are the source of payments, costs will be widely distributed within the affected society. The distributional attributes of subsidies suggest that they may be most appropriate where water quality protection measures impact low income groups or relatively weak sectors of an economy in need of support.

In addition to differences in distributional impacts, another factor affecting the desirability of the subsidy approach to pollution control is the effect on production decisions. Since subsidies reduce production costs, expansion in production within the affected sector generally will occur. Availability of a subsidy may make possible inefficient production by firms that otherwise would be unprofitable. In addition, waste dischargers may be encouraged to make socially undesirable decisions in such areas as choice of production technology where the potential exists to maximize profits through collecting the largest subsidy (Downing, 1974, p. 181).

6.1(f) Compensation of injured parties by pollution generators

Another application of economic incentives for inducing pollution control is the imposition of a requirement that generators of pollution provide compensation for resulting injuries. This approach is similar to the effluent-fee approach since both require the pollution generator to make payments as a result of waste discharge. However, the mechanics of the two processes differ. While the effluent-fee approach involves payment for each unit of waste discharged, the compensation approach requires payment based on a case-by-case assessment of damages produced. This assessment generally is accomplished through judicial or other adjudicatory processes employed for resolving a wide range of conflicts among individual parties. Implicit in this approach is the assumption that water users have enforceable legal rights to an uncontaminated water supply.

Determining legal accountability through the case-by-case approach has significant weaknesses. First, injury may be diffused such that individual parties have little incentive to act. Second, evidentiary problems in proving a cause-and-effect relationship between the activities of a particular pollution generator and water quality at a given location pose a substantial obstacle to the success of such actions in many cases. Third, any uncertainty in the status of the legal right to uncontaminated water will discourage initiation of legal actions by injured parties.

The value of such actions as a deterrent to water pollution is directly dependent on the probability that legal accountability will be imposed and compensation required. Under conditions where compensation for injury is likely to be imposed, pollution generators will have an incentive to invest in control measures up to the point of expected compensation. However, the obstacles to successful action confronting parties suffering pollution injury create doubts concerning imposition of accountability and weaken the deterrent value of such actions. This approach therefore generally will be viewed as a supplemental approach to pollution control rather than a primary management device.

6.1(g) Education and persuasion

Water quality degradation can occur as a result of lack of knowledge concerning the impact of certain pollution-causing activities or the availability of control measures; therefore, educational programs to increase awareness of problems and knowledge of solutions has potential as a control strategy. This approach has the greatest chance of producing positive results where new practices can be identified that combine improved water quality protection with direct benefits to the responsible party (e.g., use of improved farming practices that reduce water quality degradation while increasing productivity). Peer pressure within the target group can be an effective means of extending the impact of initial gains achieved through education. As the sole mechanism for achieving water quality protection, education and persuasion have limited potential, but they can be an important component of combined approaches.

6.2 Developing a comprehensive water quality protection program for application of control strategies

Development of comprehensive controls for water quality protection requires a program (or set of coordinated programs) of proper scope for applying necessary control strategies to each of the multiple sources of water pollution. To provide the necessary basis for applying specific control measures, the program must have the capacity to conduct water quality inventories for identification of problems and planning capabilities for projecting future wasteloads and other conditions affecting future water quality. A primary management function is the assignment of priorities, both among waters in need of protection and among sources of pollution affecting each body of water. Coordination among control programs addressing different sources of pollution is important to ensure the best use of limited resources. For example, continuing to place emphasis on point source controls under conditions where greater water quality gains could be attained through focus on nonpoint source controls would be a waste of program resources that program coordination should avoid.

Once priorities are determined, detailed plans for protecting or restoring desirable quality levels in different bodies of water can be prepared. Such plans will identify the appropriate control strategy or combination of strategies for each pollutant category significant to water quality within each body of water. Strategies for differing sources of pollution must be coordinated but devised separately because of differences in the nature of the activities involved and in the processes through which pollution occurs.

General categories of sources requiring differing control strategies include point source effluent discharges into surface waters; land-based waste storage and disposal systems with potential to pollute surface and groundwater; manufacture, handling, and use of products with pollution potential; land development and use activities serving as sources of nonpoint pollution; water project operations altering water quality; and activities involving generation of gaseous emissions that contribute to contaminated precipitation or dry deposition.

6.2(a) Point source control

Effluent discharges from point sources such as industries and sewage treatment facilities have been the traditional focus of pollution control efforts; control strategies therefore have seen their greatest development in this area. Essentially the entire range of controls have been applied. Regulatory approaches based on combinations of water quality standards and effluent standards have been widely used for a substantial period of time, with effluent fees having grown in application in more recent years.

Although significant improvement in water quality conditions in many bodies of water can be attributed to implementation of point source controls, significant problems continue to exist because of inadequate treatment of wastewater. In areas of concentrated population and economic activity, wastewater production often increases faster than implementation of necessary treatment measures. Significant investments in treatment facilities and other forms of control will continue to be necessary.

6.2(b) Control of land-based waste management systems

Development of controls for land-based waste management systems generally has occurred at later dates than controls over waste discharges to surface waters. One of the results of controls on surface water discharges has been growth in use of land-based systems. Generation of residuals from treatment operations has increased, and the need to find alternatives to surface water discharges has developed. Land-based systems include landfills and various waste burial operations, waste injection wells, septic systems for disposal of sewage, land application of wastewater and residuals to cropland or other land, and surface ponds and lagoons for waste storage (United States EPA, 1977).

Such systems are of special concern since they are often employed for storing or disposing of hazardous substances. They generally are intended to operate as waste containment systems that prevent escape of waste products to usable surface or groundwaters. Control measures therefore usually consist of imposing a "no-discharge" policy supplemented by requirements for use of special equipment or procedures (e.g., a requirement for use of impermeable liners at certain types of landfills) and operation of monitoring programs for detection of unintended discharges of contaminants.

Since complete assurance of containment generally is not possible, management involves determination of acceptable risks of escape and incorporation of such risks into the design of facilities. Determination of an acceptable level of risk may involve benefit-cost analysis and other attempts to evaluate consequences objectivity, but such decisions ultimately must be a relatively high-level policy decision due to the importance of value judgments to the decision (Dasgupta, 1982). Long range strategy for management of hazardous substaces must include efforts to control the introduction of such substances into use and to reduce levels of production of known hazardous substances rather than relying solely on control of disposal operations.

6.2(c) Control of the use of chemical products

An important source of water pollution not involving waste disposal is the manufacture, handling, and use of chemical products with the potential to cause serious polluton problems if allowed to escape. While water quality management programs traditionally have focused on the disposal of wastes associated with the production of such products, attention also needs to be given to the potential of chemical products themselves to cause pollution. Escape can occur at a variety of points beginning with manufacture and extending through final use. In the case of widely used products such as gasoline, leaking storage facilities and accidents during transportation and handling can result in substantial surface and groundwater pollution. Some chemical products are significant pollutants because of their hazardous nature. Pesticides are an especially significant class of chemicals due to their high risk to human health and natural environmental conditions (Holden, 1986).

A comprehensive program for control of chemical substances involves several components, including procedures for testing of new products to determine possible adverse effects prior to manufacture and distribution. For chemical substances currently in common use, a key management objective is to prevent escape to the environment. Potential control strategies include periodic inspection of related facilities and imposition of special requirements for handling procedures and equipment. Management must also consider more fundamental steps such as limiting the production and sale of certain products or at lease encouraging development and use of alternatives with less potential for harm. As in the case of land-based waste disposal systems, management of chemical products requires an assessment of acceptable risks of escape as a basis for adoption of a management strategy.

6.2(d) Control of nonpoint source pollution

Control of pollution resulting from general land development and use is made difficult by the diversity of activities encompassed and the diffusion of responsibility for the various activities. Land-use activities vary in their potential to generate water contamination, but many can produce substantial water quality alterations through normal runoff processes. Such nonpoint source pollution can be the major cause of water quality problems and therefore must be a focus of attention within water quality management programs.

Because of the diffused nature of runoff, control methods based on measurement of effluent discharges (such as effluent standards and effluent fees) generally are not available. One approach to overcome this limitation is to require collection of runoff from certain areas considered to be important nonpoint sources, in effect converting such runoff to a point source discharge and allowing imposition of point source control strategies. Where collection of runoff is not feasible or treatment of runoff not practical, imposition of land-use controls is a primary management strategy. Such measures may include limitations on density of development, incorporation of specified practices into land-use activities, or the prohibition of development of certain lands. Required practices focus on control of erosion and preventing movement of pollutants to offsite locations. Because of the wide range of individual nonpoint sources of pollution to be addressed, education is an important component of management. Where necessary controls involve low income groups, public financial assistance to subsidize related investments may be desirable.

6.2(e) Control of water quality degradation from water project operation

Substantial water quality alterations can result from operation of water projects; two primary examples are quality deterioration resulting from reservoir operations and groundwater quality problems resulting from movements of saline or other low quality water in response to groundwater pumping. In the case of reservoir operation, quality impacts depend on such factors as design of water intake structures and operating procedures, and resolution of existing quality problems may require structural and operational changes. Reservoir releases conceivably could be subjected to effluent limitations or other strategies applicable to point sources since measurable discharges are involved. In the case of groundwater movements, control generally requires restrictions on location of wells, well design, and pumping rates.

The potential for water quality problems to result from structures and operations focusing on the quantitative dimensions of water management emphasizes the importance of coordination between the quality and quantity components of management. Without such coordination, management of quality problems associated with flow altering structures would is possible.

6.2(f) Control of airborne pollution

The need to protect water quality from airborne contaminants illustrates the importance of a comprehensive view of environmental protection. Isolated focus on individual components of the environment does not properly consider interactions and can result in lack of adequate management capabilities for addressing problems. Control of water resources problems such as acid precipitation requires that such effects be evaluated within policy and programs focusing on air quality. Control of the acid precipitation problem is complicated by the considerable distances often existing between sources of contaminants and occurrence of the problem.

Atmospheric transport processes often cross a variety of political boundaries, including those between nations. The continuing debate over the specific causes of acid precipitation and the necessary control measures indicates the importance of an adequate base of scientific knowledge for management purposes.

7. Preservation of selected water environments

The value assigned to natural water environments has substantially increased in recent years. This increased value has been reflected in an expanded scope for water planning to ensure appropriate consideration of natural environments in water development decision making. While this expansion in planning has increased the level of protection given to natural water environments, continuing growth in demand for water and water services has in some cases resulted in establishment of preservation efforts as a water management activity to provide relatively complete protection to certain natural water environments as a balance to program elements that advocate water resources development (Goodell, 1978).

The decision to preserve selected natural environments requires a determination that maintenance of natural conditions is the highest and best use of the resource in question. Since preservation displaces all uses dependent on substantial alteration of the resource, the costs in terms of opportunities foregone can be substantial. Preservation programs therefore generally are highly selective in nature and focus on resources with attributes that are unique or at least rare in occurrence. Such attributes may include both natural and cultural features with exceptional aesthetic and recreational value. Where ecosystems are important in production of food supplies such as fish or other natural products, preservation may have more materialistic goals.

7.1 Program operation

The specific approach to preserving natural water environments varies among alternative forms of political organization. Within political systems where natural resources are publicly owned, the primary mechanism of preservation is withdrawal of the resource in question from development and adverse use by public management entities responsible for such activities. In the case of preserving water environments, activities of special concern include major hydrologic modifications such as dam construction, extensive channel alterations, and large changes in flow rates or water levels. The preservation program must place appropriate restrictions on the department of government implementing or controlling these activities with respect to the waters to be preserved.

Within political systems where land and natural resources are privately owned, preservation programs are likely to require a combination of public acquisition and private property regulation. Complete protection from use adverse to preservation of natural values may require public ownership and classification for preservation purposes. Legal limitations on regulation of private property within such political systems may preclude total protection by use of this mechanism. Nevertheless, regulation can provide a degree of protection. Major water development activities within the private sector generally require governmental approvals, and the objectives of preservation programs can be incorporated into such approval processes. Necessary approvals can be conditioned to ensure compatibility between proposed development and preservation objectives, or approval can be denied where basic incompatibilities exist. Regulation, while limited in its ability to achieve total protection of natural values, therefore can supplement preservation programs based on public ownership.

Although program operations vary among nations, all preservation programs share certain general characteristics. One common feature is the need for a standard process to designate waters to be preserved. First, potential candidates for preservation must be identified. While certain waters may be obvious choices, others may possess unique attributes not generally recognized. Because of the need for a broad perspective at the identification stage, general water management policy and operational procedures should include a directive that natural values potentially worthy of preservation be considered during surveys and preliminary planning activities by all water management agencies. Second, responsibility for definitive assessment of the values and characteristics of potential candidates for preservation must be assigned to an agency with appropriate personnel and resources. Third, the results of the assessment and associated recommendations must be presented to an appropriate decision-making body for final action regarding preservation. The final decision must generally be made at a high management level because of the need for a broad perspective for resolving associated value conflicts.

Programs to preserve selected water environments generally can be coordinated with preservation efforts of broader scope. The body of water to be protected may exist as part of an exceptional natural setting with other features worthy of protection because of their own intrinsic values. The water resource may be closely related to these other values as in the case of wetlands or may be only generally related as in the case of a wilderness area or an area containing special physiographic features. Preservation of certain water environments in some cases may be central to international efforts to preserve endangered species of plants and animals.

Management of waters designated for preservation generally involves integration of the area involved into broader land management programs. Where preservation is accomplished through public ownership, inclusion in an existing system of parks, sanctuaries, or other public land categories is generally appropriate. Where preservation goals are pursued through regulation of the use of privately owned lands, management depends primarily on full consideration of preservation objectives within implementation of relevant control measures. This approach therefore requires institutional mechanisms for systematic notice of proposed development activities to agencies with appropriate expertise to evaluate the likely impact of the activity and provide input to the responsible regulatory bodies.

The need for a program to preserve selected water environments generally increases with advances in socio-economic development. As development decreases the availability of unaltered environments, higher standards of living increase interest in their maintenance. But preservation efforts cannot be viewed solely as a water management activity for the developed nations. Natural water environments contribute to social welfare at all stages of development, and efforts to prevent excessive destruction may become necessary at an early stage.

8. Enhancing knowledge and awareness

Water resources management potential is directly dependent on the state of related knowledge and its diffusion among those involved in the management process. Knowledge is reflected in the skills and capabilities of a variety of technical specialists who must plan, implement, and operate water projects and programs. Knowledge is also reflected in skills of administrators who must coordinate technical and other activities into workable programs and in policy making by government officials.

The existence of adequate knowledge within departments and offices of government responsible for water resources management must be supported by general awareness of water management problems and issues among planners and other personnel within all departments of government and among the citizenry in general. Broad awareness within government is necessary because of interactions of water management and other governmental activities and the resulting need for consideration of potential interrelationships in decision making. General public awareness is necessary because political feasibility of management activities is related to widespread public attitudes and perceptions. Political decisions not consistent with such attitudes and perceptions are possible in individual cases, but continuing political support depends on general approval within the population. In addition, the success of many water management activities depends on active cooperation of large numbers of affected people.

Because of the dependence of water management on knowledge and awareness, the management program itself must include enhancement efforts. Attention should be focused on at least four areas: technical education and training, education to enhance administrative skills, research, and enhancement of citizen awareness.

8.1 Technical education and training

Water resources management involves a wide range of activities requiring professional personnel and rained

technicians. A 1981 report (Unesco and WMO, 1981, p. l02) indicates that, in spite of recent manpower surveys in many countries, reliable information on the current status of water management personnel is not available on a global scale. The report notes a shortage of personnel in the majority of developing countries, with the shortage most acute at the middle and lower level positions. The absence or insufficiency of training facilities and in-service training programs at the middle technician level is seen as a "crucial deficiency."

Several factors affect the current personnel situations in developing countries. In some countries, an overall inadequacy in the number of secondary school graduates may substantially restrict the pool of candidates for advanced education and special training. Where overall numbers of secondary school graduates are adequate, an inadequate proportion may choose engineering and other professions whose skills are necessary in water resources management. Problems of retaining qualified personnel in public sector positions in the developing countries include non-competitive salaries and lack of challenging projects and research opportunities. These problems cause movement of personnel away from governmental employment, possibly to other countries providing greater personal opportunities (Unesco and WMO, 1981, p. l07).

Addressing personnel problems in technical program areas must begin with an assessment of the causes specific to a particular country. Where the sources of the problem relate to basic educational conditions, the solution required is a broad one extending beyond considerations of water resource management alone. Where the problem is lack of specific training programs for technicians, the solution is more limited in scope and attainable in a shorter time period. Problems of inadequate enrollment in advanced educational programs in engineering or other areas of deficiency can be addressed by publicizing the opportunities and importance of careers in the particular area. Provision of financial assistance for related education may be necessary to encourage enrollment in areas where significant shortages exist. The selection of certain careers can also be encouraged by attractive salaries, an approach with potential to assist in the retention of qualified personnel as well.

A common remedy for national deficiencies in education and training programs is use of foreign expertise or use of foreign education and training programs. This solution is likely to be essential in the short run, but excessive reliance on imported expertise has disadvantages. While scientific principles are readily transferable among nations, transfer of applied science in the form of technology is not without limits. In addition to the issue of appropriateness of technology, the ability of a foreign national to interact with the socio-cultural dimensions of water manage-ment is a potential problem. The technical elements of management must be considered in relation to these other dimensions, and the inability to interact can be a significant limitation on effectiveness.

Education and training programs, while focusing on a variety of technical skills necessary in water resources management, must emphasize the interdisciplinary nature of water management and its broad context. Exclusively focus on the technical dimensions of management creates barriers to interdisciplinary communication and coordination necessary in an integrated approach to management. In addition, water-related education and training must encompass environmental issues as a fundamental component of water management. Only by instilling recognition of the environmental and social contexts of water management can the educational process develop personnel with adequate managerial perspectives (Dumitrescu, 1983).

8.2 Enhancement of administrative skills

A traditional weakness in water resources management, especially in developing countries, has been lack of efficient administration. The state of scientific knowledge generally outpaces its application, with administrative weaknesses one of the factors responsible for the discrepancy (United Nations, 1974, p.64). Administrative effectiveness is of major importance in water resources management due to the scope of activities involved. Because of the dependence on a wide range of interactions between activities and specialists of differing backgrounds, effective administration is as important as proper performance of the specialized tasks.

Administrative effectiveness is dependent in part on structural organization of the management program, but a major determinant is the performance of individuals within the organizational structure. Administrative proficiency generally has not been viewed with the same importance as scientific or technical proficiency. In addition, measurement of administrative performance is more difficult than is performance of a technical activity. As a result of these factors, a self-fulfilling prophesy of low expectations may attach to administrative responsibilities.

Improvement in administrative performance requires enhancement of both special administrative skills and administrative drive. Special skills such as personnel management are important administrative responsibilities that cannot be ignored. Promotions within an organization can result in specialists with narrow backgrounds moving into administrative positions requiring a diversity of skills. Such problems can be minimized by recognizing the importance of special administrative skills within organizational structure and providing special training in such skills for appropriate staff. Administrative drive is a somewhat intangible quality difficult to assess, but efforts to improve administrative performance must be viewed as a basic component of enhancing management.

8.3 The role of research

Research is the mechanism for extending knowledge for addressing water problems or taking greater advantage of potential contributions of the resource to socio-economic development. Although strict delineation between research and routine program activities such as planning and data management is difficult, research generally is undertaken from a somewhat broader perspective and tends to focus on evaluation of general issues and development of analytical methods and procedures rather than on specific problem solutions. Responsibility for research therefore is likely to fall outside the boundaries of traditional management agencies. Institutions of higher education generally are participants in the research process because of the availability of relevant expertise and equipment. Potential research topics are as broad as water management activities, but several priority areas can be identified.

An obvious area of research need is the development of means to extend the utility of existing water supplies by reducing water demand. Because of the magnitude of existing water use for agricultural production and the severity of food shortage problems in certain regions, development of more efficient irrigation practices and crops with lower water requirements (or greater salt tolerance) should be a major focus. Possibilities for reducing water use in industry and other supply categories should be investigated, including potential for recycling and reuse. Research for reducing water pollution and for improving the treatment of existing low quality waters also offers potential to protect and extend supplies.

Basic climatological research should be intensified. Better understanding of hydrometeorological processes is necessary for improved weather forecasting and for management of special problems such as acid precipitation. Such research should include investigation of the potential for climatic change and resulting impacts on water availability.

Research should not be limited to the scientific and technological aspects of water management but also should focus on sociological and managerial issues. Research focusing on the sociological aspects of water management is important because of the traditional lack of proper attention to this essential dimension. Policy-oriented research assists the policy formulation process by identification of alternative courses of action and evaluation of their respective impacts. Institutional analysis can assess the effectiveness of existing laws, administrative organization, and other aspects of management and evaluate the desirability of institutional modifications.

8.4 Increasing citizen awareness

General levels of awareness of water resources problems and issues vary substantially among nations. Awareness has risen substantially in recent years in some nations but remains low in others. Commonly held perceptions about water may contain substantial inaccuracies even when apparent awareness is high. This situation emphasizes the importance of communication as part of water management activities. The scope of communication needs and the necessary program for meeting those needs must be determined on the basis of individual national circumstances.

In order to conduct necessary communication with other departments of government and the public, the water management program must acknowledge the importance of this function and make necessary arrangements for its performance. Communication to increase awareness is not a traditional function, and little emphasis is likely to be reflected in administrative organization and personnel. Overcoming this traditional neglect requires assignment of explicit responsibility for communication to an administrative unit staffed with appropriate personnel. Necessary skills can be achieved through acquisition of personnel with appropriate education and training and by development of necessary skills among traditional staff, but the qualifications issue must be addressed.

For a detailed discussion of communication techniques and their application to increasing awareness of water problems and issues, the reader is referred to the companion report to the current study (Sadler (ed.), 1987).

9. Physical water management infrastructure

Water management facilities such as dams, canals, wells, locks, drainage works, and levees that control the movement of water are the most visible component of a nation's water management system. These physical structures are a direct product of all the less tangible aspects of management such as legislation, policy, and planning. These supporting activities produce decisions defining the need for structures and the particular form they are to take. Improvements in these other components of management may in some cases result in less reliance on implementation of structural measures. Nonstructural management options have received emphasis in recent years, with the result that the previous tendency to equate water management with hydrologic modification has declined.

Nevertheless, modification of hydrologic processes remains an important management device for enhancing the contributions of water to social welfare. Increasing water supplies in areas experiencing shortages during time periods of natural scarcity, providing water for crop production in areas without adequate natural precipitation, removing excess water from lands needed for food production, and protecting centers of population that experience serious flooding are but a few examples of situations where a continuing need for construction of water management facilities exists.

9.1 Constructing new facilities

The continuing potential for water control structures to contribute to socio-econmic development will result in expansion of existing facilities, but growth in facilities will likely be slower than in the past in many cases. A comprehensive approach to management can be expected to result in greater attention to the adverse social and environmental impacts of water project construction, making approval more difficult. Funding additional water projects will be difficult because they typically involve large capital investments in direct competition with other expenditures for social needs.

Funding may be hindered by recognition that expected benefits have not always been achieved from past projects. Broader recognition of these factors creates a somewhat hostile climate for additional water project construction.

But the water management system should continue to pursue structural options where a comprehensive analysis, including consideration of a full range of associated benefits and costs, indicates such an option to be the most meritorious approach. Water managers must protect their credibility by avoiding endorsement of poorly conceived projects but should advocate approval and funding of desirable projects. This function involves development of proposals that clearly present the full range of attributable benefits and costs and their relationship to other courses of action, including identification of the consequences of the no-action option.

9.2 Maintaining and increasing the effectiveness of existing facilities

In addition to its focus on construction of new water management facilities under appropriate circumstances, the management program must also ensure the continuing effectiveness of existing facilities, including implementation of measures to improve effectiveness where possible. To ensure continuing effectiveness, management programs must systematically assess operation relative to intended performance and initiate actions to remedy deficiencies in a timely manner. Performance of routine maintenance is an important consideration since neglect can substantially shorten the useful life of facilities and thereby eliminate many of the expected benefits. Post-construction appraisal of facilities also should identify the development of unanticipated obstacles to performance since forecasting of conditions is subject to inadequacies. Early identification of such obstacles may allow implementation of necessary mitigation actions that preserve expected benefits.

Improvements in the effectiveness of existing facilities can take several forms. Reduction in physical waste of water may be possible through such means as detection and control of leakage from canals and other water handling facilities. The utility of existing water supplies in some cases can be extended by adoption of a broader management perspective that integrates previously independent sources of supply into a unified system. For example, integrated management of run-of-river withdrawals, storage reservoirs, and ground-water withdrawals generally offers greater flexibility than independent management and results in improved capability to respond to droughts. Increased integration of management facilities also offers potential advantages with respect to other water-related services such as hydroelectric power generation and flood loss reduction. Treating a group of hydrologically related facilities as a system allows application of optimization techniques with potential for increasing the total benefits produced.

Another potential means of improving the use of existing water management facilities is change in the purpose of operation. For example, water from a storage reservoir constructed to supply a particular purpose could be reallocated to a different purpose where changed conditions have increased the relative importance of the second use, provided that such issues as water rights and contractual obligations can be satisfactorily resolved.

The decision to undertake such changes in the use of water management facilities depends on the relative magnitudes of the benefits and costs associated with such modifications. Only those with potential to produce benefits in excess of resulting costs generally are desirable. An important function of water management is an on-going effort to identify and evaluate potentially worthwhile changes.

10. Financing water management

Operation of a water management program is dependent on availability of adequate resources for constructing necessary facilities, employing needed personnel, and meeting other costs associated with management activities. Modification of hydrologic processes to enhance the contributions of water to socio-economic development generally is a capital-intensive activity involving large investments. Even within political systems where substantial private sector investments in water development are made, water management facilities and programs can be a major component of social infrastructure requiring significant levels of public funding. Such investments are in direct competition with public expenditures for defense, transportation, health, education, and the whole range of other social needs. The allocation of public funds among alternative investments ultimately depends on value judgments concerning the relative priorities of social needs.

Investment in capital-intensive components of infrastructure such as reservoirs with returns distributed over long periods of time may in some cases appear to be unattractive relative to alternative investments offering immediate results, especially where alternative expenditures directly improve human health and welfare. For example, provision of relief to the victims of famine at least in the short run is likely to take precedence over investment in irrigation facilities to help prevent famine. Similarly, dispensing medicinal remedies for the victims of disease is a more immediate concern than is the improvement of water supply and general sanitation as a means of reducing the incidence of disease. But funding of infrastructure with potential to address multiple dimensions of welfare over an extended time period must be a part of the overall strategy for addressing social problems such as hunger and disease.

The difficulties of funding water management activities are generally greatest where related problems are most severe: in the developing nations. International aid to such countries has tended to focus on infrastructure improvements, with water management activities a major focus of attention. While no general assumption can be made that water resource investments are the best use of such funds in all cases, substantial focus on this area is likely to continue. Allocation of internal funds within the developing nations to water management activities will also continue to be necessary, for both continuing management programs such as data collection and investment in physical facilities.

An important financing issue within nations with a federal form of government is the sharing of water management costs by the different levels of government. While a major share of management costs may be assumed by a national government due to widespread benefits of resulting national economic development, special regional or local benefits may justify assignment of some portion of costs to subnational units of government. Provisions for sharing costs and associated transfer of funds are important aspects of the institutional framework for intergovernmental relations within such nations.

10.1 The role of user charges

A special issue in water management financing is the extent to which users of the products and services of water management activities are required to pay a fee for the product or service. Practice regarding user fees is not uniform but encompasses a range of approaches. This variation is due to several factors, a major one of which is the existence of conflicting objectives within user-charge policy (Warford and Julius, 1977).

A primary objective embodied in user charges is revenue generation. Such revenues can be a major component of the funds needed for meeting repayment obligations and operating costs associated with water management facilities and programs. This role of user charges tends to be more predominant where the economic viability of the enterprise is less secure, as in the case of management activities of local governments or other relatively small organizations. Where user charges serve in this capacity, unit charges are set equal to at least the average cost of producing the product or service in order to avoid revenue deficits.

A second objective sometimes incorporated into user-charge policy, which may result in charges substantially different from those developed under the revenue objective, is income redistribution. The primary application is the provision of products or services to certain income groups free of charge or at a fee lower than the costs of providing the product or service. This approach would likely be adopted in a basic needs approach to socio-economic development in such areas as domestic water supply.

A third objective that may be adopted in user-charge policy is prevention of excessive use of the product or service provided. User charges are a potential control on use if applied on a cost-per-unit-of-service basis. To encourage economic efficiency in use, prices should be set equal to the costs of producing the last unit of the product or service under consideration. If prices are set below this value, users will not be confronted with the full costs of a decision to use another unit, and excessive use will likely result. Such behavior will create incentives for premature investment in facility expansion.

Since peak demands during certain seasons and certain times of the day are a major factor in the need for expanding facilities in areas such as water supply and electric power, use of variable pricing can be an important management tool. Use of pricing schedules that impose higher charges during peak seasons or hours of the day has potential to reduce peak demands. However, the need for more sophisticated metering is a constraint on use of variable prices for efficiency purposes.

These three objectives can produce conflicting approaches to the establishment of user fees. User fees established for income redistribution purposes will likely be inadequate for revenue or efficiency purposes. A price based on average costs designed to satisfy revenue requirements is not likely to achieve efficiency objectives, which generally requires pricing based on marginal costs (marginal costs may be either higher or lower than average costs, depending on the type of activity and its scale of operation). In some cases, one objective may be of overriding concern, with the others dropped from consideration in a determination of user charges for a particular activity. For example, revenue considerations may take precedence where the activity is forced to be self-supporting, or the income redistribution objective may lead to disregard of efficiency and revenue production in a basic needs approach designed to quickly upgrade living conditions for the poorest segment of a society.

In other situations, compromises that consider more than one objective may be possible. For example, a pricing schedule could be applied that involved a subsidy at low levels of consumption but converted to marginal cost pricing at higher levels of consumption to control inefficient use. An increasing block rate for water supply with the first increment of use priced at a low rate provides an example.

Discriminatory pricing provides another compromise approach. If total revenue needs must be met from user fees, subsidies for certain classes of users can still be achieved if lost revenues are offset by assigning higher prices to other classes. For example, a subsidy for agricultural water supply can be offset by higher fees for industrial water if public policy calls for special concessions to the agricultural sector.

A third compromise approach is useful where marginal cost pricing results in revenue deficiencies. The efficiency advantages of marginal cost pricing can be maintained through use of a two-part fee, with one part consisting of a flat fee imposed on all users to cover the deficit in revenue resulting from continued use of the marginal cost as the price of each unit of consumption (James and Lee, 1971, pp. 541-549; ESCAP Secretariat, 1981).

In addition to complications arising from conflicting objectives, user fee practice is also influenced by the price elasticity of demand — a measure of the change in quantity demanded that results from a given change in price of a particular product or service. The use of pricing as a means of controlling demand is feasible only where demand is elastic to some degree. Demand elasticity varies significantly among water uses and locations (Goodman, 1984, pp. 99-100).

Another potential obstacle to use of pricing as a management mechanism is the non-marketable nature of many water services, a fundamental reason for governmental provision. In such cases, a governmental provider of a public good such as flood protection will confront special difficulties in imposing user fees on beneficiaries. The decision to impose a user fee must be based on a determination that collection is physically practical and economically feasible when revenues and other benefits of imposing the fee are compared to the associated costs.

11. Administrative framework for water management

Water management decisions are made and implemented through an administrative framework generally consisting of separate but interacting administrative units. The most prominent feature of water resources administration is the organizational structure defining the individual management units and their location within the governmental structure. Individual water management activities encompass application of a variety of professional specialities such as hydrology, engineering, economics, sociology, and the biological sciences. Assignment of such responsibilities among different levels of government and among individual departments at the various levels is the basic step in defining administrative structure. In addition to organizational structure, a second basic aspect of an administrative framework consists of mechanisms for coordination among individual water management units and between water management and related programs.

Administrative organization for water resources management cannot be considered separately of overall national political organization. A key constraint on administrative structure is the general division of authority among different levels of government. In a federal system where significant powers related to water management are held by subnational levels of government such as provinces or states, potential for structural centralization of water management responsibilities may be limited. For example, components of management such as water allocation may be assigned to subnational units of government. In such cases, the diffusion of responsibility requires special emphasis on coordination. On the other hand, a general centralization of governmental authority at the national level creates greater opportunities for adoption of a centralized administrative structure for water management.

Because of such variability in basic institutional arrangements among nations and the wide range of administrative approaches available, recommendation of a universally applicable administrative organization for water management is impractical. Each nation must develop an administrative approach compatible with its general institutional framework and suitable for addressing its particular water management situation.

The following sections focus on discussion of general issues that must be addressed and the characteristics of alternative approaches.

11.1 Division of responsibilities among levels of government

Since the nation is the basic unit of socio-economic organization, the national level of government is assumed to be the appropriate level for exercise of a wide range of water management responsibilities. The extent to which responsibilities are exercised at other levels of government within a given nation depends substantially on the overall structure of government and general principles of intergovernmental relations. Where substantial centralization of power in the national government exists, water management is likely to be primarily a function of national government. But variability in local conditions generally necessitates exercise of certain management responsibilities at subnational levels. At the same time, problems of greater than national scope may result in some degree of surrender of national sovereignty with respect to water management to an international body.

The potential for subnational and international organizations to exercise certain water management responsibilities is considered in the following sections. The most significant of these additional levels of government often is an intermediate level existing directly below the national level. These units of government, known by such names as "provinces," "states," or "republics," often exercise major water management responsibilities. A variety of other subnational governmental units also may be involved, including general purpose local governments, special utility districts, and river basin authorities.

11.1(a) Intermediate levels of government

The intermediate level of government directly below the national level often exercises significant governmental powers likely to include various water management functions. In some cases, the majority of water management responsibility is exercised at this level. In Australia, for example, the individual states conduct comprehensive water management programs encompassing a full range of relatively independent management activities (DRE, 1983, p.5). Under these conditions, involvement of a national government may be relatively indirect except in special areas such as interjurisdictional issues affecting two or more of the subnational units of government.

Other nations provide illustrations of a relatively even distribution of powers between national and intermediate levels of government. In the United States, for example, both the national and state governments traditionally have exercised substantial management responsibilities. A primary responsibility of state governments is the allocation of water supplies among competing interests. Certain national water development programs (such as the irrigation program in the western states) have been implemented with significant

deference to state powers of water allocation, including the payment of compensation for state-created water rights displaced. On the other hand, the national government exercises superior powers with regard to navigation development, including the destruction of state-created water rights without compensation (NWC, 1973, p. 459).

A third approach involves exercise of primary authority by the national government. While total consolidation of management responsibilities within the national government is not likely to be feasible, substantial national control is possible. An illustration is provided by the Soviet Union where water legislation establishes comprehensive authority for national control and protection of water resources. However, certain management responsibilities are shared with the Soviet republics (Voropaev, 1986, pp. 37-40).

11.1(b) General purpose local governments

The local level of government generally is not considered a major participant in water management, but certain significant activities can be delegated to this level. A primary limitation on the power of local government to participate in water management arises from the restricted perspective associated with the small geographic scope of the typical local government. While small watersheds or groundwater basins may be totally encompassed within local political boundaries, local governments are less likely than other levels to view hydrologic units as a whole. Management decisions based on such limited perspective are likely to give inadequate attention to effects of the decision external to the decision maker and therefore give inadequate attention to general social welfare.

An area where local authority is common that can have significant impact on water resources is land-use control. Due to the importance of local impacts such as noise, congestion, and safety, land-use decisions are often considered primarily a local matter. But land use has substantial impacts on runoff characteristics and water quality. In addition, development patterns adjacent to bodies of surface water determine exposure to flooding and possibly to water-related disease. A comprehensive approach to addressing such problems therefore must include consideration of land-use controls among alternative management strategies and therefore involves powers often exercised by local government.

Local governments are also significant in the water resources management structure because of their frequent role as provider of utility services, including water and sewerage services. In this role, local government can be a major water developer and a major discharger of wastewater. Furthermore, decisions made by local governments regarding such factors as level of service and rate structure can be a significant determinant of demands placed on the resource. The importance of such factors within water management indicates the need for integrating local governments into the management structure.

11.1(c) Special utility districts

Many services often provided by general-purpose local governments can also be provided by special-purpose forms of local government created to operate within designated geographical districts. Water supply and other water-related services are often the focus of special district operations. While some districts provide multiple services, many focus on a single activity such as drinking water supply, sewerage, irrigation water supply, drainage, or flood protection.

Special districts have both advantages and disadvantages as an administrative organization for provision of water-related services. A primary advantage is the ability to conform management boundaries to logically defined service areas without regard to local political boundaries that are often arbitrary from a functional perspective. But their narrow functional base may restrict revenue potential, management capabilites may be limited, and lack of coordination with other local governmental functions may be a problem (Corbridge (ed.), 1983).

11.1(d) River basin authorities

The river basin authority is a regional water resources administrative unit that may encompass an area totally within a province or other subnational unit of government or may include portions of two or more of these political units. Although variation in function is possible, river basin authorities are often viewed as an administrative organization for comprehensive water resources management within a given watershed area.

The comprehensive river basin authority offers two principal advantages as an administrative approach to surface water management. First, the basin is a logical jurisdictional area since it represents an isolated surface water system within which water resources conditions and potential impacts from water development and use can be viewed as related parts of a single system. Second, the consolidation of all management functions into a single administrative unit eliminates many problems of coordination affecting most other administrative approaches. Combination of these two factors maximizes the opportunity for applying scientific concepts of management within a systems approach.

The same factors that create the unique strengths of the basin-authority approach also produce special weaknesses. While the jurisdictional boundaries of a basin authority coincide with the boundaries of the surface water resource, they may not agree with the boundaries of other natural systems and socio-economic patterns relevant to water management. Boundaries of groundwater basins do not necessarily coincide with watershed boundaries, and demographic patterns that determine demands for water-related services are unlikely to be defined by watershed boundaries. Because of their specialized nature, river basin authorities are likely to be relatively isolated from the institutional framework through which most socio-economic activity is conducted. Therefore many of the advantages of treating surface water as a unified system will be negated by the basin authority's inability to consider interactions between the water resource and the socio-economic system in the same comprehensive fashion (United Nations, 1975, p. 8; United Nations, 1970, p. 27).

The practicality of the basin authority as the administrative approach to water management will likely vary with the level of socio-economic development. At a low level of development when social institutions generally are lacking or incomplete, a basin authority may be feasible as an organizing framework. As other activities and institutions develop independently of basin boundaries, however, feasibility is likely to decrease. Under a high level of general institutional development, an alternative administrative structure for water management that is more compatible with general socio-economic organization may be more effective.

11.1(e) International organizations

Although national boundaries delineate the most commonly accepted units of socio-economic organization, meteorologic and hydrologic processes transcend such boundaries and create the need in some situations for a management perspective broader than that of any single nation. The international perspective becomes important in two principal contexts: (1) coordination of data collection and research relating to better understanding of meteorologic and hydrologic processes and (2) development and use of water resources shared by two or more nations.

The need for international cooperation in data collection and research has long been recognized. Ongoing programs such as Unesco's International Hydrological Programme and the activities of the World Meteorological Organization have made significant contributions to scientific knowledge and to improving collection and analysis of data necessary for water resources management. The need for continuance of international efforts in support of national activities is indicated by the currently unresolved status of such questions as the nature and extent of climatic change and continuing data deficiencies in many regions of the world.

Water development and use often have international aspects because a substantial portion of surface and groundwater supplies exists in systems that cross national boundaries. Approximately 200 first order streams are shared by at least two countries, with some shared by as many as ten nations (United Nations, 1975, p. 271). An even greater number of lesser streams and groundwater systems fall within multiple political jurisdictions. Significant examples of international cooperation for resolving water problems and realizing management opportunities associated with water resources shared by two or more nations exist. These experiences involve a range of management issues such as navigation, fisheries, water quality protection, flood damage reduction, and allocation of supply. They also illustrate a range of alternative administrative structures for achieving international management.

Administrative arrangements for international water management activities generally must be specially tailored for the individual situation. Existing guidelines for management of internationally shared waters provide general recommendations for conflict-resolution procedures. One of the best known statement of principles is "The Helsinki Rules on the Uses of the Waters of International Rivers" (United Nations, 1975, pp. 188-194), prepared by the International Law Association. These rules, which provide that each nation whose territory includes a portion of an international drainage basin is entitled to a "...reasonable and equitable share in the beneficial uses of the waters..." (United Nations, 1975, p. 188, art. IV), suggest several alternatives for resolving disputes. These alternatives include negotiation, referral to a joint agency, submittal to an arbitral tribunal or the International Court of Justice, and formation of a conciliation commission.

Guidelines for creating the recommended conciliation commission provide for each state to appoint two members who together are to choose one additional member to be president of the commission. Provision is made for appointment of the final member, upon request of any concerned nation, by the President of the International Court of Justice or by the Secretary-General of the United Nations in the case where the representatives of the concerned states do not agree on the final member.

Ad hoc arrangements for international water resources and by the individual nations involved, not all agreements accepted by the international body will be implemented. But the process of developing recommendations will increase available information and, in some cases, identify opportunities for mutually advantageous courses of action that might otherwise have been overlooked. This approach based on use of information and persuasion is probably the best available in view of the general reluctance of nations to relinquish governmental powers (Uttn by the individual nations involved, not all agreements accepted by the international body will be implemented. But the process of developing recommendations will increase available information and, in some cases, identify opportunities for mutually advantageous courses of action that might otherwise have been overlooked. This approach based on use of information and persuasion is probably the best available in view of the general reluctance of nations to relinquish governmental powers (Utton, 1978).

11.2 Functional organization

Decisions regarding the division of water management responsibilities among the different levels of government partially define administrative structure; the remaining structural issue is the assignment of functional responsibilities to agencies or departments within a given governmental level. Interdepartmental assignment would be largely unnecessary if the comprehensive river-basin-authority approach were to be extensively employed. However, the basin-authority approach has seen limited application. Where adopted, the basin approach is likely to be adopted for certain regions while several separate agencies are given administrative responsibilities in the remainder of a nation.

A key issue associated with the assignment of a range of management functions to individual departments is the degree of centralization desirable. In the approach favoring centralization, all water management functions, or perhaps all natural resource and environmental management functions, are combined into a single department or ministry. Within this large agency, separate divisions will be assigned individual program responsibilities. In a less centralized approach, such programs will be the responsibility of relatively independent departments of government, an approach requiring greater emphasis on coordination. Coordination generally becomes more difficult with increasing independence of components of the management system; however, coordination can be inadequate even within the divisions of a single ministry and must be of concern under any organizational structure (United Nations, 1974, p. 40).

In addition to issues associated with centralization of water management responsibilities, special concerns arise with respect to relationships among certain program elements. In some instances, a degree of independence may be necessary for maintenance of objectivity and prevention of potential conflicts of interest. A special case is administration of the water quality and general environmental protection program. Administrative responsibilities generally should be separate from or suitably balanced with responsibilities for promoting water development activities due to inherent conflicts. Similarly, the water allocation function should generally be administratively separate from programs involving development and use of water for specific purposes to avoid bias, or the perception of bias, in the allocation process.

Administrative organization for water planning is an issue of special concern. The need for common procedures among different program components suggests the need for a centralized planning function. However, separation of planning from the management agency responsible for plan implementation will produce undesirable effects. This consideration indicates that specific project and program planning should be conducted by the agency with direct management responsibility, subject to planning guidelines applicable to all components of the water management program. Such guidelines should be developed at a high level of authority, with opportunity for input from all departments with management responsibilities. The agency with authority for developing planning guidelines can be given authority to oversee planning activity to ensure compliance with the guidelines if desirable.

Administrative arrangements for data management can have a significant impact on suitability and availability of data for the various components of the water management program. The varied uses for data suggest a separation of the data management function from other program components. Attachment of the data management function to an agency with narrow program responsibilities may lead to overemphasis on certain types of data and neglect of others. The agency responsible for data should engage in basic data collection programs but should also receive data collected by other administrative units for coordination and storage as part of an integrated data system. Provision should be made for convenient retrieval in a variety of forms as required for different water management purposes.

11.3 Coordination

Because of the complexity of water management and the many interactions between water and man's activities, coordination is a major concern in the design of an administrative framework for performing water management functions. Coordination involves both the interactions among organizational units responsible for various water management responsibilities and the interactions between the water management program and a range of other socio-economic activities that generate water demand or otherwise impact the water resource.

11.3(a) Coordination among elements of the water management program

Proper performance of individual water management responsibilities cannot ensure an effective management program unless individual program elements are coordinated as parts of a coherent, unified effort. Such coordination is essential to the realization of potential complementarities among actions and avoidance of potential conflict because of physical interdependencies within hydrologic systems.

The extent of the need for coordination and the necessary form of coordination within a water resources management program are directly dependent on the administrative structure adopted. The need for formal coordination mechanisms is generally less in the case of a centralized administrative structure relative to a decentralized one. The need also is less in the case of consolidation of primary management responsibilities at one level of government relative to a situation involving substantial intergovernmental division of authority. Thus, administrative structure and coordination among individual administrative units are intertwined issues that must be jointly considered whenever alternative administrative frameworks are evaluated.

Within a national or other level of government where administrative responsibilities are relatively decentralized, a basic coordination mechanism is a coordinating committee or council made up of representatives of administrative units exercising water management responsibilities. In order for this approach to be effective, the status and authority of the coordinating committee must be clearly prescribed by law. Established departments of government can be expected to resist actions detrimental to departmental interests or contrary to traditional practices, and lack of a clearly defined mandate is likely to make the committee's efforts meaningless. This coordinating body can be assigned various responsibilities such as policy formulation and review, development of planning guidelines, review of agency plans, evaluation of program effectiveness, and budget preparation.

Depending on the responsibilities assigned, the coordinating body will likely require at least a small independent staff.

Coordination on a regional basis can be provided by a special regional organization. A primary example is a river basin commission that, unlike a river basin authority, has no direct responsibilities for implementing management activities but is limited to coordination and perhaps other specific functions such as certain types of planning. This type of organization can provide coordination among levels of government as well as among various water management functions at a given level. A river basin commission also provides a potential mechanism for coordination among governmental units of equal status such as provinces or states that share a river basin within a given nation or independent nations that share an international river basin.

Within a nation having a substantial division of authority among levels of government, intergovernmental coordination is an important concern. In addition to the previously discussed river-basin-commission approach, other mechanisms are needed. Various ad hoc arrangements such as advisory committees can be adopted for use in cases involving special studies or management activities, but establishment of standard procedures to ensure systematic coordination on a day-to-day basis is necessary.

Because of the broader perspective and generally superior position to effect coordination, the national government exercises a primary role. One potential mechanism available to a national government to achieve coordination is the delegation of certain administrative responsibilities to lower levels of government where related authority is exercised. For example, coordination between a water quality control program developed at the national level with a water allocation program operated by a lower level of government could be achieved by delegating administrative responsibilities for the quality control program to the lower level. Such delegation of administrative responsibility does not necessarily imply relinquishment of control over program content. Guidelines for program operation can be imposed, and authority for eliminating the delegation in case of improper administration can be retained.

A second intergovernmental coordination mechanism is full consultation by national program administrators with lower levels of government regarding significant decisions. Such consultations would include regulatory approval of major water projects by the national government, approval of development projects to be undertaken by the national government, and provision of national financial assistance to a water development activity. Subject to considerations of the national interest, varying degrees of deference to the views of subnational governments can be shown. Necessary consultation can be achieved in part by reliance on procedures for conducting environmental and social impact assessments. General review procedures can be supplemented by individual consultations in specialized areas such as fisheries management.

11.3(b) Coordination of the water management program with related programs

The complexity of interactions between the water resource and socio-economic activities requires close coordination between water management and decision processes in many areas outside the scope of the water management program. Water management activities are not ends in themselves and therefore cannot be isolated; they must be integrated into a variety of socio-economic processes. Improvements in drinking water supplies and waste disposal operations are likely to be components of broader efforts to improve health, housing, and overall living conditions. Irrigation operations must be coordinated with a variety of related activities in the agricultural sector that collectively focus on increasing crop production. Navigation improvements must be integrated into overall transportation planning. These examples of the need for water management activities to be planned and implemented as part of broader socio-economic activities illustrate the essential nature of coordination between water management programs and related program areas.

Coordination with activities external to the water management program is affected by the organizational structure adopted for water management. Such external coordination is likely to be enhanced by a decentralized administrative organization for water management because of the greater opportunity for individual water management activities to be closely associated with related programs. For example, responsibility for irrigation development in a decentralized approach may be located within an organization with broader responsibilities for agriculture. Centralization of water management responsibilities (perhaps to achieve better coordination among elements of the water management program) can have the negative effect of separating water management functions from related water-using sectors and activities. Adoption of a centralized approach to provide greater unity for water management considerations therefore may lead to greater fragmentation of decision making from other perspectives. In order to overcome resulting problems, special mechanisms for coordination with activities external to the water mangement program are necessary where a centralized administrative structure for water management is employed.

An essential factor in achieving coordination between water management and related areas is broad-based communication between the programs involved. A free exchange of information, with each program providing input to the others, should be standard practice. Water managers must have information concerning planned activities in other sectors that generate water demand and otherwise impact the resource. Similarly, managers in other sectors need information concerning future water availability and actions necessary for averting unacceptable impacts on the water resource. Coordination also must include efforts to provide complementary inputs necessary for realization of the potential benefits of water management activities. For example, provision of irrigation water must be coordinated with efforts to provide fertilizer and other necessary agricultural inputs. Exchange of information or other coordination cannot be left to chance but should be ensured by formal institutional arrangements. The appropriate form of such arrangements will vary among individual situations, but they should require adequate inter-organizational consultation and interaction for mutual awareness of program activities. Such awareness is essential to implementation of an integrated water management program that avoids conflicting actions and achieves complementary effects among program components.

12. References for section III

Baram, Michael S. "Cost-Benefit Analysis: An Inadequate Basis for Health, Safety, and Environmental Regulatory Decision Making." *Ecology Law Quarterly*, 8(1980), 473-531.

Beckman, Norman. "The Planner as a Bureaucrat." *Journal of the American Institute of Planners*, 30 (1964), pp. 323-327.

Bokhari, S. M. H. "Transglobal Variations in the Planning Objectives and Critiques." *Water Supply and Management*, 5(1981), 377-389.

Bower, Blair T., Remi Barre, Jochen Kuhner, and CLifford S. Russell. *Incentives in Water Quality Management. France and the Ruhr Area.* Washington: Resources for the Future, 1981.

Bowie, Norman E., ed. *Ethical Issues in Government.* Philadelphia: Temple University Press, 1981.

Bryson, R. A. "A Perspective on Climatic Change." *Science*, 184(1974), 753-760.

Cano, Guillermo J. "Water Law and Legislation: How to Use Them to Obtain Optimum Results from Water Resources." *Water Supply and Management*, 1(1977), 313-334.

Corbridge, James N., ed. *Special Water Districts: Challenge for the Future.* Boulder: Natural Resources Law Center, University of Colorado School of Law, 1983.

DRE (Department of Resources and Energy). *Water 2000: A Perspective on Australia's Water Resources to the Year 2000.* Canberra: Australian Government Publishing Service, 1983.

Daneke, G. A. and J. D. Priscoli. "Social Assessment and Resource Policy: Lessons from Water Planning." *Natural Resources Journal*, 19 (1979), pp. 359-375.

Dasgupta, Partha. "Environmental Management under Uncertainty." In *Explorations in Natural Resource Economics.* V. Kerry Smith and John V. Krutilla, eds. Baltimore: The Johns Hopkins University Press (for Resources for the Future), 1982, pp. 109-139.

Davidoff, Paul. "Advocacy and Pluralism in Planning." *Journal of the American Institute of Planners*, 31 (1965), pp. 331-338.

Downing, Paul B. *Environmental Economics and Policy.* Boston: Little, Brown and Co., 1984.

Dumitrescu, Sorin. "Report on Education and Training in Hydrology and Water Resources Management." In *Water for Human Consumption: Man and His Environment — Proceedings of the Fourth World*

Congress of the International Water Resources Association. Vol. 6 of Water Resources Series. Series ed. Asit K. Biswas. Dublin: Tycooly International Publishing (for the International Water Resources Association), 1983, pp. 47-57.

Dyckman, John W. "What Makes Planners Plan?" Journal of the American Institute of Planners, 27 (1961) pp. 164-167.

ECAFE (Economic Commission for Asia and the Far East) Secretariat. "Criteria of Economic Evaluation in Water Resources Development." In Planning Water Resources Development: Report and Background Papers of the Working Group of Experts on Water Resources Planning Convened at Bangkok, Thailand From 29 August to 9 September 1968 (Water Resources Series No. 37) (ST/ECAFE/SER. F/37). New York: United Nations, 1969, pp. 71-80.

ESCAP (Economic and Social Commission for Asia and the Pacific) Secretariat. "Water Pricing: Principles and Problems" (prepared for the Secretariat by Charles B. Aldelmann, Consultant). In Proceedings of the Expert Group Meeting on Water Pricing (Water Resources Series No. 55 (ST/ESCAP/SER.F/55). New York: United Nations, 1981, pp. 48-54.

ESCAP (Economic and Social Commission for Asia and the Pacific) Secretariat. "Some Aspects of System Planning." In Proceedings of the Expert Working Group Meetings on Water Resources Data Systems and Water-Use Data (Water Resources Series No. 53) (ST/ESCAP/SER.F/53). New York: United Nations, 1980, pp. 11-16.

ESCAP (Economic and Social Commission for Asia and the Pacific) Secretariat (2). "The Requirements for Water-Use Data." In Proceedings of the Expert Working Group Meetings on Water Resources Data Systems and Water-Use Data (Water Resources Series No. 53 (ST/ESCAP/SER.F/53). New York: United Nations, 1980, pp. 83-88.

Eckstein, Otto. Water Resource Development: The Economics of Project Evaluation. Cambridge: Harvard University Press, 1958.

Etzioni, Amitaï. "Mixed Scanning: A 'Third' Approach to Decision-Making." Public Administration Review, 27 (1967), pp. 385-392.

Faludi, Andreas. "Towards Comprehensive Planning?: In A Reader in Planning Theory, Ed. Andreas Faludi. Oxford: Pergamon Press, 1973, pp. 113-126.

Freeman, III, A. Myrick. "The Health Implications of Residuals Discharges: A Methodological Overview." In Explorations in Natural Resource Economic. V. Kerry Smith and John V. Krutilla, eds. Baltimore: Johns Hopkins University Press (for Resources for the Future), 1982, pp. 140-164.

Goodell, Scott K. "Waterway Preservation: The Wild and Scenic Rivers Act of 1968." Boston College Environmental Affairs Law Review, 7(1978), pp. 43-82.

Goodman, Alvin S. Principles of Water Resources Planning. Englewood Cliffs, N.J.: Prentice Hall, 1984.

Holden, Patrick W. Pesticides and Groundwater Quality. Washington: National Academy Press, 1986.

James, L. Douglas. "Economics of Water Development in Less Developed Countries." Water Supply and Management, 2(1978), 373-386.

James, L. Douglas and Robert R. Lee. Economics of Water Resources Planning. New York: McGraw-Hill Book Co., 1971.

Khator, Renu. "Environment as a Political Issue in Developing Countries: A Study of Environmental Pollution in India - A Viewpoint." International Journal of Environmental Studies, 23 (1984), pp. 105-112.

Kneese, Allen V. and Blair T. Bower. Managing Water Quality: Economics, Technology, Institutions. Washington: Resources for the Future, 1968.

Lamb, James C. Water Quality and Its Control. New York: John Wiley and Sons, 1985.

Lindblom, Charles E. "The Science of 'Muddling Through.'" Public Administration Review, 19 (1959), pp. 79-99.

Love, Ruth L. "Responses to Innovation: A Perspective for Social Profiling on How to Avoid the Laundry List Syndrome." In Social Scientists Conference Proceedings. Vol. I, Memphis, Tenn: U. S. Army Corps of Engineers Institute for Water Resources, 1977, pp. 200-213.

McAllister, Donald M. Evaluation in Environmental Planning: Assessing Environmental, Social, Economic, and Political Trade-Offs. Cambridge, Mass: The MIT Press, 1980.

Meyerson, Martin and E. C. Banfield. Politics, Planning, and the Public Interest. Glencoe, Ill.: The Free Press, 1955.

Mishan, E. J. Cost-Benefit Analysis, New York: Praeger Publishers, 1976.

NSF (National Science Foundation). "A Report on Flood Hazard Mitigation." Washington: National Science Foundation, 1980.

NWC (National Water Commission). Water Policies for the Future: Final Report to the President and to the Congress of the United States by the National Water Commission. Washington: U. S. Government Printing Office, 1973.

OECD (Organization for Economic Co-operation and Development). Pollution Charges in Practice. Paris: Organization for Economic Co-operation and Development, 1980.

OECD (Organization for Economic Co-operation and Development). Technology on Trial: Public Participation in Decision-Making Related to Science and Technology. Paris: Organization for Economic Co-operation and Development, 1979.

Ortolano, Leonard. Environmental Planning and Decision Making. New York: John Wiley and Sons, 1984.

Petersen, Margaret S. Water Resource Planning and Development. Englewood Cliffs, N.J.: Prentice-Hall, 1984.

Rau, J. G. and Wooten, D. C. Environmental Impact Analysis Handbook. New York: McGraw-Hill Book Co., 1980.

Riggs, James L. *Engineering Economics.* (2d ed). New York: McGraw-Hill Book Co., 1982.

Sadler, B. S., ed. "Communication Strategies for Heightening Awareness of Water" (Unesco Studies and Reports in Hydrology). Paris: Unesco, 1987.

Samuelson, Paul A. *Economics* (9th Ed.). New York: McGraw-Hill Book Co., 1973.

Scherer, Donald and Thomas Attig, eds. *Ethics and the Environment.* Englewood Cliffs, N.J.: Prentice-Hall, 1983.

Seneca, Joseph J. and Michael K. Taussig. Environmental Economics. Englewood Cliffs, N. J.: Prentice-Hall, 1974.

Sewell, W. R. Derrick *et al. Forecasting the Demands for Water.* Ottawa: Department of Energy, Mines and Resources, 1968.

Teclaff, Ludwik A. "An International Comparison of Trends in Water Resources Management." *Ecology Law Quarterly,* 7(1979), 881-915.

Torno, Harry C., ed. *Computer Applications in Water Resources: Proceedings of the Specialty Conference.* Buffalo, N.Y.: American Society of Civil Engineers, 1985.

Trelease, Frank J. "New Water Legislation: Drafting for Development, Efficient Allocation and Environmental Protection." *Land and Water Law Review,* XII (1977), 385-429.

Trelease, Frank J. "Policies for Water Law: Property Rights, Economic Forces, and Public Regulation." *Natural Resources Journal,* 5(1965), 1-48.

Trelease, Frank J. and Dellas W. Lee. "Priority and Progress — Case Studies in the Transfer of Water Rights." *Land and Water Law Review,* 1(1966), 1-76.

Unesco (United Nations Educational Scientific and Cultural Organization) and WMO (World Meteorological Organization). *Water Resources Assessment Activities: Handbook for National Evaluation* (Draft) (SC-81/WS/122), 1981.

UNIDO (United Nations Industrial Development Organization). *Guidelines for Project Evaluation.* New York: United Nations, 1972.

Unger, Stephen H. *Controlling Technology: Ethics and the Responsible Engineer.* New York: CBS College Publishing, 1982.

United Nations. *Management of International Water Resources: Institutional and Legal Aspects— Report of the Panel of Experts on the Legal and Institutional Aspects of International Water Resources Development.* (Natural Resources/ Water Series No. 1), 1(ST/ESA/5), New York: United Nations, 1975.

United Nations. *National Systems of Water Administration.* (ST/ESA/17), New York: United Nations, 1974.

United Nations. *Integrated River Basin Development: Report of a Panel of Experts* (Revised ed.) (E/ 3066/Rev.1), New York: United Nations, 1970.

United States EPA (Environmental Protection Agency). "The Report to Congress: Waste Disposal Practices and Their Effects on Ground Water." Washington: Environmental Protection Agency, 1977.

Utton, Albert E. "Some Suggestions for the Management of International River Basins." *Water Supply and Management,* 1(1978), 355-364.

Voropaev, G. V. *Socio-Economic Aspects of Water Resources Development in the USSR* (Unesco Technical Documents in Hydrology). Paris: Unesco, 1986.

WMO (World Meteorological Organization). *Hydrological Network Design and Information Transfer* (Operational Hydrology Report No. 8; WMO Publication No. 433). Geneva: WMO, 1976.

WMO (World Meteorological Organization). *Casebook on Hydrological Network Design Practice* (WMO Publication No. 324). Geneva: WMO, 1972.

Warford, Jeremy J. and DeAnne S. Julius. "The Multiple Objectives of Water Rate Policy in Less Developed Countries." *Water Supply and Management,* 1(1977), 335-342.

Whitlach, Jr., E. E. "Systematic Approaches to Environmental Impact Assessment: An Evaluation." *Water Resources Bulletin,* 12 (1976), pp. 123-137.

Wiener, Aaron. *The Role of Water in Development: An Analysis of Principles of Comprehensive Planning,* New York: McGraw-Hill Book Co., 1972.

IV. Conclusion

The water resource has played a major role in past socio-economic development and will continue to be intimately related to human welfare in the future. Many current water problems demonstrate a need for improving existing relationships between the resource and human activity. Increased irrigation and improved operation of existing irrigation projects are viewed as an essential aspect of reducing hunger. Improvement in domestic water supplies and sanitation services is a basic component of programs to improve health and general living conditions. Reduction in loss of life and property from flooding and reduction in the occurrence of water-related diseases are essential components of welfare in many nations. Accompanying these material needs is increased recognition of the importance of natural environments as a contributor to psychological welfare as well as the basis of ecological stability on which human health ultimately depends.

Recognition of the value of natural environments creates significant conflict within water management efforts. While alleviation of a variety of water-related problems will require construction of facilities to modify natural hydrologic conditions, resistance to such construction has accompanied recognition of the potentially adverse economic, environmental, and social impacts of water development. The perspective of water management consequently has expanded and now generally involves considering a greater range of alternatives for addressing a given problem and assessing a more complete range of impacts during the evaluation of alternative approaches.

The increasing scope of management considerations, together with increasing demands and impacts on the resource resulting from continuing socio-economic development, magnifies water management deficiencies and emphasizes the importance of efforts to enhance management capabilities. Increasing conflict among competing interests requires development and refinement of coherent policy to provide overall guidance. Water legislation should provide a clear statement of basic policy and must define a framework for decision making consistent with policy. Planning capability is essential for analysis of problems and potential solutions to ensure translation of policy into necessary programs and activities. A water management system must also include a water allocation program for establishing legal rights to use water, a data collection and analysis program for developing a sound information base for decision making, a water quality management program to prevent unacceptable degradation of supplies from waste disposal operations and other socio-economic activities, a program for preserving natural water environments possessing exceptional attributes, a program to promote broad awareness and understanding of water management issues and problems, physical infrastructure consisting of properly designed and operated water control structures and other facilities, and financing arrangements to support program activities at an adequate level.

Implementation of these various management functions requires an administrative framework through which necessary decisions can be made and actions taken. Variability in national political systems and institutional arrangements makes impossible the identification of a universally applicable administrative framework for water management, but common functional characteristics can be identified. Organizational arrangements must assign unambiguous responsibility for individual management functions to competent and adequately funded managerial units. At the same time, they must provide necessary coordination mechanisms to ensure proper integration of individual water management functions with one another and with related socio-economic decision processes outside the water management program.

While coordination within the water management program is essential to its proper functioning, coordination of water management with many external activities is critical to full realization of the potential of the water resource to contribute to socio-economic development. Water resource management is not an end in itself and generally cannot ensure socio-economic development in the absence of a variety of other conditions on which development depends. On the other hand, water shortages or other adverse water resource conditions can become a major constraint on development if not adequately considered within a given development program. The fact that water resource conditions are complementary to many other development inputs indicates the ultimate futility of viewing water management in isolation and mandates a close relationship with many other socio-economic factors essential to the development process.

43. *Manual on drainage in urbanized areas.* (English only.)
    Vol. I: *Planning and design of drainage systems.* 1987.
    Vol. II: *Data collection and analysis for drainage design.* 1987.
44. *The process of water resources project planning: a systems approach.* 1987. (English only.)
45. *Groundwater problems in coastal areas.* 1987. (English only.)
46. *The role of water in socio-economic development.* (To be published.)
47. *Communication strategies for heightening awareness of water.* 1987. (English only.)
48. *Casebook of methods for computing hydrological parameters for water projects.* 1987. (English only.)

29 100